A Fireman's Story

ABC Movie 1977 The Quinns, author as himself.

Actor Barry Bostwick and Joe Regan.

35 Engine streaching a line, truck works the fire escape.

All hands at work.

Responding

Harlem fire escape. Author then and korea, 1950.

Cutting off the fire, second due truck the floor above.

Buffing syracuse riding with Chief Tom Laun,he lead this girl out.

Search. Tap your way engine stop fire, protect stairway

Operation in the rear, Ladders and ropes

Tower ladder 14 bronx fifth alarm.

Vent roof, pull ceilings, wet stuff on the hot stuff.

A Fireman's Story

First 10,000 Alarms

Joe Regan

Copyright © 2010 by Joe Regan.

Library of Congress Control Number: 2010900632
ISBN: Hardcover   978-1-4500-2963-6
                Softcover   978-1-4500-2962-9

All rights reserved. No part of this book may be reproduced or transmitted in any form or by any means, electronic or mechanical, including photocopying, recording, or by any information storage and retrieval system, without permission in writing from the copyright owner.

This is a work of fiction. Names, characters, places and incidents either are the product of the author's imagination or are used fictitiously, and any resemblance to any actual persons, living or dead, events, or locales is entirely coincidental.

This book was printed in the United States of America.

To order additional copies of this book, contact:
Xlibris Corporation
1-888-795-4274
www.Xlibris.com
Orders@Xlibris.com
68479

Contents

Chapter 1	The First Ten Thousand Alarms	17
Chapter 2	The Overhaul	20
Chapter 3	The Chief's Paperwork	25
Chapter 4	Back To Fire Department Party	30
Chapter 5	Bill Faces His Past	37
Chapter 6	Reporting For Duty	41
Chapter 7	Car Pool	45
Chapter 8	Captain Mac's Drive-in	47
Chapter 9	Roll Call	51
Chapter 10	Roll The Wheels	57
Chapter 11	Listen And Learn	59
Chapter 12	Chief Walsh On The Air	64
Chapter 13	Brownstone Fire	71
Chapter 14	Tully Battlefield Commission, Almost!	77
Chapter 15	Rest Between Tours, And Egg In My Tea	84
Chapter 16	Another Fly In The Ointment, The Cane Mutiny	89
Chapter 17	When The Cat Is Away, The Mouse Will Play	96
Chapter 18	The Fat Cats	101
Chapter 19	Tower Ladder 14 On The Air	105
Chapter 20	The Nuts And Bolts Of It All	110
Chapter 21	Responding	113
Chapter 22	End To The Chief's Meeting	119
Chapter 23	Kitty Is Taken To Harlem To See Tully	121
Chapter 24	Grace And Captain Mac	127
Chapter 25	Kitty And Tully's Drive Ends	129
Chapter 26	Captain Mac's Drive To Astoria	130
Chapter 27	Home Sweet Home	138
Chapter 28	Slow Tour, But Always Something To Learn	146
Chapter 29	Making Calls And Remembering	149
Chapter 30	A Mix-up With A Punch	151
Chapter 31	Buss Man Holiday Boy, They Got Good Stuff	158
Chapter 32	Oh, What A Beautiful Morning	160
Chapter 33	Worry And Trouble Are My Middle Name	165

Chapter 34	What A Difference A Day Makes	171
Chapter 35	Day On The Town	175
Chapter 36	The Longest Night	187

I AM WRITING of a time few of any firefighters in FDNY of today worked in; it was a time we were stretched very thin. This caused a stress on all who tried to perform their duties. These are fictional characters in a work of fiction, but these times did happen. If you served then or now, I hope the story makes those times come alive for you and you recall the courage and the call of duty that you and your brothers may have answered. Thank you. All our brothers were valiant in their dedication. This is in memory of all our fallen heroes of 9/11, members of the Twelfth Battalion.

> Chief Fred Scheffold, my friend
> Chief Joseph Marchbank Jr.
> Lt. Glenn Perry
> Lt. Robert Nagel, Engine 58

And I will never forget the little girl who took my hand on December 3, 1999, in Worcester, Massachusetts fire scene and asked if I was going to get her daddy. At Box 1438, six heroes of Worchester Fire Department never returned home that night.

God hold you all in his hand.

CHAPTER 1

THE FIRST TEN THOUSAND ALARMS

FROM A VANTAGE point high in the night sky, a glimmer of light is breaking just under the dark purple horizon to the east. We are above the landmass called Manhattan, inhabited by four million people. The base of this island is granite, which has helped it to resist the cutting tidal flow of the Hudson and Harlem rivers as they reach for the Atlantic Ocean. The lights on the major thoroughfares, bridges, and skyscrapers outline the famous profile of the city of New York. The city that never sleeps is at rest.

Suddenly several red flashing lights appear at different locations in the northern quarter of the island, racing in different directions at first, but converging on the same destination within minutes.

The news chopper banks in the direction of the lights. "We're in luck, Nick," said the news spotter. "We got an opener for our traffic show."

"That's a roger," answered the voice of WNEW radio.

"If the fire guys don't put it out before we get more light."

The flashing lights are correctly identified as belonging to fire trucks. A small band of fire grenadiers in black garb scurry to enter the burning building. A silver aerial ladder rises from its red bed, rotates, and extends to the fire building's roof. Two men climb the portable staircase to the top and disappear in the billowing clouds of smoke above the rooftop. Spotlights and red emergency lights reflect off the frightening fire scene. It is clear to see that this five-story building is in dire distress as the engine men enter her cavities dragging their hose lines in after them. Some people stagger and stumble into the street, unashamed of their half dress and nakedness. Others struggle frantically to free themselves of the smoky maze that moments ago was their shelter, their homes, but now threatens to become their tomb.

Angry orange flames of fire in the heavy black smoke warns, like lightning in a dark storm cloud, of impending doom. Inside firefighters battle heat and smoke inch by inch to ground zero and hell in hopes of a heavenly outcome – extinguishment and salvation! God seems to stand back and watch their sacrifice as they do God's work – unlikely candidates for the priesthood – but then again, doesn't God always seem to choose sinners for his most important tasks?

This motley crew, sweating and swearing and crawling through their own puke as they gag and spit in the oxygen-depleted atmosphere, push on through unbearable heat and advance to the moment of truth.

The ladder men have self-deployed to preassigned areas of responsibility, to the roof to relieve the superheated smoke trapped at the upper reaches of the building and to the rear of the building. They utilize the fire escape to rescue and to ventilate new openings to let out heat away from the interior of the building.

The firemen make their way to the seat of the fire; their only light is an orange glow up ahead down a long dark hallway. From a kneeling position, the nozzle man flushes the floor in front of him; this clears burning debris and cools their path. The water pools, indicating the floor is intact. It gives them the last view of their battleground before the thermal balance is broken by water application. From here on, they will be in total darkness with only the sounds of the solid stream hitting walls and ceilings as their guide as to the reality of the room. The sweeping hose stream blows out a window with its force. Now the superheated gases mushrooming on the ceiling light up as the heated fuel meets the oxygen it needs. The expanding flames exit the window; it's over your head and all around with the nozzle. The steam produced forces them lower to the floor. The temperature is up to 212 degrees; this is a wet blistering heat that scalds unprotected skin. The nozzle man directs the powerful hose stream across the room where he hears a second window break out, improving ventilation. The heat is still intense. It's grin and bear it and one Our Father and "I pass through the valley of death, I know no evil," mumbled by rote.

Cooler, lighter air is drawn in the back of the engine company as the heat and smoke are blown out the windows and up and out the vented roof. On the roof, firemen have started a roof-rope rescue. A woman with two small children is trapped at a shaft window on the third floor. The first fireman is lowered, and he takes the two kids and is lowered to the bottom of the closed shaft. Time is running out for the woman as the flat she's in starts to light up. The second fireman on the roof snaps his safety harness to the rescue rope and rappels into the shaft and snatches the woman from her window as the room behind her lights up. In the safety at the bottom of the shaft, she embraces her two children.

Outside, the color of the smoke is changing from black to gray and then to white. The firefight is nearing an end, but the search is on for hidden pockets of smoldering embers and unconscious tenants. Luckily, this time there aren't any, only burnt offerings. But all this is not news in the big town; the chopper peels off for a look at the bridge traffic. It is so common it is a nonnews story; it happens thousands of times per year to these same units. Oh, there will be entries in the fire journals that will be stored in a dusty firehouse attic and only dimly remembered by those who fought the battle as time blends one fire into another.

Still, there is a story here to be told. One of uncommon valor, dedication, and satisfaction of a job well done at a time that is past and a day that is yet to come. This is a story of the men of the New York City Fire Department. This story focuses on a small band of roughnecks who helped to turn the tide on the most hellish period in the history of the New York City Fire Department, now referred to as the war years by all who follow the fire bell. These are the men of the Twelfth Battalion and Harlem's Tower Ladder 14.

This is their story. The time is 1970, one year after the Martin Luther King riots. Your scribe was there.

CHAPTER 2

THE OVERHAUL

THE SMOKE AND the heat hung about five feet off the floor like a surreal steam room from hell. The morning sunrays were entering the room through a broken windowpane, reflecting through the smoke and tiny dust particles that floated through the heavy air. The room smelled like a burnt garbage pit; the walls were stained black from the ceiling to three feet above the floor. From there on down, it was a dirty wet gray in what was once a living room used as a part-time bedroom for a boarder.

The point of origin of the fire was clearly defined by a black V-burn pattern working its way up from the couch that subbed as a bed at night. One fireman was wetting burnt stuff down as the other two were throwing it out the window. Another was pulling down the lath and plaster ceilings with a six-foot wooden handle with a steel hook at the other end, looking for hidden fire at the point where the steam pipe entered the ceiling in a corner of the room. A fourth fireman was trimming a burnt window frame down to bare red brick in a methodical manner. New window frames and windows could be reset by carpenters this evening, the room sheet rocked, taped, and painted by the end of the week. This flat was an investment that had served its different owners from 1910 and would be put back in service quickly. Any delay and squatters would move in and use it as a base of operation to burglarize the rest of the apartments in the daytime as the tenants went to work. The fire department had saved the old building one more time.

After conflagrations in New York, Chicago, Boston, and Baltimore at the turn of the century, building standards of the cities were adjusted so that buildings were able to withstand the destruction of fire for a longer period of time, giving the fire department more time to put out the fire inside before it spread to neighboring buildings. The structural integrity was improved starting at the apartment door with a steel covering on the wooden construction and self-closing to keep the smoke and heat from entering the public hallway. Steel staircases replaced wood, and a bulkhead door was added to the roof to aid the fire department in ventilating the public hallway. If a fire could be stopped at an apartment door, tenants could then leave by using the stairs as an escape route, and the fire department utilized them to attack the fire. These old tenements continued to serve each new wave of immigrants as each generation moved up the social ladder and the vacancies were filled by the next group, who added in turn to the melting pot that New York City was famous for. However, building construction had started to go the other way after World War II as the population moved outside the city limits and away from its building codes. Homes were built with unprotected wood that was easier to work with and cheaper.

Chief Walsh popped into the room.

"How's it look, boys?"

"I think we've got it, Chief," said Captain McLaughlin, "but I'll check the floor above one more time before we take off."

"Good, give it a good bath and take up," said the chief. "I'm heading back to quarters, my relief is in and that will give me a shot at last night's paperwork."

The chief stopped to watch Tully trim the window frame. He thought to himself about asking Tully about his roof-rope rescue, but there wasn't really that much time. Tully was lost in his work. His coat was off; he was wearing a heavy duck shirt, no undershirt. He was wet through to the skin. Steam raised from his muscular body and trim waist. He reminded the chief of a truck horse in harness on a cold winter morning doing its work without complaint, driven hard and put up wet. Would the next generation of firemen be as good? Only time would tell. He was a craftsman, that was for sure, and he was now showing the new man the trade.

The chief turned and headed down the stairs, dodging debris and skipping over hose lines that snaked their way out of the building. This fire would not be investigated; it was too routine, the loss of dollars too small, and the fire marshals too few and their workload too heavy. In the room of origin, the firemen's faces were unintentionally camouflaged by black soot and gray plaster dust for a finishing touch. Were they young or were they old was undistinguishable, but they were wet and tired after fifteen hours, all spent in the saddle.

Smithy cleared his nose in an archaic manner, by placing one finger on one side of his nostril and blowing out the other, aiming out the window. He was quite proud of his ability to place his shots and in the production of his sinus cavities.

This feat was only possible after a particularly snotty fire; hence the term *snotty job* was quite literal. The life of a fireman had the ability to corrupt genteel behaviors that had been groomed over a lifetime by well-bred mothers and wives. Dirt was a mark of valor that separated the shining knight of fiction and the ragged monks of the poor. The ghetto firefighter.

"Romeo, we need to talk up a new color TV for the firehouse," said Smithy. "I went over to my sister's the other night, the brother-in-law got one. It looks great, real color."

"No kidding. That meathead got a color TV? What did you see?" asked Romeo.

"The Mets game, and it was a duzie, the grass was so green," Smithy said as he threw a burnt cushion out the window as the conversation continued. "You know, I've got to give him credit, he's really making something out of himself. He started to do the books for bars and grills, and now he's worked his way up to appliance stores, and he does them on location, carries an adding machine with him, and they love this for some reason."

"Will you two beauties get that crap out the window so we can get the hell out of here by nine o'clock," said Skitter from Engine 35, holding the controlling nozzle.

"Anyhow, as I was saying before I was so rudely interrupted by the runt," said Smithy, "he, the brother-in-law, can get us a break on a new color TV from one of his accounts if we can just get that cheap bastard torch to spring for some of the money out of the commissary."

"There's a fat chance of that, he's tight as a crab's ass, and that's watertight," said Romeo.

"Well, I've got a plan. All we've got to do is be civil and, in a reasonable manner, put a case together."

"And then, of course, he'll say no," said Romeo.

"Yeah, and that's when we call him a cheap Scottish dick."

"You know, Smithy, that just might work. He seems to be overly sensitive about being Scottish for some reason."

"Yeah, but we need a two-prong attack, so we also bring up the fact that they love to wear dresses and all."

"That'll get him," said Romeo, shaking his head.

"Anyhow, he quits, as planned," continues Smithy. "Hence, I take over, we get the money, and we purchase a beautiful discounted color TV for the brothers, and we're all happy."

"Yeah, but how about Burns?" said Romeo.

"No problem," answered Smithy. "We get Ducky to cook up some boiled crap, and we call it a Scottish festival, we sing 'Bonny Lass' a few times, and we'll let the poor sucker take the commissary back minus its money."

"Will you two morons throw the last of that crap out the window," said the engine officer Sanchez.

"Why is it necessary for you to call us names that you know in your heart have no truth or basis?" retorted Smithy.

"You know, Smithy," continued the engine officer, "you were transferred to 14 from 1 Truck. You were touted as a great catch for the battalion, an army ranger officer, a Bennett medal winner, and a college education, but you're not showing the leadership we expected and hoped for, but the reverse."

Smithy thought and threw a burnt article out the window before replying. "When I came up here, Lieutenant, no one spoke to me for one month. I went to see Captain Mac about transferring back to 1 Truck with this concern, and he said to me, 'Don't worry about it, laddie. After a while, you'll pick up some dirty, filthy habits, and you'll fit right in with this bunch. They're just slow to warm to you because of your refinements.' And he was so right. When in Rome, do like the Romans." Skitter, from the engine company, gave him a Bronx cheer from the rear of the room.

"That's the last of it," said Captain Mac, coming back into the room from the public hallway. "Let's back out, men, and let the engine men wash it down," he said as he turned and headed down the stairs. Smithy continued with his chatter since it met with a degree of agitation from the engine. "If we could just get the engine to move in a little faster and do their water thing, we wouldn't be detained from our other important activities. This city is in danger every minute the tower ladder is out of position, and our important services are needed, but these little munchkins are so cute it's hard not to love them," said Smithy, and he blew them a kiss as he walked toward the door and passed Skitter with the nozzle. Skitter started the water before they cleared the door, hitting the ceiling overhead and drenching Smithy and Romeo before they got out the door.

"Sorry about that, don't let the door hit you in the ass, you big hairy burley truckies," says Skitter.

It only took a few minutes to wet down the room, driving the water into the places that fire could hide and preventing a rekindle later on.

"OK, Skitter, shut down and let's take the line up," said the engine officer.

The engine company went about their work and broke the hose down in the street first so the water would empty there at the lowest point and outside the building. They began to work and repack the hose on the pumper and talked at the same time.

"Hey, Skitter," asked Marty, "are you riding home with Tully and Smithy today?"

"With Smithy. Tully is going to his mother-in-law," Skitter said, folding the hose in the hose bed.

"I bet you'll hear an earful on the roof-rope rescue."

"No, I wouldn't bet on it. Most of the time, they don't say anything about rescues."

"Really," said Lieutenant Sanchez.

"You know, what Smithy said is the truth in a way," said Skitter. "He did change to fit in. He is quiet, and so is Tully, that's why they really like each other."

"Skitter, what are you saying, Smithy never shuts up."

"OK, OK, he bats his lips a lot, but he's never really saying anything about himself."

"Skitter, you're deep. You're riding with those guys too much, son," said Lieutenant Sanchez.

CHAPTER 3

THE CHIEF'S PAPERWORK

BILL WALSH LOOKED up from the old manual typewriter at the clock on the chief's office wall. It was 1030 hours; it was time to head out to Brooklyn. From 125th Street in Harlem, it could take forty-five minutes or more to get there, even on a Saturday. The occasion was a retirement party for the assistant chief of Brooklyn, Matty Cortland, a legendary good guy who had been a grunt for twenty years before taking any test for promotion and then went to deputy chief in ten year's time.

Now that he was retiring as assistant chief, there were some who were saying, if only he had started to get into the books earlier, he would have made chief of department easily. This was probably true, but twenty years of carrying the tools and doing the job had made him a fireman's fireman whom all officers worth their salt relied on and turned to when the going gets tough to hold the units together and come up with the insight that only experience produces. For Matty Cortland, his twenty years were not spent in vegetation but in incubation for what he would become – a great leader. He had passed on his experience to all who showed any interest. Bill Walsh had been lucky to have served under him when Cortland was a captain, battalion chief, and deputy chief. He was Bill's model, despite the fact that he was a proby fireman under Lieutenant Mann who was now chief of department of New York City. The difference was Matty had what might be termed *sweet power*, the mystifying ability to give orders that men would follow to their death if need be. Napoleon, Grant, Patten all had it, field commanders who led their troops into battle only asking their men to do what they would have done in similar situations that had worked safely in the past. Matty's judgment was gold; he had never lost a man in a fire. Now, sadly, Matty was leaving, and with his departure would go his counsel, and there was the loss that could not be measured in a manpower slot. The Matty Cortlands of the job did more than put out fires; they passed on the torch, the knowledge, which illuminates the way long after they have gone.

The chief took a notebook out of his shirt pocket. Captain McLaughlin would make out the meritorious report for Tully's and Smithy's roof-rope rescue. He began to type on a plain sheet of paper some of the facts from the notebook before he misplaced them.

> Box 1532
> Time: 0410 transmitted
> Second alarm: 0420
>
> Ladder 30 was first to report trapped occupants in shaft on third floor of a five-story building. Tower Ladder 14 took roof rope to the roof in their bucket. The rope was tied with department knots per department evolution on fireman Smithy who was lowered into the shaft. Fireman Tully had on the safety harness and controlled his descent into the shaft, Ladder 30 assisting. The woman gave Smithy the children, and he was lowered to the bottom of the shaft, then the rope was secured to a chimney on the roof, and fireman Tully went into the shaft single-sliding with the safety harness. He retrieved the woman from the windowsill and rappelled with her to the bottom of the shaft.

The chief sat back in his chair again. He would recommend a class 1 for each man. The roof-rope was a cut-and-dried class 1 award. The fireman exhibited competence and bravery, enabling him to save an endangered life above the fire, with normal escape cut off by the fire, without the aid of a mask or hose line. In this case, they saved three lives. Both men had other rescues before coming to Ladder 14 but had been overlooked in the past. As of late, because bucket rescues were so common, they were now not being considered unless the firemen went into the fire. Tully had found two old people above the fire by the direction of the crowd in the street. It was a very smoky fire, and he found the couple on the fifth floor. He was not cited for the rescue by the covering officer, but the chief had spoken to him later about the rescue, and Tully had said, "OK, forget it, that grab was a thrill. The crowd cheered when I pulled those two old folks out of the smoke." *It all works out in the end,* thought the chief. Perhaps unnoticed acts were the only ones that would be accredited by Saint Peter at the pearly gates.

The department phone rang and brought Bill back to the present. "Twelfth Battalion, Chief Walsh speaking."

"Chief, I'm glad I got you, this is Arty Cummins, Ladder 105."

"Yes, of course, Arty. I was going over a fire report, and I guess I started to daydream of the fires of old," said Chief Walsh.

"Tell me about it," said Arty. "It's an occupational hazard. I'm starting to feel that I only occasionally have flashbacks back to reality once or twice a day. I just called your home, Chief, and Margaret told me you weren't coming home today, you were going to the party this afternoon from the firehouse."

"Yes, Arty," said Bill. "What can I do you out of?"

"Well, Chief, I've got a favor to ask. I've got this fireman high on the lieutenant's promotion list, name's Tom Burke. He'll be sitting at our table tonight."

"Yes, Arty, what can I do?"

"Well, I see your driver just got promoted, this kid's got twelve years on the job, he's been in my group the last four years. Well, I was wondering, you needing a driver and all."

"Arty, you've sold me. Let's talk about it at the racket."

"Great, Chief, you're at our table, Ladder 105, see you there."

Bill replaced the receiver and reached for the motto on his desk. "I only pass this way once. If there's any good I can do, let me do it now." It was good to see Arty turning into a do-gooder too. Bill started to laugh to himself. The sanctity of the deserted old firehouse was jolted back to life as Ladder 14 and its crew were returning. It had been a busy morning with two fires. They rolled open the steel front doors and the tower ladder backed into a long single bay where one type or another aerial ladder had served Harlem for over one hundred years, followed by the Twelfth Battalion chief's car.

Chief Walsh knew he was going to have to put himself into high gear if he was going to get to Brooklyn on time. It was now eleven ten; he wouldn't have time to talk to Chief Galvan about the report they were putting together on manpower. But Joe would understand. He had wanted to go himself to the party but could not get a change of tours.

Bill was already duded up with tan slacks and a blue oxford shirt and blue necktie. He donned his Irish brown tweed jacket and checked out the look in the mirror. It was becoming frightening how much he was looking like the old coach and less like the star college athlete he once was. Bill turned away to the office door, collected his stuff bag, reached for a twelve-inch threaded pipe capped on each end; it had the look of a pipe bomb. He picked it up like it was a dumbbell and started out the door, across the second-floor bunkroom, and down the spiral staircase, heading to the front apparatus door. Chief Galvan and Lieutenant Crimi were having a conversation.

"Bill, what you got there, an Irish walking stick?"

"This, gentleman, is a Sullivan tool used to ventilate windows from the roof. It contains a sash chain fifteen feet long. It's activated by unscrewing the red cap and throwing the pipe over the side of the roof while holding on to the cap. This action enables the operator to guide the pipe through the window ten feet below and execute ventilation."

"I think you missed your calling, Bill. You would have made a great potato-slicer salesman," said Chief Galvan.

"Yeah, it sounds like fly-fishing with a blackjack," said Lieutenant Crimi. Bill was quite pleased they liked his imitation.

"Well, I've got to blast off, firefighters, I'm heading over to Brooklyn," said Chief Walsh.

"Gee, they've still got some buildings standing over there they haven't burnt down yet?"

"Yeah, there're fine, they finally got it right after I left, Lieutenant. By the way, on the next day tour, I'd like for you to demonstrate to the men an oil change blindfolded," joked Chief Walsh.

"These guys from the Bronx are still talking about the cruelty you perpetrated on your subordinates," replied the lieutenant.

"Yeah, that's why they gave him a car when he had to leave," said Chief Galvan.

"Oh god," said Bill, "let's not bring all that up again."

Lieutenant Crimi patted Chief Bill on the shoulder. "I hope this doesn't mess up my chances to get invited to your training seminar."

"I'm leaving while I'm still technically ahead," said Chief Bill.

All three men were smiling as the chief exited.

As the chief started to make his way across 125th Street, he spied a pair of junkies. They broke their forward cadence and started to size him up. He was now standing on the center white line in the middle of the street, waiting for one more car to pass him before he made a break for his parked car. He brought the steel pipe up to the side of his head to scratch an imaginary itch. The junkies, seeing the pipe, started on their way again; this didn't look like a fair fight.

The drive to the Brooklyn banquet hall was without event. Brooklyn, then advertised as the third largest city in America with a population well over two million, just behind Chicago, was not unlike the rest of New York City. It was made up of small towns and villages that had grown together in a seamless manner, but at a closer look, they had their own identity, like Flatbush – past home of the Brooklyn Dodgers – Bensonhurst, Bedford-Stuyvesant, and "likewise," as they would say in Brooklynese. There were tight units within each town known as the neighborhoods or home turf defined by churches, synagogues, and playgrounds, with hangouts like Pop Ratner's Candy Store, the Heidelberg Bar & Grill, Mario's Pizzeria, and Kelly's Pub, all places Bill Walsh spent his growing-up years. This is where life's business was conducted, the stage and setting for adventure, folly and grand notions. The Shalimar Banquet Hall was set on the site of a block fire a generation ago. It was only fitting that the fire department patronized the hall for all their parties, paying homage to the fire gods for supplying them with a fitting background for their endless stories of nozzle men's valor and truckmen's grit.

Bill parked in the lot that was normally serviced by valets, but this courtesy was dispensed with when firemen or cops held any rackets at the hall. The parking lot would become a war zone; driving violations of the family chariot were prosecuted with knuckle sandwiches and other acts of carnage.

CHAPTER 4

BACK TO FIRE DEPARTMENT PARTY

CHIEF WALSH MADE his way into the hall and headed to the bar; he was spotted by Capt. Arty Cummins, commander of Ladder 105.

"Good to see you, Chief," said Arty. "Let's grab a cold one, I feel some parchment setting in. Barkeep, two Shafers," requested Arty.

It was an open bar, so both men put a buck in the bartender's tip glass to start the night in good faith.

"You know, Chief, I remember the first time that we inspected the Shafer Brewery and the engineer took us down to the taproom to sample the Brewer's Gold. Boy, can anything match that, I mean you just grabbed a cup and sampled away."

"Yeah, them was the good old days," said the chief. "You know, Arty, tell me about this driver before we get interrupted."

"Sure, Chief, thanks for keeping me on track. Well, this Tom Burke is a levelheaded kid, I think we did a good job with him. I was remembering back to when I got the spot as a lieutenant in 26 Truck myself. I don't mind telling you, I was over my head, I started to ask the chief driver questions at fires, and I got some good answers. I started to think that this should be an in-between position to learn this job. One day you're riding the back step, the next day you're responsible for six guys' lives and God knows what else."

"Don't get me wrong, Arty," answered the chief. "It doesn't get any easier higher up the ladder. A chief would like to ask a veteran chief's driver a question or two at the big one and not get a blank stare, so I'll tell you what, I need someone because no one wants to do it at Ladder 14. I prefer a ladderman with experience in moving around at the fire to find the fire, so let's see what I can do."

"Thanks, Chief, let's get a plate of chow and sit down at our table," said Arty.

The chief of department, John L. Mann, also made an appearance. He was also a Brooklyn fireman and a friend of Chief Walsh starting his career in Ladder 105. He sat down for a drink at the table and started telling them about Chief Walsh being one of the greats on the NYU basketball team and city champs. Chief Walsh changed the topic fast to where John was a lieutenant and Bill was a young fireman just breaking in. He spoke about being told to hold on to his coattails as they crawled down a long hallway to rescue a mother and two children in a rear bedroom on the third floor of a row of wooden-frame houses.

"What must have happened," said Bill, "was they went to the apartment front door and found heavy smoke in the public hallway. It was too hot for them, so she headed the two children to the back room, which was serviced by the rear fire escape. She heroically got them to the back window in an apartment rapidly filling with smoke and opened it, only to be hit by a blast of superheated air from the fire that was burning out of control on the floor below. She passed out, but first she put her children underneath her and shut the window. Like a mother hen protecting her chicks, she folded over them. When Lieutenant Mann located this bundle of humanity, he realized they were unconscious and needed fresh air as quickly as possible. Being on the floor above the fire meant there was a possibility that this apartment could light up at any time. There would be no second chance to come back and find anyone alive. The floor was red hot, our knees were burning. He passed me the two children. He said, 'There are two of them.' I couldn't see diddley for the smoke was so thick. 'What'll I do with my tools?' I asked. 'Leave them, get out fast.' I could just hear the lieutenant's voice through the heavy smoke, and he was only inches from his face, the smoke was that thick."

Chief Walsh looked up; all parties were focused on him. He realized he was sweating and the crowd had gathered around the table to hear the tale of how the Brooklyn fire medal was won.

"Jesus, Billy, get the hell out before this friggin' place lights up," said now chief of department John Mann.

Like a punch line that breaks the tension of a joke, his timing was perfect and started the table roaring, and Bill Walsh was surprisingly relieved. He wasn't just telling a story; he was reliving it, and he let out a sigh of relief.

The assistant chief of the borough of Queens, Patrick Hopkins, who was sitting next to Bill, patted him on the back. "You had us all gasping for air with your story. I remember it well. I was the engine officer on the fire floor. It was reported there were trapped people on the floor above. You forced the fire door for us on the fire floor, Bill, before you went to the floor above. The chief there" – nodding in the direction of Chief Mann – "said to me, 'Patty, we're going to try to make the floor above, hold the fire at this door.'"

"Then you said," interrupted Chief Mann, "'Hold it your ass, trucky, we'll take this flat like Grant took Richmond as soon as we get water,' and that's what you did."

"I believe that is the way it did happen, you're still as sharp as a tack." John Mann saluted Pat Hopkins.

It was one of those rare moments when all the characters to a well-known story were all present, telling the story of the block fire that leveled the very ground where they were now sitting. The firefighters around the table were smiling and laughing but also reflecting on their part in the story, but they wouldn't have time to tell it until another day, as the master of ceremony spoke. "Ladies and gentlemen," he said into the reverberating hum of the loudspeaker, "our chief of department will say a few words."

As the chief got up to make his way to the podium, most of those in attendance got up to applaud. He stopped and put his hand on Chief Bill Walsh's shoulder as he passed.

"Chief, could I see you before you leave?" asked Bill.

"Sure," said the chief. He trotted up to the front of the room, still in shape at fifty-eight. Before joining the department, he served in the army as a paratrooper and as a rescue officer with Rescue 3. He had written number one on the chief of department's test, but the political system had a choice of the top three, and it wasn't him they wanted. Though John L. Mann wasn't a politician, he had friends in the governor's office and who were also Brooklyn Irish Catholics from Our Lady of Sorrows. They recommended a counselor who advised the city that they would sue the city if John L. was not appointed head of department. There was a hasty reorganization; a new office – the department of personnel – was created within the department. The mayor appointed Chief Walter Berger, a bean counter, to head and control the purse strings and the staffing and transfers of the department. The chief of department would run the fire operations only. Chief Mann received full support from the Uniformed Fire Officers Association and the Uniformed Firefighters Association for continuation of the old system of civil service tests as the final rung to the top position. Chief Mann had reclaimed some of the power but not all.

The increase in fire activities had helped Chief Mann. This is what he did best, command the troops. The super pumper and tower, which seemed like overkill when ordered, turned out to satisfy the mayor and the press that something was being done about the new fire mania. That was two years ago now. The bloodletting was creating an ulcer on both sides. The new chief was holding his own by the sheer force of his personality, for now anyway.

The chief was now behind the podium, and he removed some three-by-five cards from his inside pocket that contained his prepared remarks. "If I could pick one man for the future firefighters to emulate, it would be Chief Matty Cortland," said the chief of department in his best master-of-ceremony voice. He then turned in the direction of the retiring chief and his family, bringing his hands up in front of him and paused. This gesture brought all the firefighters to their feet, and there was the usual whistles and stomping of feet. There was a good turnout of wives and girlfriends in the audience. There were no females in the department at this time. The men all wore a suit and tie, and the women wore the typical 1970s style of dress.

"Ladies and gentlemen and distinguished guests," continued the chief as the crowd started to sit back down, "I could tell you of his firefighting prowess, and if I did, it would go on all night and still would not completely cover it. I would like to share what Chief Mac's advice was to me when I was breaking in. Take care of the job, and the job will take care of you." This received a polite applause. The chief rearranged his three-by-five cards and went to the meat of the speech. "It's spring, but we have already prepared for next winter. Last year broke all records for the number of fires and multiple alarms we responded to. This was an excellent test for the super pumper and its three satellite hose wagons with three-thousand-gallons-per-minute turret nozzles. The two tower ladders in Manhattan had done an outstanding job."

"Why Manhattan?" came a rumbling from the troops.

The chief's hands were up. "More are on the way."

"They had to be tried out in slow camps first," said a fireman in a stage whisper. This got a chuckle from most.

"There will be a new tower ladder in Brooklyn this winter," continued the chief.

This brought the partisan gang back to cheering.

The chief decided to quit while he was ahead. "I would like to end with a silent prayer for our fallen brothers who passed away this year." Then the chief broke the moment of silence with "May the wind always be at your back, may the road rise to meet you, may you safely be inside the pearly gates and away from the dreaded fires and nestled at the bosom of your mother ten minutes before Saint Peter, the gatekeeper, finds your name on the list of the dearly departed. Amen." This brought back the cheers, and the chief came off the stage at a fast trot and headed for the door.

Bill Walsh was up and behind him by the time he reached the front door and entered the parking lot. The chief's car and driver was at the curb, motor running.

"Chief, could I have a minute?" asked Bill.

"Yes. Yes, yes, Bill, please get in. You remember Howard Parker?" said the chief.

"Oh, yes. How are you, Howard?"

"Well, fine, thanks to our old lieutenant here!"

"How's your wife?" asked Bill.

"Betty passed away, Bill."

"Oh my god, I didn't know." Bill leaned forward in the seat.

"We had four children," said Howard, "and I couldn't work in the firehouse anymore and leave them home alone, so the good chief here asked me to drive him."

Bill Walsh put his hand on the black firefighter's shoulder before sitting back in his seat.

"Bill, what is it that you want to talk about? Howard, please drive around the block and park," said the chief.

"Yes, sir, boss, you've got it," answered Howard.

John Mann reached for the handle on the cabinet built into the back of the front seat that opened a small but nicely stocked bar. "Drink, Bill?" asked the chief.

"No thanks, Chief. I've got a long drive home."

"Good man, Bill. I've got to watch my drinking, high blood pressure. It helped kill my old man."

"He was always really nice to me," added Bill. "I was sorry hearing of his passing. I would stop at the old firehouse and he'd put me to work. He even gave me things from time to time."

"Like what?" asked John in bewilderment.

"Well, he gave me one of your old coats you got too big for."

"Jesus!" exclaimed John Mann. "You know, he could be as hard as nails, but he was one of the sweetest guys at times, wasn't he?"

"He's got my vote. He was always proud of you, John, and he'd be especially proud of you now," added Bill. John looked like he might have a bit of water in his eye as he pulled a blue bandanna from his coat pocket.

"Shoot, Bill, what do you need?" said Chief Mann, blowing his nose.

"I'd like Tom Burke transferred from Ladder 105 to the Twelfth Battalion to be my driver," said Bill.

"Is that all?" said John Mann. "I thought you were going to ask to go to the North Bronx battalion that is going to open up in two months." The chief stopped talking and took a sip of his drink – a Canadian rye and ginger ale. "There have been five requests for that berth tonight," the chief continued. "It's not like these requests are coming from slackers, far from it. It's just that the workload is exceeding a good man's ability to stay with it. Here's a card with my secretary's phone number. If you want something, call. If there's something you think I need to know, call her and she will get the message to me," said the chief. "How's the tower ladder working out in Fourteen?" continued the chief.

"It's an outstanding piece of equipment and getting special calls to the Bronx and Queens regularly," said Walsh.

"Yes, I know, Bill," said Chief Mann, "but how does it function, and how do the people interact with it?" Bill sat up in his seat and realized that the chief was intensely interested in his answer.

"The people are very good, and a few are excellent," said Bill.

"I'm glad to hear you say that," said John.

Bill continued, "The tower ladder can do many things. There's a tendency to overuse it."

"How you mean?" asked Mann.

"Well, there's a case where fireman Tully – "

"He's the one that's a volunteer," said Chief Mann.

"Yes, I think he is," replied Bill. Bill was surprised that Chief Mann knew Tully at all, no less that he was a volunteer. This was a department of ten thousand men. He made a mental note to talk to Tully about this. Bill continued with his story. "Well, there was a good fire going in the rear of a five-story tenement. There was a man on the third floor trying to come out the window. He was distraught, and a second man was keeping him from jumping. The building was isolated, there was only light smoke in the front. The outside vent man and the roof man were in the bucket. I radioed the bucket to get the man in the window – "

"Seems obvious, life before property," interrupted the chief.

"Well, Tully didn't do it. He dropped off the roof man first and then came down and got the jumper guy. Well, it turned out that the guy tries to jump out of the bucket, only Tully brought it down so fast he takes the guy's breath away. Anyway, long story short, I talked to him back at the firehouse, and he said, 'Chief, your order would have been the easiest of the two actions, if I grab the guy as ordered, it's a rescue. But this guy is a jumper, there's no fire in back of him. If this guy is already coming out the front third-floor window, what's it like in the rear on the fourth and fifth floors, that's where the fire is. My job,' said Tully, 'is to get the roof open, this will do the greatest good for both the rescuer and the firefighter. If he had been on the ledge of the window, it would've been a different story. Plus, I was already past him and was extending for the roof – '"

"So?" asked Chief Mann. "Did he get written up for a rescue or charges?"

"Neither," answered Bill Walsh. "Well, in the old days, that would have been a medal, but with the tower ladder, it's becoming common, it's no longer a rescue. So I guess I'm saying it's a good piece of equipment that takes a good bit of judgment to use correctly if it's going to be assigned to a regular truck company. A chief needs to be careful not to reassign the truck position by his orders and put the truck out of position to perform tasks like venting the roof."

"That story gives me food for thought," said Chief Mann. "So how about yourself? How's Harlem treating you?"

"No complaints," answered Chief Walsh, "but I'd like to point out Ladder 14 had four runs the other night – "

"Well, that doesn't sound like a problem," interrupted Chief Mann.

"No, but the four alarms were two-second alarms and a third and an all-hands fifteen hours of fire work – they had no supper and never returned to quarters all night."

"Well, that's a night's work, all right," said Chief Mann.

"In two night tours, they had twenty-five hours of fire duty at structural fires, all occupied," continued Bill Walsh.

"You're saying that they're overworked?" asked Chief Mann. "Why, the South Bronx companies are doing thirty runs a night."

Bill Walsh stopped to get the right tone before he answered. "When I worked at the Twenty-seventh Battalion in the Big House in the South Bronx, my problem came about from too much work. Work needs to be defined by hours worked. The South Bronx false alarms are work, and fireman Carr paid with his life responding to one when he fell from the back step of 82 Engine. What I'm saying is, I'm responsible for the men in my command, and from the look of them, yes, they are overworked," answered Walsh.

"Now listen, Bill," replied Chief Mann, a little red in the face. "I'm between a rock and a hard place with these tower ladders, there's only two of them, and they're covering all of New York City. I have nothing to take their place. They need to be ready to go twenty-four hours a day, and that's it. Could you cut the men some slack?" asked Mann.

"They're already as loose as a one-hinged door now," answered Bill.

"How about cross-training other companies in the tower ladder operation and using fresh people to replace Ladder 14 on a bad night tour? Bill, I need you to work on this with some creativity. We have more towers on order, and I hope to have five in service by this time next year. Fourteen's got to hold out. Help is on the way!" said Chief Mann who wanted to change the subject.

He gestured with his hand as he remembered something. "I was at a conference a few weeks ago, it was a special meeting of urban chiefs. A special agent of the FBI briefed us on what they believe will be more civil unrest in the inner cities in the near future. After the King and the Kennedy assassinations, J. Edgar Hoover thinks there's a commies behind every tree looking to tear the fabric of our country apart. He may be right, who knows, if you see anything, let me know fast! And, Bill, this is important, it's your duty to keep the men of your battalion performing at the highest level. A lot depends on the success of the tower ladders to reduce manpower at alarms. The old days of putting in another alarm at a fire is over. These are changing times, and we've got to change with them! And I intend to get tough, very tough about this."

Bill didn't reply, as he didn't know what to say. The chief had very skillfully upped the ante; the issue of the tower ladder was of the utmost importance for the whole city.

"I'll do my best, Chief. Chief, thank you again."

Bill opened the car door and turned back to bid both men good-bye as the black Buick pulled away. The car had only a small Maltese cross to identify it as the official car of the New York City Fire Department – Car 5.

CHAPTER 5

BILL FACES HIS PAST

B ILL WALKED THE three blocks back to the banquet hall. He didn't envy Chief Mann's position. There were no answers to the fire workload dilemma. It was what it was. There was little chance that manpower was going to increase with the city's finances the way they were – things were uneasy in the streets since the Martin Luther King riots. More radical groups like the Mow Mows and Black Panthers had come out of the closet in Harlem, and they were more than a little scary – with sandbags and gunport windows in their brownstone headquarters. The Black Muslims were also becoming a force. While these groups were militant and at times dangerous, they were against drugs and for family, and this, in Bill's opinion, is where the real problem was. Less than a month before he had responded to an emergency for an eight-year-old boy for a heroin overdose, he was sitting on the john in a public toilet in the hallway with a shoelace tied around his arm – he was DOA at Harlem Hospital. Bill was unable to erase this picture from his mind.

His own life as a boy had not been all that easy, but this was not a life at all, this was hell! Bill found himself shaking his head and talking to himself again. He said to himself out loud, "This has got to stop!"

Turning his mind to something upbeat, he looked at Chief Mann's card, still in his hand; he was happy to have the secretary's phone number. He put it in a safe place in his wallet; it was good to know the chief personally. He had helped him out of a predicament in the Bronx, and then he was asked to take over the Twelfth Battalion – this was like jumping from the frying pan into the fire. The only important difference was, now he was in charge. He also knew not to get on Chief Mann's wrong side, which the Bronx chief had done, who Bill had a major falling-out with; only Chief Mann took Bill Walsh's side. This also was overrotating men so they could go back to quarters, wash up, and have a meal. There was no provision in the regulations for this at the time.

Walsh walked through the parking lot. Some people were leaving; it was 3:00 PM. *Smart move,* he thought to himself. He had seen a lot of old faces he was happy to see, and a few he didn't mind missing either. He entered the overdone lobby of the Shalimar Banquet Hall, decorated in early gangster, lots of red and mirrors. Bill realized he needed to hit the head, which was located close to the bar. The men's room smelled surprisingly sweet. Maybe too sweet.

Jimmy Callahan was the first person he recognized as he entered the restroom. Callahan was waiting for an open position at a urinal. Callahan was a writer for the *New York Mirror*, a morning daily. The paper was owned by Walter Winchell; he was a national syndicated writer and radio commentator. Jimmy had received a number of awards for his journalistic endeavors. Some said he was following in the footsteps of Damon Runyon, whose characterization of real gangsters sprinkled his column and were the talk of the town in the days of prohibition and the speakeasy, when hoods supplied the people's need for an honest drink. Runyon is most remembered for his characters in the musical *Guys and Dolls*.

"Hi, Billy!" shouted Callahan. "Guess who I saw the other day, Sister Rita."

"Hey, Jimmy, talking about Sister Rita in the men's room is sacrilegious," winced Bill Walsh. Luckily, a position opened up at a urinal at the far end of the white tiled men's room, and Bill walked away.

"Hey, Red," said Jim Callahan in a voice loud enough for all to hear and, turning to the redheaded six footer standing next to him, said, "you're gonna love this story. Red, you remember Sister Rita? Well, Billy over there, holding his wanger, and me and Peter Bowgeo, you remember Bowgeo? Well, Sister decided to play handball with our heads off the blackboard because of some minor infraction. Well, anyhow, Sister sticks us in each corner of the room. You know, divide and conquer. I take the first beating, she hits me with rights and lefts." Jimmy is now dancing around the men's room, his head rocking to and fro, hair in his face, reliving his black day of infamy at Our Lady of Sorrows School. "She's got me backed into the ropes, so she darts away and sails into Pete Bowgeo. He puts up a brilliant defense, he tries to run away." The john is now filling up, and the bouncer storms in because he thinks there's a real fight going on, but screeches to a halt to hear the rest of the story. "Bowgeo's down for the count, folks. One, two, three. It was a right cross, sport fans, that nailed him. Nine, ten – he's out, ladies and gentlemen! But Sister saved the real dirty stuff for last. For Billy here, a real criminal type in his youth, she grabs the pointer, you know the long wooden thing. She got a bit fatigued delivering those right crosses. She's getting ready to do a real job on his cruller. But Billy, a poor sport, takes the pointer away from her, and she comes back with an underhand bolo punch, you know, the one she taught Kid Gavilán." Jimmy demonstrates. "But Billy here puts her in a hammerlock, and all the girls start crying, 'He's hurting Sister.'" Jimmy is now wiping tears of laughter from his cheeks. "She's coming within inches of killing me and poor Bowgeo, and now she's wielding her pointer like Zorro's sword, she's out to cut a cross on Billy's forehead. I can still see those little girls' faces and crying, 'He's hurting Sister.'"

The bouncer breaks in. "Jimmy, please, give this guy a break, you've got guys lined up outside to get in here, and they're going to wet their pants, and someone's going to have to clean it up, please!" pleaded the bouncer, sounding like an altar boy. He was still holding a roll of nickels in his right fist that added weight to his punches and a wad of chewing tobacco in his jaw that he'd spit in your eye just before he coldcocked you. "Please, come out to the bar and I'll buy both you hooligans a drink."

Jimmy put his arm around Bill, and they started out. "Bill, you never gave Sister a rematch?"

"No, I got thrown out of school, remember."

"Oh, that wasn't right, that wasn't fair, Billy, wasn't fair at all."

Jimmy picked the inside corner of the bar to park his 260 pounds that he carried on a five-foot-six-inch frame. He mounted the barstool as you would a beast of burden, bracing himself with his left hand just as a cowboy would on the saddle horn and swinging his meaty right leg over the stool, then lowering his weight onto it. The steel barstool groaned and flexed under his weight then steadied under its load. Jimmy let out a sigh of relief as the union had been consummated without mishap. He was now in position to watch the length of the bar and also to be seen by its inhabitants. The king and his court. Jimmy was a showman. Barnum had nothing on Jimmy! Bill took the outside stool with a lot less fanfare; his view was three shelves of whiskey bottles. "Shafer draft with a Seagram chaser," stated Jimmy, "and the same for my friend, the fire chief."

"The Shafer's good, but hold the chaser, I feel fine," reordered Bill.

"God, we took our lumps as kids, didn't we, Billy?" said Jimmy, downing the shot of Canadian whiskey. "But, you know, we all turned out pretty good, us kids from the old neighborhood – the governor, the fire chief, and you and me – and we're on our way up, all the way from Our Lady of Sorrows. Of course, you had a few extra hard knocks, that's for sure, Billy," added Jimmy.

"No comment, Jimmy, I've got this funny feeling anything I say could end up in the newspapers," said Bill as he sipped his glass of Shafer.

"Now you're hurting me, Billy, that hurts. You're still sore about the column I did on the fix at NYU, when you were playing in the basketball tournament."

"Jesus, Jimmy, would you keep it down, you sound like you're writing a lead for tomorrow's paper," said Bill, his face turning red and grimacing.

"Bill, that's more than twenty years ago. Look, everyone knows you didn't do anything wrong," said Jimmy, now whispering. "You were the highest scorer in the game, I was a cub reporter and in school myself."

"I talked to you off the record, Jimmy, and then you used the information."

"I was a kid, Billy, I wouldn't do that today. Honest!" Jimmy said. "Look, Billy, I'm glad we're talking about it, I am sorry, really sorry, and I owe you. If I can help you, just say the word, that's the God's truth. I was hoping to see you tonight, old friends need to see each other and talk." Just then the bartender came over to set up another round.

Bill spoke to break the silence, "Did you really see Sister Rita, Jimmy?"

"Yeah, I did, and she asked for you."

"I don't believe it, but thanks for saying it anyway." Both men gestured to touch their beer glasses.

"Bottoms up, pal," said Jimmy. Both men emptied their glasses for a second time.

"OK, Jimmy, let's just forget it," said Bill. "It was a long time ago!" He had a mellow smile on his face.

"That's a good guy," said Jimmy. "To err is human, to forgive divine."

"Yeah, well, just don't try and kiss me on the lips," wisecracked Bill.

"Now that's my old Billy Boy," said Jimmy Callahan. Bill Walsh gave Jimmy a pat on the back as he left the bar.

Bill Walsh was more than ready to call it a night; things start to get sloppy after dinner, and that's where this party was at. He said his farewells. "Tell Tom Burke to pack his bags and ship out to the Twelfth Battalion as the new driver for the battalion commander, Bill Walsh."

CHAPTER 6

REPORTING FOR DUTY

TOM BURKE SAT behind the wheel of a 1964 Volkswagen. He hailed from Levittown, Long Island; it was over fifty miles one way to work. He'd had been driving one and a half hours and was just reaching the approach to the Triboro Bridge. The time was 3:30 PM. The chief's drivers relieved an hour earlier than the regular shift change, which was at 6:00 PM, so he still had plenty of time. He felt a bit edgy; there would be a lot of things that would be new. Each firehouse had a different atmosphere, a personality all its own that was created by the senior firefighters and officers of the company. They introduced a new member into the company with dos and don'ts of behavior. These things weren't written down anywhere, but they were real; they would be learned by watching and listening. The rules weren't broken by new people for good reason: all men are not equal at a fire, experience has the upper hand. This is clearly illustrated at a fire when reasonable people are running out and firemen are running in. The difference is experience and training. The experience to survive in a hostile environment is only learned from being there. Your trial by fire can, of course, be learned alone, but your chances of being alive to pass it on are diminished.

At this point in time, no one had ever tried to tell about it in a book, so a wise man listened and watched but did what he was told. On the other hand, the job of fighting fires and the basic evolutions were standardized in New York City to a degree. However, it didn't start that way. At the turn of the century, New York City and Manhattan combined with the Brooklyn and Long Island City fire departments and became one department – the New York City Fire Department. The three departments, however, were always on a different page. Some things were small, like Brooklyn had a green-color apparatus, which was a small thing. A two-volume training manual was written by Chief Harrington in 1926 where he answered questions to official officers' tests given by New York City for promotion.

What-if-you-were-in-command-type questions.

Evolution for accomplishing given tasks were included and built on by future generations. The unwritten task operations of firemen in tenement truck companies could only be learned from experienced officers and firefighters in tenement companies. This Tom had done; he had been assigned to Ladder 105 located in Brooklyn where he learned from its members and his captain, Arty Cummins. He was now going to drive in Harlem. It was explained to him that the Twelfth Battalion was also a proving ground for new battalion chiefs, a place to get your ticket punched on the way up the career ladder. It had also become a custom, added by Chief Mann, to assign new battalion chiefs to headquarters to write a paper on different types of fire operations and then assign them to busy battalions to be tested in the field. Tom was getting in the loop early as a firefighter. He considered himself fortunate to have his captain thinking about him.

Tom pulled alongside the tollbooth and threw a quarter in the toll basket. He turned into the 125th Street exit ramp. There was a stoplight at Second Avenue and 125th Street, which was red. Tom brought his car to a halt behind two other cars. Three kids were washing windshields with a dirty cloth. The guy in the Ford in front was telling the younger one to "get the hell out of here!" When he got to Tom, he streaked the windshield, and Tom gave him a dime. He would be told later that there were two tolls to get into Harlem: one you paid to the toll man, the second you paid to the squeegee man, or the rag game. He drove across Second Avenue and onto 125th Street heading west, he crossed Third Avenue; the firehouse was located between Lexington and Park avenues. He passed the firehouse, which was on his left, traveling west, the next avenues were Park, Madison, then Fifth. The numbers after Fifth Avenue were West-10 West, 12 West, etc. This was referred to as the West Side, the dividing line being Fifth Avenue. This had been laid out to him by his captain of Ladder 105, who had been a lieutenant in Ladder 26.

"Look, Tom," he had said, "if you're going to drive the chief, you've got to know where you're going. This is not brain surgery. Here's a map of Manhattan, this is the Twelfth Battalion's response area. They go from 110th Street to 135th Street from the Hudson River west to the Harlem River on the East Side. Study it, I don't want the chief calling me up and telling me that you don't know your ass from your elbow."

"Thanks, Captain," Tom had said. "I won't let you down."

"Yeah, I'm afraid of that!" said the captain.

Tom had turned around after Twelfth Avenue and before the Hudson River and headed back east on 125th Street. It was 4:05 PM before he double-parked outside the firehouse and took his well-broken, inoriginal-leather fire helmet of twelve years, his discolored and frayed fire coat of four years, his two-year-old fire boots that needed to be replaced before inspection, and went inside. Fire gear didn't last long in busy companies. Only the symbol of the New York City Fire Department – the black leather helmet – could hold up to twenty years of fire duty and hopefully a retirement spot on the mantel.

Walking in the apparatus door, while the chief's car was in front, a Ford station wagon, he put his gear in the car. There was no one at the house watch desk, but Tower Ladder 14 was in as the big Mack truck with baker boom and bucket on the end stood in testimony. There were all kinds of laughter coming from the back room. Tom just waved and went up the spiral staircase, common to all firehouses built in the city in the late 1800s. On the second floor, he made his way through a row of cots on both sides of the room and then into the chief's office, which was located at the front of the old building. It received its light from three large front windows that overlooked 125th Street.

"Hi, Chief, I'm Chief Walsh's new driver, Tom Burke," he said.

Chief Galvan was looking out the window; he never turned around. He said, "Is that your Volkswagen double-parked out front?"

"Yes," said Tom.

"That meter maid is getting ready to write you a ticket."

"But I've got my card in the window," replied Tom.

"That and twenty-five cents will get you on the subway up here," continued the chief.

Tom ran out the door, turned right and turned and slid the pole, ran into the street, opened the driver's door, turned the key, and sped away with the meter maid screaming at him. She had started to write the ticket but didn't have all the plate numbers to complete it. Tom pulled around the corner and came back to the other side of the street. A guy was running across the street and introduced himself as Neil, saying, "Your chief was in the kitchen, we relieve that way. Take my spot, you're my relief."

"Thanks," said Tom as Neil got in his car and pulled out of the fire-zone parking space, then Tom pulled his car into the spot.

He got out of his car, crossed the street and into the building, and headed back upstairs to the second floor. The telegraph alarm started to ring. "One-four-five-nine, get out, 123rd Street and Lexington Avenue." Tom turned and headed back to the apparatus floor and jumped into the chief's car and started it. Chief Walsh got in the other door.

"Turn right, Tom, then right at the first corner, that's Lexington Avenue, then left into 123rd Street." The fire radio reported all units responding to Box 1459 Engine 35 reports working fire. "Tom, go to 122nd Street, turn left there, we'll go to Third Avenue and come back up 123rd Street. This will give the ladder a clear shot at the front of the building," instructed the chief.

"Sounds good to me," said Tom.

As the wagon pulled into the fire block, there was fire out of the second-floor windows in the front. The children were running and laughing and having fun – this was just another fire.

"Tom, tell Manhattan to fill out the box, but hold rescue at this time."

"Yes sir, Chief," said Tom.

Putting on his helmet and fire coat, he looked up at the fire, a blast of glass and steam and window shades came flying out of the window. *That's a good sign,* Tom said to himself. Ladder 43 had pulled in behind the chief's car, and there was room to pass. Ladder 14's driver had dropped the fire-escape ladder. Tom could tell it was the chauffer because he had on no fire boots, but street shoes, and just a Levi's jacket and a fire helmet. Two members of Ladder 43 went up the dropped ladder to the fire escape and the floor above the fire, broke out the windows, and went in. "Twelfth Battalion to aide," the portable radio said. "Tom, tell Manhattan we're using two engines and two trucks, a third engine standing fast, probably will hold," the chief said. Tom's responsibilities were to handle the radio communications and to relay the chief's orders to all incoming companies. Tenement truck companies self-deployed, their assignments were given to individuals at the start of the tour. There were basically three teams for the truck company: the first team was inside forced entry, search and ventilation from the inside; the second team was outside vent, vent as a ladder, vent as a team from the front or rear, or as individuals; and third was the roof team, vent the roof and, when possible, drop down to the top floor and search. This was the most dangerous position above the fire, so it was only given to a senior man. This type of fire operation grew out of experience and worked very well in tenements; even when a fire had a good headway, it could be brought under control quickly by an-inch-and-a-half hose line and an aggressive inside attack. If the fire extended into the open public stairways, shaft ways, it could take the fire up these vertical passageways like a chimney flue. To get above it could only be done from the outside by aerial ladder or a fire escape until the fire's advance could be halted by the engine company at the fire door and control was regained at the stairway.

"Battalion 12 to aide."

"Go ahead, Chief."

"Tell Manhattan we're going to use one engine, two trucks, other units in service and on the air."

"OK, Chief," Tom replied.

Tom Burke's captain had told Tom, "You'll learn the job short and sweet in Harlem," and Tom was very impressed at what he had seen so far.

CHAPTER 7

CAR POOL

TULLY PULLED ONTO the Long Island Expressway at Deer Park; his six-cylinder Mustang was underpowered with four people aboard, and he floored it to get on the expressway. Tully was going to drop his wife, Kitty, off in Astoria, Queens, before going on to work. Smithy and Skitter were in the backseat and were on their best behavior. Kitty was reading her script to herself for tomorrow's shoot of the soap she had a lead role in as a young female character in the show. Her perfume filled the car. And her presence totally changed the atmosphere of the all-male car pool. The car radio was tuned to WINS news. The head of the city's sanitation workers was saying his men would hit the bricks if they didn't have a contract by September 1. "How about the Taylor Law forbidding a strike let Taylor pick up the garbage," was his answer. Tully tuned to the Mets game.

"It's the sixth inn. With luck, we'll be past the ballpark before the game lets out," said Tully. "Skitter, you driving the chief tonight?"

"No, the new guy from Brooklyn is going to drive."

"Hear he's on the lieutenant list. I thought you were thinking about driving him regular, Skitter?" asked Tully.

"In the winter, there's a lot you can say for the job," said Skitter.

"You bet the car got a better heater than the back step," said Smithy.

Skitter didn't retaliate but continued, "True. But you got the fire reports to do, and there's something to say for fire duty putting the fire out instead just looking at it."

"Kitty, can I ask you a question about the show?" asked Smithy.

"Why, yes. I didn't know you watched," Kitty said with a big smile.

"Carol is a fan, and when we're home together, we look at it. Well, because we know and like you," said Smithy.

"Why, thank you, Smithy. What's the question?" Kitty slid around in the seat. She was a beautiful young woman, which any photograph would capture, but it would not tell the whole story; her born gifts and training made her every move something extra that caught the eye and stole every scene she was in. There was a name for it, *pizzazz*. But that didn't describe it. It was something children have but lost with self-consciousness, a type of animation that moved all of her down to her toes when she moved, a slow-motion dance of all her parts. Tully caught it as she turned in the seat. And he smiled. She wasn't turning it on. She just did it.

"Sometimes you have a scene where you're so sad and sometimes you cry. How do you do that?"

"Good question. On the stage, it's a bit easier because there's no close-up, all you have to do is change your facial expression and put a hankie to your face. But on TV, the lens can zoom in, so it's harder. What I do is ask for the shot to be done at the end of all shooting when I'm tired and hungry. And I go to a dark place in my mind, and then I give it to them."

"Where is that dark place?" asked Smithy.

"That I can't tell."

"Yes, of course," said Smithy. "I understand, it's a trade secret."

"No," said Kitty, "not really. It's just that it really made me sad. So to talk about it is not fun."

The car was moving past flushing meadows, and traffic was still light at Shea Stadium.

CHAPTER 8

CAPTAIN MAC'S DRIVE-IN

MAC TURNED THE key in his black MG and it roared to life. He loved the sound of the engine and exhaust pipes as he let off the gas. It was a clean-burning engine; its tailpipes showed light-color gray of almost complete combustion. MG stood for Morris Garages of England. He was told his machine was destined to be a classic and to drive it into Harlem was foolhardy. But to Mac, a machine was to be used. Not like fine china to be kept on the shelf and to be admired. To work was an honor, and Mac took great joy in putting it through its paces.

He took one last look at his home, a two-story Cape Cod, the home that he and his wife, Maureen, had built. She had passed away now. After a very happy marriage. It was his home here in America, the US of A, land of opportunity. Mac tipped his walking hat and pulled away from the neat, kept front lawn, his plot of land. His stake in America. It was located in Brewster, New York, thirty-eight miles from the Harlem firehouse.

Patrick Francis McLaughlin, fifty-eight years old, born in County Cork, Ireland, served in WWII with the British army in Burma. He had commanded a platoon of Gurkha jungle fighters, famed for their fighting behind the lines and their ability to live off the land. They had helped keep the Burma Road open. The main supply route from India to China, this was a real road, not to be thought of in comparison to the Ho Chi Minh trail, the main supply route for the Vietcong from North Vietnam. The Vietnam War was more than twenty years later. Mac found himself thinking more of his war experiences now than he had in the last twenty-seven years. Because of the

Vietnam War, he found himself talking to Bruce Smithy about his tour in Me Nam as a ranger. Tully's war experience in Korea was similar but different.

Bruce's jungle tales brought back his memory of Burma. Bruce was very lucky, Mac thought. He took a piece of shrapnel in his stomach hitting his bladder; it was repaired surgically, but he had some difficulty getting on the job because of it. He had told Captain Mac the whole story. Smithy had received a letter from the department of personnel informing him he had been disqualified because of medical reasons from the fireman's list. It seemed to Smithy there was no justice in this world; he decided to go downtown and straighten these people out. This letter had worked him up to a high pitch, but by the time he arrived at the third-floor office, he had cooled down. There was an overweight clerk talking to his mother on the phone; his name on his desk was Ishmael Horowitch. He was speaking to his mother with a great deal of patience and understanding. Smithy had lost his mother when he was overseas. He had been a good son; his mother had told him so. Still he wish he could have had more time with her. She would have been proud of his uniform and war ribbons, but it was not to be. Smithy sat down in the well-worn wooden chair next to Ishmael Horowitch's desk and waited. When he was done with his call, Bruce poured out his heart. He had served his country; he had been decorated. He didn't take a medical discharge after being wounded in combat; he had been spit on when returning home on furlough. When he told the cabdriver at the New York airport he was returning from Vietnam, he advised to ditch thoughts, medals, and uniform; it could get dangers here. He continued to serve as a stateside instructor until discharge. He had worked hard to pass the written test and the demanding physical, and now all he wanted was to serve as New York City fireman. He rested his case.

Mr. Horowitch must have been moved by what he heard because he got on the phone and spoke to the personnel doctor. He offered no deal that Bruce could perceive but asked the doctor, "Take a real good look at the war veteran, he wants to be a fireman."

After seeing the doctor, Bruce went back downstairs to make sure he had all bases covered. The examination went well with favorable comments from the doctor. But he was willing to do anything he had to do to get the job, including paying off if he had to. When he approached Mr. Horowitch's desk, he thanked him by extending his hand, which was accepted. "Is there anything else that I need to do?"

"No, Bruce, just be a good fireman! I can tell you you'll be in the next class," said Horowitch.

When Bruce had told Captain McLaughlin this story years later in one of their chats, McLaughlin had said, "Sometimes in this life, the sweets gifts come from unexpected sources. Cast the bread upon the water, laddie, and do your best. And don't be surprised if one day, you'll be fishing and the biggest salmon you've ever seen tries to jump into your back pocket."

Both men had laughed.

"It does come back to you," McLaughlin repeated aloud.

His daydreaming and driving went together hand in glove. He loved his sports car, and for some strange reason, his car was left alone out in front of the firehouse. He logged his final mile on his trip to work. As he drove across the Willis Avenue Bridge connecting the Bronx and Manhattan at the north end of the island and entered Harlem, the MG tooled in to 125th Street, followed by a herd of angry vehicles pressuring to get somewhere fast. McLaughlin signaled early that he would be attempting to park in the middle of the block. This communication angered the charging autos in the rear as they sounded their horns to bully and discourage this needless delay. McLaughlin jammed on his brakes, causing a chain reaction of screeches of tires, but releasing the brake quickly not to be rear-ended. The herd slowed down without incident, pulling ahead only one car length and stopping. He had a spot for the little MG. But a black cab had pulled up tight and was making his parallel-parking maneuver a higher degree of difficulty. No problem; this is what sporting contests are all about. Easing the MG's four-speed transmission into reverse, McLaughlin cut the wheel hard to the right and backed into the curb. Disregarding the beeping of horns from the rear, in one triumphal maneuver, the mission was over. As McLaughlin turned off the motor with both wheels parallel to the curb, the taxicab in the rear had room to pass now, and he did so laying on the horn and giving the one-finger salute. McLaughlin paid little attention, except wishing him better luck next time with a salute of his own.

It was five o'clock. McLaughlin turned in the seat and reached in the rear for his pressed uniform shirt and trousers on a wooden hangar. On the front seat was his old ditty bag with the Gurkha regiment crest on it; it was not his original ditty bag, as they were affectionately known to the British troops, but it had been found in an army surplus catalog. And he enjoyed it.

Having few minutes to spare, he walked forward to check out Ducky O'Shaughnessy's ghetto jalopy. All the 1950 Ford needed was numbers painted on the door to be recognized as a fugitive from the demolition derby. Taking a closer look in the front window, there was a half-eaten mummified burger located on the dashboard above the hole where the radio belonged. Scattered on the front seat were the remains of other snacks. It was more difficult to discern the category of debris on the floor front and rear, except it was definably biodegradable as there was some form of life sprouting on the passenger side energized by solar energy and greenhouse effect of the car windows. Both door locks were erect, indicating an unlocked car – no need for alarms; no self-respecting car thief was going to knock off the ghetto jalopy. It was a ploy that Ducky had devised after his two other cars had been vandalized in the parking zone. Bob had slowly built this street ruse into an art form in which he added and sub-subtracted new tweaks weekly. Captain Mac in particular liked to keep abreast of the new revisions. His best by far was placing a live duck in the trunk to safeguard his spare tire. The duck would quack in anticipation to be let out of his cell to any activity around the jalopy, which activated his wings, which propelled duck dirt and its aroma through the special vent built into the trunk lid. There was no lock on the trunk; it had been pulled and now need to be opened with a screwdriver. The duck was taking for a stroll when it would cause the most commotion on the street. The duck had a collar on his neck and was very cantankerous when being walked and would attack the firehouse dog, "the werewolf," if he got half a chance.

Harlem, as most communities, has its share of brilliant inhabitants; on the other hand, the front of the firehouse had some type of magnetic ability to draw the other end of the spectrum. The fact that the firefighters of Ladder 14 seem to enjoy eccentric behavior just might have had something to do with it, and there may have been an eccentric or three being harbored in the fire company itself as Captain McLaughlin made his way across 125th Street, dodging traffic in a surprisingly nimble manner for such a top-heavy man to carry an ungainly combination of gear and apparel. Ducky O'Shaughnessy was holding court.

Outside the firehouse, with the duck perched atop the fire hydrant, Ducky was lecturing on the care and feeding of his prized golden attack eagle. The duck had soiled his feathers on his ride down from the farm in the trunk of the ghetto jalopy and started to flap them vigorously upon seeing Captain McLaughlin crossing the street; perhaps it was that the captain's silhouette resembled a big-ass bird, with his trousers and uniform shirt on their hanger flying over his back as he neared. The bird flew at Captain Mac in full mating attack. "Jesus, Mary, and Joseph!" cried the captain, with the bird picking the back of his neck. I'll kill the son of a bitch."

James Tully, Vinny Romeo, and Bruce Smithy all ran for cover from the front of the station; the citizens also left in a hurry. One was heard to exclaim as he left out of sight, "I don't know what type of bird that'd be. But he be a fool, for sure, for messing with the boss man."

"Right on," echoed his partner in crime. "I rightly don't know what type of bird that'd be either, but I do know one thing for sure – he bee dirteeeey!

CHAPTER 9

ROLL CALL

FOR TERRY PENA and Anthony Torro, this was a different start than they expected for their first tour of duty in Ladder 14 as probationary firemen (probies). The opening scene with the Ducky and his duck on leach was too far-out for Terry, though it could have fit in a *M*A*S*H* TV episode, which Terry didn't find all that amusing. Not that Terry had lost his sense of humor or his fondness for black comedy on war. It just was that they weren't real veterans, but were actors who did not have to go to war and were making fun of those who did. Making soldiers look silly was one thing, but making their doctors incompetent was another. Because to Terry, the dying had names. There was a lot that Terry didn't have right in his head about the war; he only knew how he felt, and he was keeping it to himself. He couldn't find two people that had the same view on it. So it was all best left alone. He had been drafted in the regular army. This was a very different experience from Bruce Smithy's as an army ranger because it was a different part of the war and Bruce's Special Forces unit was always talking up their experience and Terry's unit concentrated on how they were being screwed. Terry hoped the fire department would be a different experience than the service.

Proby school had covered all the basic, the evolution, the process, and the tools needed for each task at fires, but Terry and Anthony both had a lot of unanswered questions that could only be answered by real fires. They were both happy to be assigned to Tower Ladder 14, the second tower in FDNY, which was on the top ten in the '60s for structure fires. They would learn from the best, and it was also a plus to be together as they were friends from the start in their class of one hundred recruits.

The new men fell into formations in the morning in alphabetical order, and Terry's loud military ho, in answer to his name, keyed Anthony that his name was next. They had experienced and helped each other in each new step in learning their trade: climbing the one-hundred-foot aerial to the roof, the single slide from the roof, and the totally terrifying scaling ladder; climbing from the first floor of the training tower to the roof. The scaling ladder was a ten-foot single-beam affair, with the treads attached to the beam at the center to form a T for rescuers to climb on. It took a relaxed, coordinated individual to keep the ladder from swinging from side to side as they climbed, like a pendulum, ticking your sweet life away, as the top of the ladder was a hook that rested on the windowsill in a precarious fashion. Death was a possibility. Spotting a certainty in learning this skill, Lieutenant Nagel was an excellent teacher, not only in the technical aspects of the ladder, but also in the psychological need to scale the tower's seventy-five-foot front wall with the one-man scaling ladder.

In military training, Terry was pushed over the edge without knowing the reason why, this method known as "Yours is not to reason why, yours is to do or die." This had a fair amount of detractors in the Vietnam period, and Terry blamed most of the instructors for not doing a better job in preparing the troops for what they would have to face in combat. Instead there was a lot of macho nonsense and nit-picking (like a bug). Terry did learn discipline was the utmost, but you must learn to think for yourself within the team. The training instructor commands your every move in training, but in combat, that's impossible; to be a survivor, you need to unlearn this fast. You must respond to the situation, and you're responsible for yourself. Yes, men can do brave things, but they can also do stupid stuff too. If everyone stays alive, the team stays strong. And there's power in numbers in combat.

On the other hand, the fire department instructors were very practical. They taught the task clearly. One in particular was noteworthy – Lieutenant Nagel. He was the type that the expression was made for: he came from the period "when ladders were made of wood and the firemen were made of steel." He got you there and back; yes, maybe an arrow or two in your hat, but you'll be safe. The best of both worlds, alive and a hero, he inspired confidence; he was a model as a leader, and they were in short supply. In Terry's experience, it might be said that Lieutenant Nagel and the scaling ladder was a turning point for Terry. A defining moment. Step one in teaching was showing them how for Lieutenant Nagel. He had the probies assembled on the second floor of the five-story training tower. They watched from safety as the TI scaled the outside of the two floors to their second-floor position. He didn't climb into the window of the second floor but hooked his safety belt to the shaft of the ladder and lit up a cigarette.

He motioned for them to move closer; as he removed the string of tobacco from his tongue, he asked, "Is there anyone not afraid of heights?" Two recruits stepped forward. He had sympathy in his heavy-lined face and steel gray eyes as he asked, "Have you worked on high steel?" addressing both at the same time. No was the answer, both men realizing they were toast, then steeplejacks! "Riggers."

"No sir, Lieutenant Nagel, sir."

"Then, gentleman, am I given to understand that after giving this long thought, you're just not afraid of falling from heights that at the very least will cripple you and, more than likely, kill you!" There was wisely no answer. Not wishing to demoralize, he continued, "OK, at ease," Lieutenant Nagel said in a fatherly tone. "Light up if you got them!" Guys started scrambling for smokes nervously, even those who never smoked. "You need to be afraid," Lieutenant Nagel started, "because you don't know how to do this. If you fall, you're going to hit that net and bounce the hell out in the middle of the street. And your widow is going to have the city by the short hairs. But we're going to have to kiss your sweet ass good-bye." They were laughing now a nervous laugh and some were coughing. This was good. With laughter comes relaxation. "So relax," continued Lieutenant Nagel, "breathe easily and steady, don't try to muscle this ladder. I've seen people squeeze the ladder shaft so hard that sap was squirting out of the bottom of the ladder, dark sap. It smelled bad too, real bad." Their laughter was coming easier now. He was on their side; he wanted them to be successful. This was not going to be some cruel test to tear them down. It was to build them up to perform a very difficult task, and he was going to take them through it. "No one has ever fell who I trained. And I'm going to be pissed if anyone breaks my record," Lieutenant Nagel went on. "Now in this order, put out the smokes, police the area, take one lap around the training tower slow, report back here in fifteen minutes, that's eleven hundred hours. And be prepared to climb."

The first dozen climbed to the fifth floor. The climbs were slow. It was nearing lunchtime, and tomorrow would be another day. Terry and Anthony only had to climb to the third floor. And they did this with ease. The next day, they went all the way to the roof. Terry's thoughts were interrupted.

"The captain would like to speak to you both at the house watch desk forthwith," said Tully.

Captain McLaughlin was writing his six-by-nine roll call tour report in a fine hand with a straight pen, department issued, with an ink blotter in the other hand. All members were present, apparatus and equipment found in good order. He finished his writing in the company journal. He looked up. "Well, gents," addressing the two probies, "I see from your records you both served in Vietnam. Tully, Smithy, and myself all did tours in Southeast Asia. Different wars, of course. We all carry a little bit of Asia in our heads, and we left a little bit of our hearts there with brothers that didn't come home. I'm sure you did the same. Tully here was in Korea, and he makes a great kimchi and rice, and his cat spareribs are out of this world." The captain laughed. The werewolf, the company dog, liked it when the captain laughed, and it got playful. Captain Mac petted him on the head and started to play with his ears as he continued to talk. Tully moved to close the front apparatus doors so there wouldn't be any distractions. The house watch desk faced the front door with telegraph key bells and a phone on the wall to the left of the desk. The bells tapped 1111. The six o'clock test. Terry and Anthony's heart jumped. The captain and Tully showed no reaction. "Now look here, men," said the captain. "They do a good job with you rookies out at the Rock. Your military training for discipline and obeying orders will also put you in good order, but the job cannot be learned in ten weeks. You're on probation for the first six months. During that time, keep close to me. And at the start of each tour, I'll assign each member a position. Terry, you're going to be an extra man. You will be assigned depending on the incident. Anthony, you have the can! Six-foot hook and 2 ½ gallon extinguisher powered by compressed air. After each fire, it needs to be filled, if it's been used, and charged with air. Terry, you help him with this. Any questions so far?" asked the captain. Neither Terry nor Anthony asked any. "OK!" he said. "Do you both have flashlights?"

"Yes," was the answer. "Tully told us to go down to the hardware store on Second Avenue and get one before the tour started. We also went to the A&P and got the supper. Ducky made out a list for us."

"Excellent, men! Excellent!" he said. "Now, men, listen carefully. Leadership is job knowledge, and the job is fire. Therefore, the other firemen on this tour are to be listened to, they know the job. Understand? Last but not the least," finished the captain, "you men are on probation. This department will go a long way with seasoned firefighters, but termination is rapid for probationary men. Remember, you've been forewarned." The captain had been addressing the two men from the house watch chair. He stood up. His shoulders were broad and his chest wide; his stomach was thick but not fat. From the waist down, he narrowed considerably. He was carrying 210 pounds, and he fought as a middleweight in the 140-pound class in the British army. He extended his powerful right hand to both new men and wished them good luck. He turned and headed back to the kitchen to refill his coffee cup and headed upstairs to do his paperwork before it was time for the drill, which would be held at seven o'clock or 1900 hours.

"Put your fire coat, boots, and helmet on the side of the rig next to your assigned tools so you can step into your boots and put the rest of your turnouts on as fast as possible," said Tully. "The drill will be about tools tonight. The captain will ask you where a tool is and how to put it to work. The ladders are at the rear of the truck. There's a ladder lock holding them in place, it must be released before you can withdraw a ladder." He walked to the rear of the ladder. "Like this," demonstrated Tully. "Pushing the handle up, we will be the inside team. I have the irons tonight. We will stay with the captain." And he pulled out the twenty-four-foot extension. "The twenty-four is a good all-around ladder. It's our most used because most of our buildings have fire escapes, front and rear, and we drop the fire escape ladder and climb it. For taking people off the fire escape, you need to ladder the other side of the fire escape away from the drop ladder."

"Why don't you just use the bucket?" asked Terry.

"The bucket may be used to get to the roof."

"But isn't life the number one priority at a fire?"

"Yes," answered Tully, not the least perturbed by the question. "This is a tenement district. There're five-story buildings, four apartments per floor, that's twenty apartments. Average eight people per apartment, that's 160 people or more total for a nighttime fire. Eighty front, eighty more rear. There're six of us and six more firemen with the second due truck. By opening up the bulkhead door and venting the skylight, you relieve the pressure and killing smoke from the public stairs. This lets the firemen in and people out. This operation is manageable. With the number of firefighters the city have given us to do the job, you would not be put in the position to be sucked in by a lot of screaming people in the front and lose the rest of the building population in the rear, that's the chauffeur's job, and Ducky is one of the best." Both young men looked at each other. Tully didn't add anything more about Ducky. "The thirty-foot ladder is the last I'll touch on now. At the rock, they show you three men to lift it right, right?" said Terry. "OK, it's a bear, but two men can do it. You place the butt against the curb. Two men get at the end, jerk and lift together, then walk the ladder erect, talking to each other what you're going to ladder, or vent dropping the tip of the ladder through the window."

"Jezz, Tully! We never heard any of this stuff at the rock," exclaimed Terry.

"Listen, Terry, as the cap said, they do a good job with basic training. But now you're going to learn tenement work from us. The difference between training and combat at times is large because we need to get the job done any way we can. Remember, as in combat, the largest number of grunts to get hurt are in the first firefight out of the gate. The longer you stay in the game, the better your chances of not killing yourself by some dumb mistake. This is the place to ask questions, not at fires. Do what you're told there and you'll be OK. Let's go back and let's see if we can help with the meal."

"How about house watch desks?" asked Anthony.

"There's a phone in the kitchen. And Captain Pat will pick it up when he's in the office. If the chief's out, he wants you at the desk, he wants the door open as soon as he backs in. Bill Walsh is the chief tonight, and there's none better. But look, guys, you're probies, go by the book," said Tully, stopping on the walk to the kitchen to emphasize his point. "You both, in most cases, will be working under direct supervision of someone, just do what you're told, and you're in the clear. When you have watch, stay at the desk. If the department orders tell you one way to do something, do it that way unless someone tells you different. I'm personally being more productive by leaving the watch and showing you the rig and helping out a bit with the meal, the officers understand that. We will not miss a run, I guarantee, but don't try and do anything I do until you're through with your probationary period."

Terry had noticed Bruce Smithy changing the roof-saw blade while Tully was at the back of the truck showing them the ladders. His body language and expression led Terry to believe that Tully was to be listened to. They walked into the kitchen, which had fresh paint, a new sink, a dishwasher, and a big cooking range; a Formica table had been made with two-inch pipe as its base. Tully and Bill Mac Quinn – the head of the company commissar – had slowly made some improvements, with the help from all members doing the work, and paid for all the materials themselves. Tully and Bill also ran a picnic and a dinner for the company and the wives. The kitchen was small in improvements in living conditions, which makes time pass a little faster and brings the men close together.

CHAPTER 10

ROLL THE WHEELS

BEFORE THEY COULD enter the kitchen, the department phone rang three short rings. Smithy picked it up in the kitchen. The captain was already taking the message: smoke condition, Paladino Drive. The probies were already instructed on how to don their gear and mount the apparatus. And they were on their first fire call. The fire building was a fourteen-story fireproof public housing unit. Nothing was showing. Engine 35 was in ahead of them and was carrying high-rise folds, 2 ½ hose, and nozzle. The officer had a sack of tools to replace anything that may be missing from a standpipe connection, NY bent tip, which has a ninety bend in it to use in the incinerator-shaft fire, if that was the case.

"Smithy, take Terry with you to the roof!" said the captain. "Terry, dislodge a belgium block like I'm doing."

"How come?" asked Terry.

"Because I said so. Do it."

Both carried a block and their tools into the building.

"Engine 35 to Battalion 12."

"Go ahead, Thirty-five."

"It's blocked, the incinerator between third and fourth floors."

"Ten four," answered the chief.

Smithy pointed to the elevator and pressed 9 and 10 floor buttons.

"Smithy," Tully said, "it was OK to ask a question."

"At drill and in quarters," said Smithy. "At fire, just do what you're asked to do."

"Can I ask a question now?"

"What?"

"We were told not to use an elevator that was not under fire department control at a fire," asked Terry.

"This is a fire in the incinerator shaft. The only trouble is the shaft is blocked with garbage," said Smithy, laughing. "The smoke got no place to vent itself. Except the third-floor incinerator door."

"Why not just use water?"

"Because the shaft is tiled and red-hot now, water will crack it. Remember, Terry, we are not to break anything unless we have to."

"OK, Smithy, what's the blocks for?"

"To drop down the shaft, it will get going about sixty mile per hour and plow into the obstruction."

"Suppose it doesn't open it."

"Then we drop the second block. And if that does not open, it's the chief's call to use water."

Smithy opened the roof door and used his Halligan tool against the wall of the incineration stack to step on and pulled off the screen. He gave a warning on the radio to stay clear and drop the block. There was a boom, and fire and smoke came out of the stack.

CHAPTER 11

LISTEN AND LEARN

"SPAGHETTI WITH CLAM sauce is served, dig in, boys."

In self-defense, Ducky has started making a bulk appetizer so the troops could partake of some bulk carbohydrates early before they got tied up with a tower ladder job out of their district or their own fire work. The main course was a seafood stew of clams, shrimp, white fish, and pieces of chicken all steamed on rice. Bob "Ducky" O'Shaughnessy was a treasure as a cook, moralist, and top chauffeur. Thought unquestionably twisted, he was the bedrock every good unit needs to build on. His side job was as crane operator for a construction company. As a guy who does the job every day and then some, O'Shaughnessy brought something extra to the job of chauffeur – experience. He had been driving big rigs of one type or another since he was seventeen years old and in the navy. He drove for the post office and then railway express in midtown Manhattan. He didn't want to go to chauffeur school when the captain asked him at first, as the captain felt at the time that Ducky still had a lot to learn as a trucky. He then had four years on the job. But this did cause him to do a lot of soul-searching. If the captain thought he'd make an important contribution, so be it. It was a year or two before he was asked again; this time he accepted. After two weeks of training, he was at the top of the class, but still tied with a young firefighter from Ladder 105. There was no test on the tower ladders as there were only two on the job, so this wasn't taken into consideration, neither was the fact that Ducky gave a lesson on backing in the hook and ladder with the tiller man locking the rear wheels and not helping to steer the rear of the tracker into quarters, as you would a tractor and trailer driver without a tiller to help steer the rear wheels. The instructor asked if a tie was OK with Ducky, and he said, "Give it to the kid." The instructor shook his hand and said, "If it means anything to you, Ducky, you're the man! I would like to have you drive for me." When Captain Mac's chauffeur got promoted, Captain Mac picked Ducky O'Shaughnessy for top whip, a term carried over from the old horse days.

Ducky took his job very seriously. He never had a drink with a meal or after a hot night fire, to hydrate and urinate as one of his first captains would say after a smoky fire; but instead, he would cook up mounds of potatoes and eggs and bagels found at the grocers markets starting at three in the morning. The importance of breaking bread together for combat units has been employed and described from Alex the Great, Wellington dinner table, Foreign Legion, and so on. The different parts of the same battle can only be learned from those who carried out these different assignments. Though we are at the same battle, our experiences are different, and what better way to learn them than to go over the details of the last fire at dinner. Tonight Romeo was assisting with culinary duties; he did the salad and clam sauce this night. Vinny was nicknamed D'Artagnan, one of the four musketeers, as he was a swordsman of the first order with the ladies, or so his story indicated. In reality he was a good husband and father and a hard worker; his romances had some fact but little consummation. Nonetheless, it had considerable verbalisms.

"Ducky! What's this swill you're throwing at us tonight? I'm hungry enough to eat the crouch out of a rhino," taunted Smithy, entering the kitchen just in the back of Tully and the probies.

"Just shut your dirty trap and put out the plates. And do as I order!"

Ducky loves to play an insane Captain Queeg of *Cane Mutiny* fame when the captain wasn't around, and he took full charge of the details of getting the meal ready and keeping the tower ladder and all its equipment clean and in good order. Though his orders were given in ridiculous manner, they were always correct. If they were refused, Ducky would present the case to the captain. "Gee, Captain sir, I only asked the men for a hand with all the enormous responsibility that I have for the department apparatus per department regulation, in addition to accepting the arduous work of procuring and preparing and presenting substance for the men to maintain their energy for combat. Sir, instead I was met with indifference and complacency."

The only way to beat Ducky was not to eat, and this was cutting off your nose to spite your face, as Ducky was a great cook. And Captain Mac would have you thrown out of his group if you didn't eat with the company.

Tully and Smithy started to put out plates and utensils; Romeo placed his clam sauce on the table in a pot with a ladle to service yourself, and Ducky O'Shaughnessy presented spaghetti with olive oil and cheeses as an appetizer course.

"Enjoy!" proclaimed Ducky.

As all jockeyed for a plate of steaming pasta, Captain Mac who had been called from the office for chow asked Ducky, "Is the chief going to be dining with us tonight?"

"I asked," said Ducky, "but they're going to deliver the department papers and might stop in to see Father Cook at St. Mary's."

"Thank God, someone is praying for us," said Smithy.

Ducky made the sign of the cross, standing at the head of the table, putting out the garlic bread and secretly blessing everyone.

"Hey, Smithy! A military question?" asked Tully.

Smithy looked up with a mouth full of pasta and, not wishing to stop eating, signaled with his fork in a come-hither fashion that he would field the question.

"I saw this movie on the *Late Show* about Merrill's Marauders, U.S. jungle fighters in Burma in the Second World War." Tully stopped to rip off a piece of his garlic bread and another fork of pasta. They were in the mitts of some serious eating. The taste bug had kicked in, and Ducky was starting to moan, making love to his fork as he was eating.

"It's a disgrace not to service wine with this meal," said Romeo. Tully, Smithy, and the captain were drinking some kind of grape juice out of coffee cups poured from a Coke bottle in a brown paper bag. "When I visited Rome fire department, they had wine with each meal," said Romeo. "Where was that?"

"Rome, New York, Vinny," said Smithy.

"Merrill's Marauders," interjected the captain to change the subject as the chief walked in, "were misused in Burma by Vinegar Joe Stillwell!"

"Chief, are sure you won't have something to eat?" asked Ducky.

"On second thought, we will," said Chief Walsh. "This smells too good to pass up. This here is Tom Burke from Ladder 105 who will be driving me. Any help you can give him, I would appreciate."

All members looked up acknowledging, but fully engaged in eating.

"We have two new men riding with us, Chief," said the captain. "Terry Pena and Anthony Torro."

"Good luck to you both," said the chief as he and Tom found seats and Ducky put plates in front of them. "Please continue, Cap, with what you were telling the men about Merrill's Marauders, I always miss your tales of Burma."

"Well, the saints be my witness, Chief, Tully here and Smithy have been trying to bait me in to get to some storytelling for a month. But I resisted, for to tell you the god truth, I think both of them have as good, if not better, war stories. Tully's a marine, cut off in Korea and encircled by the Chinese army. And Smithy's a U.S. ranger in Vietnam training the indigenous people of the Monton yard to be soldiers and building fortifications for their villages."

"Well, I'm sure they do," said the chief, "but it's age before beauty."

"And they are indeed beauties," chimed in Ducky. "Please go ahead, Cap."

"Well, the Brits' army had been driven out of Burma retreating to India. This was a bad showing. The word had got around that the British troops, about one hundred thousand, after it surrendered Shanghai, were badly treated. Some stories said that some Brits captured in Burma were strung up with wire and bayoneted, so no one was about to give up after that. So while the British and the Americans were trying to regroup and help China from being completely overrun, a Colonel Wingate put a unit together to attack the Japanese in a hit-and-run fashion. The plan was for them to leave off the land, be supplied by air. Only this ended up giving their locations away after a while. They found themselves being pursued by relays of light rifle teams, over half of the unit was lost. But a lot was learned from Wingate's men. New units were put together. American units of the same type ended up with the name of its leader, Frank Merrill, Merrill's Marauders. The Brits were called Chindits made up of United Kingdom units, Australian, Indian, Gurkha, and tribe people. We got equipped with U.S. M1 carbine because of lightweight and army mules."

"I didn't know that. You left that out before, I thought you used the Enfield rifles," said Smithy.

"Well, it would work caked with mud, but it was heavy, and the ideal was to be as light as possible. M1 carbine had thirty-round semiautomatic clip This made difference to us in speed of fire. And it was beautifully light after carrying the Enfield."

"Our unit was one-third Gurkha riflemen. The captain brought in one of their knives to show us!" said Tully.

"I heard they were deadly fighters," said the chief.

"Oh yes, they were warriors of the first order. If they drew the knife, it had to have blood, it was their religion. The blade had a tooth at the bottom where the gods drank the blood," said the captain.

"Oh baby!" exclaimed Tully. "The best part of being with them was they had a tea for everything and poultice to drew out poison from man and beast. They knew how to feed the mules to make them calm and to purge their system to expel worms. If a mule went down in battle, they had them dressed out, butchered, smoked, and cured in gig time. When we came back in with our wounded for debriefing when the monsoon started, we were in such good shape it was embarrassing. The other jungle units had dysentery, malaria, and every bloody sickness you could imagine."

"Was it just the teas or what?

"For as near as I can tell, it was the whole program, good nutrition and herbs is the key to fight off disease."

"Even malaria?" asked the chief.

"Especially malaria," said the captain. "I didn't know it going into the jungle, but coming out, I believed the Gurkha introduced us Europeans to food we never thought of eating, like monkey, snakes."

"Sounds tasty," said Smithy. "We too had the mountain men with us to guide us. They had a type of leaf they smoked and roots to chew for pain."

"You both were like regular flower children," said Tully.

"You're telling me, Tully, you never smoked herbs in Korea. What was General MacArthur doing smoking that corn pipe coming ashore?"

"That's a different war, blockhead, let the man tell the story," said Ducky.

"Yes, please continue, Cap," said the chief.

"Well, that part of the world is called the Golden Triangle. These tribes dealt in herbs that produced drugs, including opium and heroin. They dealt with the Japs at first but didn't like their dealings, they were very bad people to cross as they had a whole bag of dirty tricks – dart, pungy sticks and snares, and a poison to go with each. They had a type of black-powered elephant gun that could be loaded with shot. This would take down the vegetation in a firefight and stop a charge, it made our M1 more effective, and as a team, we were stronger, and this made a difference."

"I do have a lot of questions I would like to ask that reflect on our job today, but we got to get on the road," said the chief, finishing his plate of food. "But let me ask you one thing. You said that Merrill's Marauders were misused. How was that?"

"Well, in my opinion, all units have their best uses and, for a time, can be misused, as in above and beyond the call of duty. But misuse will cause a breakdown in equipment and people and result in failed missions. Merrill's troops were kept in the jungle without relief. That's why in the end, they were disbanded. But this was the beginning of the Army Special Forces," finished the captain.

"Very interesting," said the chief. As the chief made his way to his car, he was thinking he wished he had Captain Mac's concise view the other night when he was talking to the chief of department. *That misuse in the end will cause a breakdown in equipment and people and result in failed missions.* But what defined overuse in people? In the military, it was called battle fatigue, and you were down-and-out. In the fire department, it's not that visible. Going off the deep end, it could start with six beers instead of two to unwind at night, crash, and be up after four hours of sleep and up the rest of the night. In the chief's experience, he would rather have three good fires than thirty false alarms. But in the long run, which was the most detrimental to the mind and body, the false alarms were a hardship on Chief Walsh in the Bronx. Tully and O'Shaughnessy were up and out to open the apparatus door for the chief to leave the quarters; the old doors were opened by manpower. O'Shaughnessy slid the right door. Tully then left Ducky and walked over to speak to the chief as the car was rolling out.

"Chief, be sure to ask the good father to bless us. If you see him tonight."

The chief nodded. Tully smiled.

CHAPTER 12

CHIEF WALSH ON THE AIR

"Twelfth Battalion to Manhattan."

"Go ahead, Twelfth."

"Left quarters and on the air, K."

"Ten four," answered the Manhattan dispatcher.

The chief hand-signaled to Tom for a left-hand turn onto 125th Street at the same time he was talking on the radio. "OK, Tom, we stay on 125th until Lenox. Then take a right onto Lenox Avenue. Go to 133rd Street, turn left, that's our first stop. Engine 59, Ladder 30, and squad."

It was still daylight, and the people were out in force; there were street peddlers with pushcarts selling direct to the public. Sustenance was being furnished ready to eat in the form of hot buttered corn on the cob and traditional hot dogs, the original fast food. Fresh fish for the evening table were displayed on a bed of ice, vegetables of all types on carts and open pickup trucks, and of course, ice cream trucks that took food stamps and sold more than just dairy products. In business, it is often said that there're three important things to consider: location, location, and location. The pushcart handled this premise to perfection. They went to the people and the best locations; they could change locations as the day went along. Subway entrances and bus stops early morning, and again later in the day as workers come back home from a long, hard day and they emerge from the dark hole in the ground. A cup of shaved ice with a sweet flavoring added or a soda to quench the thirst for the walk home, a reward for a good day's work, a celebration for getting through it all. Dealing in five and ten cents was not that bad of a business; after all, Woolworth had made millions this same way.

"What's wings and things and mambo sauce?" asked Tom.

"Spying a hand-painted sign artfully done and placed in the window of a butcher shop. 'They'd be good eating,' as Mrs. Edwards would say, whom you'll meet at St. Mary's in a bit."

Bill Walsh had a fond feeling for Harlem and its inhabitants. Harlem was not a traditional neighborhood. Its population of people of color had originated in the early 1900s. Harlem had the flavor of different countries in some ways; though it's very overcrowded and parts qualified as a first-class slum, it was not without its charm! Only you had to look with a kind eye for it. It was situated on a very important and valuable piece of prime real estate state in northern Manhattan. It has an excellent bus transportation and two subway lines running through it and is flanked by a highway, which run along the Harlem River on the east side and the Hudson on the west side and Central Park to the south.

"There's the Apollo Theater up ahead, and over to the left, the Martinick Hotel, Castro is staying there now," said the chief.

"Why here?" asked Tom.

"I believe he mistakenly thinks he's a saver up here than downtown. Rumor has it that he's killing and plucking fresh chickens so he won't be poisoned by the CIA."

"People with paranoia sometimes live longer," said Tom.

They were now traveling north on Lenox Avenue.

"It's a grand avenue, wide and separated by islands of trees in parts, this is the epicenter of uptown 125th Street and Lenox Avenue. This section of Manhattan is left out of most travel guides for now. That's not because there is not a lot to see, it's just maybe a little more dangerous to see them. So was the perception since the '69 riots. Most people, of course, were decent and hardworking and industrious, but watch your back and walk fast was still the order of the day in 1970. These large arteries lessened the chance of conflagration and added airiness to the city. It is not surprising that the main water supply run below this same thoroughfare from Upstate New York, some of it coming more than two hundred miles through tunnels that would swallow two trains side by side. The basic supply lines on the water grid in Manhattan were sixty-four inches, it was estimated that the city uses or misuses over one billion gallons of the wet stuff per day."

"Question, Chief! These buildings are a lot like downtown Brooklyn."

"Right, they were built under the same building laws, basically. Tom, New York's strengths were in their building trades and steady stream of immigrants in the 1800. Which came first, the chickens or the eggs? I guess historians would say the harbors made New York, I say it was the people. But anyhow, New York downtown and Brooklyn connected by the Brooklyn Bridge caused the population to spill over and things even out, and the population moved uptown in Manhattan to the newer apartment, and new immigrants moved in to the old. The 1907 Old

Law and New Law Tenements are the primary housing here in Harlem with the projects in third phase. The old law was an award-winning design. It encouraged light and air movement to fight TB, the city's big killer of that day. It did away with the wooden interior staircases and added fire-retarded hallways and apartment doors and bulkhead doors at the roof and steel fire escapes, that was pretty good for 1907. Tom, I almost talked us past our turn. Left turn here on 133rd Street. Tom, this is the Big House! Home to 59 Engine and 30 Truck and squad."

It was newer than Fourteenth and Twelfth Battalions' quarters. A two-story brick building. Tom parked the Ford in front of the quarters.

"Tom, you stay behind the wheel and I'll take the bag in," said the chief.

Tom had not had a chance to check out the chief's car; it was a bomb. The pollution stuff on it caused it to run poorly. The design at this point in time was to try and have the motor eat its own poop, which it could halfway do at about forty-five miles per hour, cruising and taking in a prodigious amount of fresh air; but at idle and stop and being driven off the city, the motor gets obstructed exhaust ports and couldn't get out of its own way. The chief opened the door and jumped in.

"OK, Tom! Find your way to 126th Street and Madison Avenue."

"OK," said Tom, sharing his thinking, "we backtrack and make a left turn on Madison, cross 125th. Then right on 126th Street."

"You got it," said the chief.

The dispatcher transmitted Box 1613 Eighth Avenue and 143rd Street.

"We don't go," said the chief, holding up his hand. And in the next motion, pointing to a parking spot at the curb on the left, said, "But they do, let's get out of their way."

Watching the engine and truck and the squad flew by caused Tom to feel like a colt left in the starting gate, and the starting gate didn't open.

"Feels like we should go," said the chief. "But in the fire department as in the military, Tom, we have our positions to cover, the Sixteenth Battalion is just across the street from that box," said Chief Walsh.

The car fire radio interrupted the conversation.

"Battalion 16 to Manhattan."

"Go ahead with your message, Sixteen. Transmit ten seventy-five. For Box 1613, we still don't go!" said the chief. "Let's take it back to Spanish Harlem and our home turf."

"Do you still want to go to 126th Street and Madison?" asked Tom.

"Yes, let's take it that way," answered the chief. "I don't believe we do anything on that box. But they will let us know!"

"Have you known this priest for long, Chief?"

"Yes, I met him one night up here standing in a doorway at 3:00 AM. Buffing a fire, I had to do a double take. Then I stepped into this dark doorway to escape the cold wind that night. It was positioned across from the fire building. He was dressed all in black. What I could see of his face was illuminated with the red flashing lights of the fire trucks. I jumped back, startled. And he said, 'Hey, that tower ladder is doing a job, Chief.' And he held out his hand. 'I'm Father Cook of St. Mary's,' and we've been friends ever since.

"OK, Tom, make a right on 126th Street and go slow, just turn on your gum-ball roof light on. And Father will come out and unlock the gate.

"These old churches were built like fortresses. About 1830, there was a Catholic church burning in Philadelphia. Cardinal Hughes of New York put out a statement that if that were to happen in New York, he'd have every Protestant church in Manhattan fired."

"Oh boy, he was wicked," exclaimed Tom.

"Yes, wicked times produce wicked ways. It was believed the Irish would revolt given half a chance and the blessing of their church and might burn the whole city down."

"So you're saying the fire department's job is the same today as yesterday, only there're different burnee today."

"Oh, you developed a wicked edge on yourself, Tom," said the chief. With a note of respect, he added, "You'll enjoy Father."

Father was using all his 150 pounds to move the six-foot gate. Tom backed in slow, and the chief got out and helped the priest to close the heavy gate. The fading evening light added a splash of highlights to the church's salad garden, rosebushes, and herb plants, all laid out in front of a statue of Our Lady of Victory.

"The garden is coming along," said the chief.

"Yes, I had help from Ducky. He helped turn the soil over, and he had this wonderful natural fertilizer he brought down from the farm."

The chief and Tom looked at each other. And the chief spoke to cancel out the picture of Ducky's golden eagle taking a dump.

"Oh yes! He sent his sentiments, Father. Father, this is Tom Burke. He is my new driver, he is on the lieutenant list."

"Oh, good luck, what company did you come from, Tom?"

"Ladder 105," answered Tom.

"You have a tiller rig."

"Yes, that's right," acknowledged Tom.

"That's on Dean Street, and you're with Engine 219."

"Right again," said Tom.

"And your captain is Art Cummins, and he was a lieutenant, up here in Ladder 26."

"Holy mackerel, Father, gee, I'm impressed." Tom started to laugh to himself on his restricted verbiage. He probably would have said, "Holy shit, you nailed it, bro."

His four years instructed by the Jesuits at Yorkville was all coming back in a flash. He being the only black in the school, he needed to be an example of correctness.

"Well, let's go in and grab a bite to eat," said Father.

The kitchen was off the side entrance of the rectory. A young black male was coming out, and then eating something, he nodded and did a double take at the black face of Tom Burke. They followed the priest around and in the side door. The aroma of cooking food was appealing. A small dust mop type of dog was barking and darting and sliding around the floor happily, bumping into the tables and chairs.

"Now you leave those firemens alone," said a well-endowed black woman in her late twenties. The fire radio was going in the background. "Now that's a shame, a real shame," she said, pointing at the radio with her wooden spoon. "Your people don't get a blessed minute rest, no rest at all. Now you all sit! An' start eatin'," she ordered.

Tom didn't need to be told a second time. Mrs. Edwards put out three plates of barbecue and collard greens with hot sauce on the side and a hot pan of fresh biscuits,

"Father, would you please sit down, you're making me nervous." The priest sat down and said a blessing on the food. And they continued.

"It's easy to see," proclaimed the priest, "that Adam's sin in the Garden of Eden may have been circumstantial."

"Like accessory to the fact, get over here and eat this apple," said Tom, enjoying the barbecue.

"Exactly," responded the priest, enjoying Tom's quick response.

"Then, Father, what was his sin?" asked Tom.

"That is a very good question, Tom, very good," said Father Cook, carefully savoring the joy of a biblical intellectual discourse and breaking bread.

"Greed!" bellowed Mrs. Edwards, turning to face them and holding her wooden spoon up in the air. "The grandddaddy of them all, they had it all. They weren't hungry, they sure enough didn't have to ride the subway to work. And fact that they were strutting out there naked as jaybirds give us to believe dat de Lord wasn't fretting on how they was spending their afternoon under the fig tree."

They were all laughing. "Well, you go ahead and laugh, but it's just the way it's said in the Good Book, plain and simple. Greed."

Father Cook had his mouth open and looked like he might say something, but Mrs. Edwards continued with this afterthought. "They needed that apple like they needed a hole in their head. Now, Chief Bill, you eating like a bird. Is something wrong with my cooking tonight?"

"Well no, Mrs. Edwards. I'm ashamed to say we had a bit to eat before leaving the firehouse."

"What's that, we all don't feed you enough here?" said Mrs. Edwards, folding her arms across her chest-pronouncing cleavage that could be frighting to a timid soul.

"No, no," said Bill. "It's just that we've been very lucky tonight. I lost track of all the meals I missed in this job. And I took advantage of the opportunity to have Tom here meet some of the men he will be working with."

The fire radio in the kitchen announced a second alarm, Box 1613. "We don't go, Tom! Unless Special called," said the chief. Both Tom and the chief reached for a second glass of iced tea, to cool the hot sauce and perhaps the thought of the second-alarm fire.

"Well, we better get hitched up and get on the road," said the chief. "Would you like to ride, Father?"

"Oh, God bless you, I'd love to, but I have to finish a report for the bishops committee. But to tell you the truth, if you were going to the second alarm, I couldn't resist."

"No, I don't believe we'd go on this, but it looks like a busy night," said Chief Walsh.

"Would you like a sip of spirits for what ale's you?" asked the priest of the two firefighters.

"Thank you, Father, another time perhaps," answered Chief Walsh.

"Well, thank you, Mrs. Edwards, you're a great cook," said Tom. "I haven't had barbecue and collard greens since my grandma cooked them for us. Could I ask where your people were from, Mrs. Edwards?"

"Waynesboro, Georgia."

"Well, that explains it," said Tom. "My grandma was from Burke County too. It's a small world, Mrs. Edwards."

"Jasmine, please call me Jasmine, Tom."

"Thank you again, Jasmine," said Tom, "and if you were Eve, you would keep Adam right, that's for sure."

"Now that's there's one a smart man. Is you marry, Tom?" asked Mrs. Edwards.

"Oh yes. Hog-tied and branded!"

"Oh, too bad, all the good ones are spoken for," said Mrs. Edwards.

* * *

On their way back to quarters, Tom Burke stopped the car at Park Avenue and 125th Street for a red light.

"You know, Tom," said Chief Walsh, "you brought something out in Mrs. Edwards I've never seen before, a softer side. When she told you her name was Jasmine, I realized I didn't know that! And I've known her for years."

"Well, to tell you the truth, Chief, she brought something out in me too, a curiosity for a home I've never known, the South. My mother would say when I did something wrong, 'Now, Georgia boy, you better do right and not shame your people.' I never knew exactly what that all meant."

The signal light changed green. The department radio broadcast, "Box 1535, Madison Avenue and 131st, Ladder 14, Engine 36, and the Twelfth Battalion, respond. Units responding, this is a working fire, phone calls reporting occupied building with entrapment."

"That's us, Tom," said the chief. "Turn on the warning lights."

Tom made a U-turn onto Park Avenue. Tom could see Tower Ladder 14 was pulling out of quarters, and Ducky spotted the chief's car making its turn. Engine 36 is located on Park Avenue and was on the box and was pulling out of their station in front of the chief's car. Ducky would make a turn directly onto Madison. He would have to watch out for the chief's car. It would turn back on Madison with Engine 36 beside them.

CHAPTER 13

BROWNSTONE FIRE

CAPTAIN MCLAUGHLIN SLID the cab window open between the jump seats.

"Now, laddies," he said, "this most likely will be a brownstone, and there in a row, it's the devil to get to the rear to vent, so our roof man will swing a tool off the roof to vent the window below."

The two probationaries listened intently and were amazed that the captain would take time to talk to them in a matter-of-fact way as they were responding to a fire. But of course, they had no idea what he was talking about!

"Tully will be in charge of you. If we get split up, do what he tells you."

"We got a job, Cap," said Ducky.

The Twelfth Battalion car and Engine 36 pulled out and in front of the tower ladder and onto Madison Avenue, two blocks ahead. Fire was out the front door, and smoke on all floors of the brownstone.

"Twelfth Battalion to Manhattan."

"Go ahead, Twelve."

"Ten seventy-five the box. Heavy fire showing, report to follow."

All the firemen and officers of Ladder 14 and Battalion 12 and Engine 36 saw and computed their impressions of the fire differently. The probies Terry and Anthony saw the fire as a blur of fire and smoke and brownstone and brick and cement front steps leading to the second floor. Terry heard his heart pounding in his ears; the diesel motor was racing. The air smelled of smoke and was blowing by his now-wet-with-sweat face. *This is it. I made it though Vietnam to die of a heart attack in Harlem,* thought Terry.

Tully saw the fire as a possibly cellar fire or first-floor fire. From past experience with this type of building, the front stairs lead to what was called the parlor floor, which was in fact the second floor and the main hallway, which had unprotected wood staircase leading to the third floor and an unprotected stairway down to the first floor with closed stairways and a door to the cellar. Each room could be made into a boarders' room if the brownstones had been converted from a private town house. But without sprinklers or fire escapes being added – unless there were legal single-room occupancy, in which case they would have a sprinkler in each room – these were very dangerous buildings for sleeping tenants. It was early in the evening. Tully knew that didn't matter; his first action would be to check the first-floor door that was located under the front steps. The first due truck had the fire floor, and first order of business was to find the fire, unless ordered otherwise. He saw his job was to supply the officer with information to formulate an attack, a point man position.

Bruce Smithy knew the captain's comments were for him and not the probies. It would be his job to vent the rear and the roof because Romeo, the outside-vent man, would not be able to get a ladder by himself to the rear, and there were no alleyway fire escapes or rear porches as in Chicago or Boston three-deckers, which he read about recently. He put the Sullivan tool in his pocket. The pipe boomed. He would make the roof by the adjoining building, reaching the roof by the scuttle ladder located on the third floor inside of the stairway; he would be carrying a six-foot hook and a Halligan bar, his personal escape rope, and the radio.

Ducky gave Engine 36 room to drop two attack lines, 1 ½ open-bore controlling nozzle with two lengths of 1 ½ attached to a brass. Two and a half underwrites controlling nozzle with 1 ½ thread at the barrel and 2 ½ hose. This would be the first line the pump operator would make up to the pump. The engine officer was thinking the same as Tully. First-floor attack with the 1 ½. The second line was a 2 ½, the big line for the second-floor main hallway. He had four hose men, the chauffeur, and himself. He sent one hose man to the hydrant to help the chauffeur break hose and connect to the fireplug. He and one Jake on the first line on the first floor; the other two firemen on the floor above with the second line. He had confidence in Skitter Blake to lead that task.

Tom moved the chief's car forward after the engine took off for a hydrant and the chief had stepped out and into his fire gear. Harlem fire company was self-deployed under the direction of their officers. This left the chief free to oversee the big picture and to identify what was different from standard that study and experience had taught. The fire was on the first floor; that he could ascertain not from the visible flames, but from the heavy brown smoke pushing out around the first-floor window and door frames. This much fire this early in the evening, it was most probably a fire in the rear of the first floor that had extended up in the open stairway and was pushing out in the hallway on the second floor.

"Tom, check out the rear for me," asked the chief.

He walked back to the chief's car, studying the building and fire intensity and the color of the smoke. As he walked back to the red car, the smoke was dark brown on the first floor, and gray and black mixed above the fire on the second floor. There may be a sprinkler head or two going off in the individual rooms, but if so, it's not touching the main fire.

The chief reached for the car phone and stepped back outside the car where he could see the fire building. As he talked on the radio, he said, "Battalion 12 to Manhattan."

"Go ahead, Twelve."

"We have a working fire at Box 1535, it's a three-story, nonfireproof brownstone. Fire on the first and second floor, two lines stretched. Exposure 1 is a street, 2 is similar construction, 3 is rear yard, and 4 is similar. We need this box filled out, and I want an additional engine and a truck on top of that. K?"

"Ten four, Battalion 12," answered the Manhattan dispatcher.

Heavy fire traffic had drained off the other units that would have normally responded on this alarm. This box was assigned three engines, two trucks, a squad company, a battalion chief, and a rescue company. With the seventy-five signal for the box, the chief dispatcher knew he had been stealing from Peter to give to Paul all night, and the rent just came due at Box 1535. Captain Mac picked up on the engine officer Bob Sanchez's tactic. They did not need to talk. Sanchez was splitting his manpower into two hose teams: one for the first floor and the other for the second floor. Captain Mac would send Terry with Tully as a forcible entry team to the first floor, and he told Anthony to leave the extinguisher, take a Halligan tool and a six-foot hook. They were going to the second floor along with the second line.

Bruce Smithy had no difficulty in gaining entry to the adjoining building, exposure 2. He made his way to the third-floor ladder that led to the scuttle cover and the roof. It was chained and locked. He hung his six-foot hook on the ladder rung drove the fork end of his Halligan bar up and in the back of the hasps and lock that held the case-harden chain and lock, and the wooden screws came out of the wood like toothpicks leaving cheese. *Looking for and attacking the weakest link is the key to force entry,* thought Bruce. It was hot and stuffy in the roof space under the cover, but that was typical, all heat rises; and it was enclosed and protected so fire could not enter from below and into the roof space, or cockloft as it was called. Next door, the fire building (to his right) would be the same; he pushed up and the cover opened. He was met with blue sky through the heavy smoke. *Break the skylight first, it's the biggest opening and the easiest to vent being only glass,* Bruce thought as he climbed onto the black flat roof.

There was still good visibility on the fire roof. He crossed over the divide and, driving the hook through the glass of the skylight, pushed down; this dislodged a panel underneath. Superheated smoke bellowed up and out. He continued to work breaking out all the glass with the six-foot hook. He stood with his back to the wind, his eyes and nose starting to run, placing the Halligan adze end of the bar under the scuttle cover lid and pulling back, like a knife under a jam jar lid. This action popped off the scuttle cover of the fire building. He retreated as the engine opened the 2 ½ nozzle in the hallway below him. Approaching the rear of the roof slowly and the last few inches on his hands and knees, he looked over the roof's edge; there was heavy smoke under pressure pushing out from around the window frames. There was a lot of gray in the smoke color. He guessed both hose lines were in operation now, on the first and second floor. Most people who die in a fire do so due to smoke inhalation. Venting windows lets the smoke out and helps the firemen move in. Here was Captain Mac's tip: the rear is tough to vent. It was of course right; only the roof man would be in the position to do both the roof and the rear. Reaching in his pocket, he pulled out the Sullivan tool, unscrewed the cap, and holding it in his left hand, he lobbed the pipe containing a sash chain over the roof hand-grenade style, crash, pay dirt, second-floor windows. He retrieved the pipe like he was pulling in a bluefish and let it sail again. He was able to pull out a cross member of a windowpane on the second try. *Good but not spectacular,* thought Bruce. Tying his rope to the Halligan tool, he cleaned out the top-floor windows with the Halligan and rope, using his six-foot hook to help clean out the top-floor windows frames. He was proud of his work; the rear was vented, and steam from the hose streams was pushing out the vented windows now, and smoke was billowing out of the skylight and scuttle opening. His job was done. Bruce reached for his radio mic inside his fire coat.

"Ladder 14 roof to Twelfth Battalion."

"Go ahead, Bruce," answered Chief Walsh.

"The roof is open, rear vented, no jumpers in the yard that I can see. Looks to be progress on all floors, K."

"Good report, roof, K."

All the officers of each company had radios, also the ladder driver and outside vent. They heard Bruce's transmission. This gave them a picture of the top and rear, which was helpful, especially for the troops still inside the fire building. They were still in total darkness and surrounded by heat and fire to the front of them.

* * *

Ducky had raised the tower ladder, and Romeo, from its platform, had vented the front windows, second-and third-floor front. Tully had forced the ground front door; Engine 36 moved their line in. Tully vented the first-floor windows from the outside. He took Terry with him into the front room and searched in the back of the engine company. As they moved their attack line to the rear of the building to kill the fire, Captain Mac and Anthony helped Engine 36 with the 2 ½ line and searched the room off the hallway – in the back of the line, in the front room, second floor – and found an old woman dressed and overcame by smoke. Mac instructed Anthony to remove her from the building. The hallway had been on fire, Waynes coating on the walls, wooden stairs, and carpets. The 2 ½ hose line was a bear. Two hundred fifty gallons per minute had darkened the fire down fast, but the two doors to the rear of the hall were closed, so there was no place to push the fire, heat, and smoke. Captain Mac made his way to these doors and forced them with his lock-puller tool, a small crowbar; there was fire in the room to the right, which Engine 36 knocked down. The units that were especially called were in and at work; Truck 26 laddered exposure 2 and sent two men to the roof. The inside teams searched the second floor and third floor with the officer covering the third floor. Engine 58 stretched a third line to the front of the building but did not charge it. Truck 40 sent two men to exposure 4, two to the rear yard to check for jumpers and extension check and was used for overhaul. Engines 91 and 37 were used for relief and mop-up. All other units returned to services. Ladder 14 was not put back in service neither was Engine 36. Captain Mac had cut his hand and burned the back of his neck. Tully located the gent who had fallen asleep on the first floor with a cigarette never to wake again. In the room of origin. Romeo went in on the top floor after venting the window and searched without a mask and took a shellacking. Lieutenant Sanchez, Engine 36, had also taken a beating as did Tully. All were transported to a joint-diseases hospital by Rescue 1 to be looked at by the department doctor. Ducky took the rig back to quarters with Bruce Smithy in charge with the two probies. The chief had left Engine 91 and Truck 40 with the responsibility to open up and wet down and take up.

Tom stood by the chief's car; he had been taking notes of what the companies had done for the fire report. Addresses, names of owner, the DOA, and the woman who had been removed, who had been given oxygen and taken to the city ambulance.

The chief came out of the fire building and got in the car and said, "Let's go." He radioed Manhattan, filling them in on who was and who was not in service.

"Chief, can I ask a few questions?" asked Tom.

"Oh yes, of course, Tom. Shoot," answered the chief.

"Why not just put in a second alarm from the get-go?"

"Well, that would have been a second alarm or more in a row of wooden frames with a common cockloft because of the probability of the fire extending to the exposures, but in brownstones, there's a brick wall dividing each building up to the roof. There are no shafts as there is in tenements between building to communicate fire. Time of alarm when people are sleeping is also important. And no one was hanging out the window, 14 roof man would have reported it from the rear, and I sent you to take a look as a backup report. My first request was actually what I felt I needed and hoped I get. When I asked for it, which was four engines and three trucks, that was a second alarm, on top of what we had then, one engine and one truck," answered the chief.

"One more question, Chief. Thirty-six stretched 1 ½ line!"

"Well, that's OK," answered the chief, "by the regulation, it was the first floor, and they were going to operate two lines, I could not ask for more. In fact, I was considering writing both companies up for a unit citation. For an outstanding effort and excellent tactics."

"Chief, you are unbelievably good at this stuff."

"In all fairness, Tom, it's the firemen who put the fire out, and they were working shorthanded. Above and beyond, as the captain said at dinner tonight. You cannot make regular practices of overextending yourself without having failed missions and getting someone hurt."

"Chief, I had no idea Captain Mac was talking about the fire department with his Burma stories."

"Tom, there's a great deal of similarity between army battlefield tactics and the fire department, that is why it's called a firefight. Captain Mac's warning is becoming a fact here! We're skating on thin ice, and we all know it, you can only push the envelope so far before something gives," finished the chief.

CHAPTER 14

TULLY BATTLEFIELD COMMISSION, ALMOST!

TOWER LADDER 14 was parked in the street in front of the quarters. Truck 13 located in the Yorkville section of Manhattan had relocated to Ladder 14 and was parked in the quarters. Ducky gave orders of what needed to get done to the probies. With the tools, Bruce was in charge. With the captain, Romeo and Tully being looked at the hospital. Bruce spoke to his three men as soon as he got to the house watch desk.

"Gentlemen, the first order of business is to attend to your needs, we're out of service until the chief puts us back in. As soon as our people get looked at, they will call, and we will go get them. Ladder 13 will respond to our calls, any questions?"

"No, sir," answered the probies.

"Bruce, should I heat up dinner?"

"Yes, thanks, Ducky, and we'll just play it by ear. I guess we'll be back in service one way or the other in an hour's time."

Truck 13 had two runs before Ladder 14 had picked up the captain, Tully, and Romeo. The captain was put on medical leave with lung congestion, and Tully and Romeo told the doctor they could go back to work. Tully became the acting lieutenant, having the most time on the job.

They were all sitting around the kitchen table. Ducky had heated up the main course, clams and chicken on steamed rice. He did this with chicken soup. He also had sent the probies for the newspapers.

"You think there's any chance that Mets will win the pennant?" asked Anthony.

"Not a chance in hell," said Terry.

"You've got to believe," chimed in Smithy. "You'll never know!"

"Were you an officer in the army?" asked Terry.

"Yes," answered Smithy.

"I could see you had no trouble taking right over. That's leadership," finished Terry.

"Not really," answered Smithy. "It's job knowledge. If you know how the job is supposed to work, it's easy to lead it. It's hard when you do not have a clue. Tully here is a born leader, he's always thinking."

"Thanks, Smithy. But like you said, if you know the ladder, the saw, the tools, etc., then it's easy to tell people how to use them. There are some guys that are best in combat. I think that's because they stay calm and focused on what has to get done. But get me back here, and I do not care for it."

"There's one other thing, come to think of it, I learned how to give orders by watching others make mistakes. It's just maybe a disadvantage to be promoted too fast. You've only worked under a few officers. In maybe only one company. In the service, a young lieutenant is totally lost without a good sergeant to help him find his way."

"Yeah, you're right! A second louie looks great back in camp, but in the field, the whole picture starts to break up. In combat, nine out of ten is a washout. If a new officer is smart, he puts his trust in the sergeant."

"In some respects, the fire department system seems to be superior, they utilize experienced personnel to test and promote from within," said Anthony.

Tully gave Anthony a look of respect. "Hey look, guys," said Tully, pointing at Anthony and Terry, "you're my forcible entry team. If we get a job, you stay with me. Smithy, you stay with the roof, and Romeo, outside vent. Ducky knows what he's doing. OK, I am going upstairs and see what fire reports I need to do."

There were three short rings on the department phone, a signal there's a fire. Ducky answered it.

It turned out the fire was at 250 East 126th Street. There was no smoke showing in the street in front of the five-story tenement, but there was strong odor of mattress cooking at the third floor. The door was locked, and smoke was coming out around the door frame.

"Force the door, Terry," said Tully. "Anthony, you use the axe to drive the Halligan in above the lock. OK, Terry, now flex that door by pulling on the tool and lean into the door with your back."

The door popped open, and black smoke came blowing out with mild heat. Tully got on the floor and made his way down the hallway. He bumped into a pair of spindle legs standing erect.

"Grandma, are you OK?" asked Tully. No answer. "You're right," Tully replied to the mute form. "That is one dumb question. Terry, you there?"

"Yeah, Tully."

"Take this old lady out of here! Tell Anthony to come up here with me and bring the can before this place lights up."

"Is it going to light up, Tully?"

"Hell no. Just tell him to come up here."

Another five feet and Tully found the doorway to the bedroom, and he took the can from Anthony and started putting water on the burning mattress.

"I'll get the window, give me your hook."

Tully, still on his knees, used the hook to tap the wall like a blind man to find the window by its sound. *Crash, bang!* Anthony was coughing. Out went the window, in came fresh air, and the mattress started to light up. And bed broad was going good, and a weak orange flame was running up the wall.

"OK, Anthony, back out and give me the can, tell the engine to bring in the line." The engine knocked down the room easily. After the mattress was wet down, Tully showed his probies how to open the mattress so water could get inside. "Tie it up and throw it out the window." He told them that bedding could light up. Taking it down the stairs, form rubber is petroleum based and have done just this and caused a second fire bigger than the first.

On the street, the chief told Tully to take up. They returned to quarters and were backing in as they received message to respond to another fire. The tower ladder pulled back onto 125th. With flashing lights and siren wailing like a motherless child, Tully in the officer's seat reported to the dispatcher they were responding. The company proceeded to Lexington Avenue and made a left turn and then a right turn on 123rd Street. There was no fire showing. Engine 36 had gotten in first but had not stretched a hose line. Tully and his forcible entry team went into the hallway of the building. The lights were flickering. Tully turned around and went outside with his team following.

"We are going to force the lock on the cellar door. I think this is an electrical problem! Hear that sixty-cycle hum? That could indicate that there was an electrical malfunction someplace in the building."

Upon investigation, it turned out that the problem was in the electrical-service connection in the basement. The electrical service was grounded to the gas pipe. And the ground had gone too hot, meaning all ground locations were cherry red and humming. This situation from 1 to 10 was a 10 not just because of the electrical fire with the BX electrical cable running hot through the walls and floor of the building, but also the gas lines involvement had the possibility of explosion. Tully used the radio and told the dispatcher to fill out the box. The troops had self-deployed to their preassigned positions. Smithy reported from the roof that there was a smoke condition, and it was definitely a wood-burning smell. Tully now had a full assignment.

"Fourteen to Manhattan."

"Go ahead with your message, Fourteen," answered the dispatcher.

"We need to have Con Edison respond to Box 1459. We have electrical condition in a five-story tenement. BX has gone hot throughout the building. We are evacuating the building and conducting the search for fire. K."

Ladder 26 was second due truck, had the floor above the fire, which was the first floor. They removed the lock from the hardware-store door and found fire on the wall. They used a pressurized extinguisher to cool the hot spot from a distance indirectly. No chief was on the scene. Twelfth Battalion was in the Bronx on a vacant-building fire. Tully, being in command of the first unit in, had taken charge of radio transmission. The captain of Truck 26 had aggressively put his company to work to stop the upward spread of the fire. Tully, after his last radio transmission, decided to look up the captain.

"Hey, Cap! Captain Mac went sick after the last job."

"Yeah, I know, Tully! Ducky clued me in as we pulled in."

"Yes, he's got great confidence in me. Well, do you want to take charge of this thing or what?" said Tully.

"Tully, you're doing fine. If the shit hits the fan, I'll take it," answered the captain. "As I like to get the hell out of here at first chance. We had supper on the table for the third time tonight," continued a Ladder 26 officer.

"Yeah it's got the makings of a toll disaster of a night," said Tully.

Tully made his way back into the cellar; conditions were the same. There was a hum and smell of hot metal; the way the electrical service had been grounded to the gas line was a common thing. The fittings on the gas meter were lead. The gas pipes themselves were black pipes. If the lead fittings on the meter failed, the meter would drop, and the gas would escape to the atmosphere. With the pipes being cherry red, there was more than a good chance for fire or, worse, explosion. Tully backed everyone out of the cellar and warned his men that if an explosion takes place, it would come out through the cellar doors, so stay clear of them. When Con Edison arrived, the last thing they wanted to do was cut power in the street because it would disrupt service.

"I can understand your not wanting to shut off all the power in the street," said Tully. "But if you don't, there's a real possibility that this building will burn down or it may get lifted off its foundation by the explosion. That's when those gas meters in the cellar drop to the floor," said Tully. "Let me take you into the cellar, and you assess the situation," said Tully.

"Look, pal," said the Edison boss, "the last thing in this world I'm gonna do is going to that cellar."

"OK, it's simple then. Cut the power to that building in the street. With the electric off, 90 percent of the problem is over."

"OK, OK. You got it." The Con Ed boss realized the buck stopped with him.

This building had a real-life super A, Mr. Gonzales, and he was very helpful. As the power was disconnected, this returned the gas pipes to their normal color. Con Edison had a second crew on the scene, and they shut off the gas services in the street after the chance of electrocution from contact with the gas line had ended. After the power was cut, Chief Walsh rolled in and took charge. The officer from Ladder 26 went over to fill him in. Tully made his way over too.

"Twenty-six said you took charge and did a good job with Con Ed," said the chief.

"Yeah, well, after I threw up and pissed my pants. I was very competent."

"Well, good job. We're going to take up," said the chief. He would have laughed in most cases, but the night was wearing on him. "Check the building out again. I think we're going to be OK on this," said the chief.

"Yes, sir," said Tully. "The super is going to stay with it, he lives in the building and has a job with the hardware store, and the guy who owns the building is on his way, responding from uptown. I give you all the information, Tom, back in quarters."

* * *

As Ladder 14 was backing into quarters, the phone was ringing. No one picked up the phone and until the doors were shut and the motor was turned off. Tully picked up the phone and answered, "Acting lieutenant Tully, 14 Truck."

"This is Chief Berger! Why was Fourteen out of service?"

Tully closed his eyes to try and think. "OK, we had two fires since the all hands. We were out of service then because of injuries at a fire," answered Tully.

"Why wasn't I notified?"

"Well, Chief, I was at the hospital with smoke inhalation. So I guess I'm not sure! But we're back in service now." Silence on the other end of the line.

"Well, I'll be sending a real officer up there to take charge."

"Very good, sir. Is that all?" The phone clicked off. "Well, so much for the field commission now, that's one sweetheart," said Tully to no one in particular. "OK, guys, take care of your personal needs. I'm heading upstairs to see if I can get some of these fire reports done." The department phone rang again. "Acting lieutenant Tully, 14 Truck."

"Tully, this is the dispatcher, is the truck in service?"

"Yes, sir, I was just going to call, I think," said Tully.

"I just got a call from Chief Berger, he wants a report why he wasn't called when you were out of services."

"Did you ever see that cartoon with a monkey in the shit house with toilet paper wrapper around his head? Anyway, the caption is, 'The job ain't over till the paperwork's done.'"

"Ain't that the truth," said the dispatcher. "OK, Tully, take care," said the dispatcher. "You've had six hours of fire duty so far tonight."

Tully looked up at the clock; it was 12:30 AM. As Tully was walking up the stairs, he realized he was going to be sick. He just made it to the head at the top of the stairs before he let go of what was left in his stomach out the open window. *That was handy,* Tully thought, and that started him laughing, only this was short-lived as he had bad pain in both of his temples. He made it to the offices on the third floor, washed his face, which was red. He had taken too much smoke tonight. This not wearing a mask was taking its toll. They had MSA filter mask that were less than ten pounds, but it was taken out of services when two firemen in Boston and New York were killed with it on. If only they could invent a twenty-pound mask that lasted sixty minutes in a real fire. That would be great. The standard argument again. The present thirty-pound-plus mask. It would last about twenty minutes truth time. This would be fine for 90 percent of fires. The problem with that is running out of air and you don't have the fire out, or worse, having found the fire and you're twenty minutes into the belly of the whale.

Tully had been working about an hour when the covering captain showed up. It was Captain Cane. Tully was lost for a greeting. "Good to see you, Cap! You can take over this paperwork. I've made all the notes and boxes and time out and addresses, you only have to run it through the typewriter."

"I'm not taking over anything until all this paperwork is complete."

"Yes, that's funny, Cap. I had the same reaction when they said I had to take over two fires ago with no extra pay. But here we are," said Tully.

"This is no joke," said the captain.

"OK, Cap, that's fine. But I had six hours of fire duty so far tonight, and I threw up two meals. And my fucking head is pounding. So I think I am going to take it personal and sit down before I fall down."

"I'm giving you a direct order."

Tully for a second just stared at him in disbelief. "Sure, that's true, but you got no witness! So kiss my Irish ass." And Tully walked out. The captain sat down. *This was going to be too easy. These people are totally out of control.* He picked up the department phone, called the Twelfth Battalion; the house watch picked up the phone. "I want to talk to the Twelfth Batt – "

"Chief Walsh, Twelfth Battalion chief."

"We have a very serious situation here! Fireman Tully is guilty of insubordination."

"Who is this?"

"Captain Cane, covering officer in charge."

"In charge of what?" asked the chief.

"Well, Ladder 14."

"Get off the department phone and report to me on the second floor now," said the chief, slamming the phone down.

Captain Cane was intimidated by the chief's tone; he thought of calling Chief Berger. But he had just received an order, so he went down the stairs. He knew of Chief Walsh's reputation; he would defend his men, right or wrong. There was even a story he attacked a chief over his men's treatment. He formulated his plan. All he had to do was stand his ground. The man broke the rules, that's that. He would have the backing of Chief Berger. They would make short order of this bunch of roughnecks. Any man that would work up here had no respect for himself to start with. As he reached the second floor, Tully was coming out of the chief's office and slid the pole to the apparatus floor. Captain Cane looked for a chair to sit.

"Remain standing, Cane," said Chief Walsh. "This will be short. Why didn't you report in to me before going upstairs to Ladder 14 office? You had to pass it."

"Well, I don't know."

"Do you think that you were above protocol of reporting into the officer in charge?"

"No, no, I just didn't think – "

"That's it exactly. You didn't think. Let me make this clear. You're not coming up here and piss on my parade, Cane! I'm writing Tully up for a performance award for his actions tonight, and I suggest you forget what you think happened in your first minutes of your appearance here in my command. This is my ship! You report to me when you board her."

"Oh no! Hold on. I know what happened, and Tully is going to receive charges for insubordination."

"OK, now listen closely," said the chief. "Tully is charging you with being under the influence of alcohol or drugs or both. So I'm going to take you both to the hospital to draw blood. It will become part of charges and countercharge."

"Now hold on, you can't do that."

"Then you're refusing to be tested, Cane?"

"Well, I might have had a drink before I knew I was going to be called to work tonight."

The chief stood up. "Tully will do what I tell him and drop this. We will end it before it starts. If you go on with this, you will not come out clean, Cane. I guarantee that if this foolishly continues."

Captain Cane was in a bad position. He did have a drink while on the phone with Chief Berger and a second one after that to brace himself for working with this bunch of outlaws. He had to refuse the blood test, and this would give a false impression. He was not in full control.

"Now go downstairs and sign in the house watch book. It's 2:00 AM. Case closed, and we start over."

"Yes sir, Chief Walsh," said Captain Cane. He had to think of himself, he thought, and not take a chance. The hospital records would be public records and Chief Berger would not be able to help him. *If Tully tested clean and I refuse to be tested, it would look bad. They won this one.* Cane was thinking he had to think long and hard before he came up here again. And that's how tour went all night; only Chief Walsh responded to the rest of the calls and kept the captain in line. Tully was glad to see the tour come to the end. Too much smoke had hurt his judgment.

CHAPTER 15

REST BETWEEN TOURS, AND EGG IN MY TEA

TULLY LOOKED FOR a parking spot, but it had to be the correct side of the street. The city had alternate street parking for snow and garbage removal. He went around the block two or three times without finding one. It was ten minutes to eleven. He decided to take a chance and parked on the wrong side of the street for the ten minutes left on the restriction. He had hit the proverbial brick wall for endurance. His eyelids felt like swollen blankets closing over his red eyeballs. He was sitting on empty for staying awake gas. He put his firefighter's union card in the window and went into the H-type six-story apartment house. This class of apartment house was the next step in the evolution of housing for the upper-middle classes in the 1900s. This unit was constructed at the end of the 1920s. It was called H-type because its layout was in an H. There were two housing units side by side with a throat unit, which connected the two outside buildings in the middle. Kitty lived here with her parents until Tully and Kitty were married and found an apartment in this same building. This was helpful with Tully working night tours as Kitty could visit her family by taking the elevator from the fifth floor to the third. There was Sunday dinner and football or baseball games that Tully watched with Kitty's dad, and he enjoyed it. Kitty bagged a summer beach house for them after she landed a meaty role on a daytime soap. It was located in Storyville. The small town had nice sandy beaches and an inlet on the Sound where Tully clammed and fished. Their days there had a honeymoon quality. It was slowly becoming their regular home. Smithy and Skitter, who also moved out to the area, made up a carpool they could all take into Harlem. Tully and Kitty's place was a small cape with a dormer and a nice new back porch room that overlooked Long Island Sound, with a pool built into the back deck. Tully had joined the volunteer fire department and laid down roots for the day that they moved out there for good. For now, with both of their jobs being in the city, they kept their city apartment on the fifth floor, and Tully visited Grace, his mother-in-law, in between night tours, when Kitty was working.

Tully took the elevator to the third floor, something he never did, except now he was so tired. His legs felt like cement. He got off the elevator, walked down the white-and-green tile floor, and he rang the doorbell of apartment 310. A fish eye appeared behind a peephole in the center of the door. Some mumbling sounds came from behind the door and a series of locks, dead bolts, and a fox locks. A steel rod in the center of the door, thirty-six inches from the floor, angled into the floor, was unlatched and unfastened.

"God Almighty, Tully, I've had never seen you look so bad. That job is killing you! How could they even call it a job, it's beyond me."

"Please, Grace, my head's killing me," said Tully, making his way into the apartment.

"Do you want breakfast, honey?" asked Kitty's mother, trying to soften her tone.

"No thanks, Grace, just a hot shower and a chance to get some sleep."

"Do you need your clothes washed, Tully?"

"I'm OK, Grace," said Tully.

Tully didn't make it to the shower but lay down in Kitty's old room. The pillow had the scent of Kitty's perfume. She had slept there last night when he was working. The walls were decorated with pictures of Kitty's acting roles. Tully's tired eyes focused on his favorite picture. It was Kitty in a wet T-shirt at a cowboy bar in Long Island. She had worked there on her way up. He took in a deep breath of her scent, and he was asleep. What would seem like an instant, he was awakened by Grace calling his name.

"Tully. You ought to be ashamed of yourself. You didn't even take your clothes off. It's time to get up," said Grace.

"Oh no, it can't be. I just went to sleep!"

"It's 4:00 PM. I'd made coffee. Do you want eggs?"

"Yes! That's good, just let me go catch a shower," said Tully.

"OK. I'll be ready when you're ready," said Grace. "If you want me to scrub your back, just give me a holler. After all, that's what mothers-in-law are for."

"You're a wild woman, Grace," said Tully. Grace's kibitzing put a smile on Tully's face. Grace was the perfect mother-in-law: one part mother, one part platonic girlfriend. She was still a nice-looking woman. She was long and lean and trim like her daughter.

His thoughts turned fondly to Kitty. He was ten years older than she. She was his best friend's little sister. Michael and he had enlisted in the marines together and been shipped overseas and landed at Inchon, Korea, with General Macarthur. It had been a glorious landing and a magnificent advance to north. And then the Chinese entered the war, and so did the early winter, and young man's glory turned into freezing hell on earth. Michael didn't make it home.

Tully's family had moved to New Jersey at the end of the war, and the McCarthys became Tully's second family when he returned to New York. When Kitty was to graduate, she needed a date for her prom dance. Grace had called Tully and asked him to please take her. Tully obliged. She was a good-looking skinny kid at the time, and he fell in love with her at first kiss. But he kept his feelings to himself; she was too young. There was a big difference between seventeen and twenty-seven. She went away for summer stock and then to Europe to tour with a play she was doing with an Off-Broadway theater group for the state department. She had a few boyfriends and many adventures.

Tully was on the fire department and got on with his life. His social activities were mostly the bar scene and sports. He did meet a woman or two, but it just didn't work out. Tully stayed close with the McCarthy family. Kitty's father retired from the Long Island Rail Road and started selling mutual stocks, the first step into the stock market for the little guy in the 1960s. This enterprise had gone over big with his fellow workers, and he had made a modest killing. Just when everything was coming up roses, he died suddenly from a heart attack.

Kitty was now nineteen, and her first love was still the theater. The men she dated from the theater groups were either too fast or sweet but gay. For the hometown boys, her image as an actress didn't foster confidence that she'd bloom into the wifely type in the near future. Kitty turned her "side interest" to horses and took up with a semiwild bunch of Long Island cowboys from the racetrack. Tully came back on the scene again with Grace asking him to please check on Kitty; she had not been home in a week. Tully found Kitty in a cowboy bar winning a wet T-shirt contest and riding a mechanical bull. The ride had just started and was easy to stay on. Kitty's and Tully's eyes met, and Kitty pulled her orange wet T-shirt, monogrammed peanut cups, two tasty treats, and hit Tully slap in the face with it. Kitty had grown up, and she was wild and unbridled as a young mustang. Tully got Kitty home, and they became best friends long before they became lovers. But when the cork came out of the bottle, Kitty felt deliriously in love with Tully. For Tully, it was like opening an artery, frightening and final. He never loved anyone else.

"Tully, your food is gonna get cold," called Grace.

Tully was jolted back to reality, hot water running down the back of his neck. Sleep and hot shower was the lenexa needed to restore him to the living. He dressed quickly and had a wake-up cup of coffee and egg sandwich.

"Grace, do you got something on your mind?"

"Why do you say that, Tully?"

"Because you're standing over me like a cat waiting to pound on a mouse, that's why."

"Tully, do you know what today is?"

"No, Grace, tell me."

"Mr. McCarthy is gone four years."

"Im sorry, Grace, I didn't know," said Tully.

"And I'm thinking I feel responsible for you and Kitty."

"Grace, you sound like you're talking about a car wreck."

Grace continued with an intensity that surprised him. "Tully, remember it was I who asked you to take Kitty to her prom and she was only a kid?"

"Grace, I remember all too well, you asked me to do you a favor and take her, and I did. So what's your point?"

"She told me that you kissed her."

"Well, that was a long time ago, Grace! But yes, I did."

"Well, the point is sometimes all a girl needs is a kiss."

"OK, Grace, you win. I guess I'm a lecherous old man where your daughter is concerned," Tully said with a smile, "failing to see the harm." And wishing to move on, he said, "Where is this all taking us, Grace?"

"We want you to quit that job as a fireman."

"Grace, this is you talking, not Kitty," said Tully.

"I know, as a woman, in her heart she feels the same as I. And you know perfectly well that this so-called job is killing you. Even in war, you have only so many missions to fly or stay in a combat zone only so long. In New York City Fire Department, you just keep going to fire after fire until you get killed or come out cripple."

"Boy, Grace, you should run for union president, that was good."

"This is no joke, Tully, we couldn't stand to lose you! We love you," said Grace. Tully looked at his watch and felt for his gym bag. It was time to go, but he gave Grace another minute.

"First, I lost my dear son, Michael!" Grace continued. Grace was a beautiful woman, thought Tully, looking at her talking with so much passion. She had on a pale green sweater, camel hair slacks, her auburn hair was combed straight back and hung down her back, her green eyes were flashing, her lashes were wet. She turned and pointed to a picture, which sat on top of the refrigerator. "And that's Mr. McCarthy," she pronounced. "He was a saint!"

Tully would have, in most cases, said something like, "He had to be to put up with you." But Grace was now whimpering; Tully had never seen her like this. Tully got up and put his arms around her, and they faced each other.

"Listen, Grace, I love you too, and there's something to say for putting yourself in harm's way for no reason. As Michael and I did in the war. But this is not the same, and I am not killing anyone! I am saving people, doing good, and it makes me happy to do it." Grace wasn't hearing Tully anymore but was pulling his body closer to hers. Tully continued talking, "No, this is different, it's not the same as war. I miss Michael too. He was a beautiful person." Grace held Tully's face in her hands and kissed him gently on the mouth. Tully kissed back. Grace moved her head to a new position and kissed him again with her mouth open, and suddenly, like awaking from a dream, she pushed him away.

"You're a beast for kissing me like that, Tully, a beast."

Tully's head was spinning. He felt light-headed and hot, very hot. "I'm sorry, Grace, I didn't know what I was doing. It just happened."

"Don't you know how lonely I am?" said Grace, who was wearing a bra under her sweater. But it didn't help cover her nipples that were standing out prominently.

Tully took a step back and knocked over the kitchen chair. "Grace, I have a good suggestion for you."

"I already have a vibrator, Tully, I need someone to hold me and make love to me."

Tully picked up the kitchen chair and put it between them. Grace pushed it out of the way. "Grace, I was talking about Captain Mac."

"He's twenty-five years older than me," said Grace.

"No way! Grace, he's fifty-eight," said Tully.

"I just heard him tell the doctor the other night at the hospital his age. Oh God in heaven, what was he laid out on a stretcher at the time!" said Grace.

Tully put his hands up in front of him; his back was now against the wall. "You said you already had love tools! What does his age matter? He has arms to hold you and a mouth to kiss you."

Grace pressed her breasts against Tully's hands and kissed him again. "But he's a fireman like you, Tully," she spoke into his mouth. "I couldn't stand to lose him."

"Didn't you say it was better to have loved and lost than never to have loved at all?" Tully said inches away from Grace's face. Something was happening for Grace as she pressed into Tully and she started to cry and kiss him on the neck. Tully managed to remove his hands from her breasts. She put her face in the crock of his neck; she was smiling and crying at the same time. Tully was left out of the experience. He felt like he just took a beating. The sweat was running down his back. He stood rigidly against the wall; he feared any move would be wrong.

"Tully, I am so ashamed of myself, this is all my fault. Please don't tell Kitty. No, no, god, no."

This caused him to relax. "Grace, listen, I'll talk to Captain Mac. Don't worry, I'll be discreet."

"Yeah, sure, I can hear it now! Listen, man, I got this old babe who wants to get laid."

They laughed. "Trust me, Grace, you're still a babe."

"I've always trusted you, Tully, that's why I put my daughter in your arms."

"And no man has had a greater gift," said Tully.

CHAPTER 16

ANOTHER FLY IN THE OINTMENT, THE CANE MUTINY

TULLY QUICKLY RAN down the three flights of stairs. He felt 100 percent better physically than five hours before when he needed the help of the elevator to get to the third floor. But now, something in the pit of his stomach was not right. He was confused by Grace's (his mother-in-law) actions and what part he had played in the whole mess. He was the first one to get up and put his arms around Grace; this was a comforting embrace. But it had triggered something else. They had both crossed the line. Tully hit the outside air, and he realized his T-shirt was wet with perspiration. He crossed the street to his car, and there was a fifteen-dollar parking ticket on his windshield. He took the ticket and put it in his pocket, opened the door to his Mustang, turned the motor over, and burned rubber all the way down the street.

By the time he reached Astoria Boulevard and crossed it and made his approach to the Triboro Bridge, he had cooled down to the point he was capable of rational thought. Grace was right; sometimes all it takes is a kiss to fall in love. Tully had kissed Kitty that night of her prom. But it was not to take advantage of her. She was seventeen years old, and he was twenty-seven. It was a total mismatch not just in years, but also in what type of life they had up to this point in time. It had been an outstanding night, and they had come to the next-to-the-last couple from being picked on the dance floor, which would have made Kitty prom queen. She was still very happy. Tully had thought at the time it had to be him who kept her from winning, because she was so beautiful and it all seemed to happen at once. One minute she was his friend's little sister who was killed in Korea and he was doing a favor for the mother. But from the time they entered the ballroom, she came alive. Like the unexpected bubbles in opening your first bottle of champagne, like the second before sunrise on a tenement roof when you have lost track of time. The smoke clears like a fog, and you know the fire is out, and now everyone gets a chance to live one more day, and then the sun rises. Kitty was Tully's new day. She caught everyone's eye and stole Tully's heart that night. He was defenseless against her charms. When she slid across the car seat at night's end, she kissed him and whispered, "Take me, Tully. Please!" He regained control. It was wrong for every reason he had been taught, and right for every fiber programmed in his male body. But he fought that side of himself for the day that it would be right. He knew he loved her from that minute on, and yes, Grace was right. Sometimes it only takes one kiss. Somehow he got her home and had one drink that Grace had poured for him, and he left. The irony of this whole situation, their love and their life together, Grace was responsible for. She had a hand in building the foundation from the beginning, and now she could destroy it all.

Yes, he would give up his job for Kitty if she wanted it. But Kitty knew the importance of their careers. They had talked about it endlessly. Acting and what she wanted. It was not a lark for Kitty. She had discovered her calling. She did not pretend to understand Tully's vocation, but she respected it. He was happy, and he was doing good work; that was enough for her and, more importantly, for them as a couple. Tully had been able to put aside things that other men who were less comfortable with their manhood might have worked on their egos. Kitty made four times the salary that Tully made, and as part of her contract, she was giving the beach house they lived in. Kitty's role as home wrecker and Western trollop deluxe, whose job it was to kiss all the cowboys and shoot out all the lights and show the most skin, that helped to build the male watchers who tuned in daily. This might not be so bad had half of the firehouse in the city tuned in to drool over Kitty's charms each day, including Tower Ladder 14. But Tully and Kitty had something few lovers never have; they were happy with each other just the way they were. They liked each other and were glad that the other was happy in their work. Tully knew he had to do everything in his power to keep things the way they were.

But how?

* * *

Tully made his way into the firehouse kitchen to grab a cup of coffee. He is greeted by Smithy with, "You got the first watch."

"I think I know that," said Tully.

"The bad news is they're ganging up on us tonight," said Smithy.

"How's that?" asked Tully, taking a second sip of hot coffee.

"Well, we got a covering chief and killed Cane is back as captain."

"Oh boy," expressed Tully.

"And I think they are asshole buddies," said Smithy. Tully took the parking ticket out of his pocket to take a look at it. "Do you want me to take the first watch so you can stay away from each other?" asked Smithy.

"That's a good idea, thanks, Smithy," said Tully, putting away the ticket.

"Well, I think the best plan is to lie low tonight, let them make all the calls, and if things go wrong, oh well, the ball is in their court. And y'know what's the joke? That some people in this job think they can put out the fires without firemen. Like all they got to do is stand outside in some magical spot and then stick a finger up their ass and scream and the fire goes out," said Smithy.

"Let's hope they don't kill anyone," added Tully.

The tour started very slow, and Ducky decided on something simple for supper like hamburger and french fries and a salad. The word was out that the orders were to batten down the hatches and weather the storm. The first incident with the covering captain started after his roll call. He told the crew that he didn't believe in preassignments and that he would assign tasks at each fire. No one add any information like, "You're endangering the other truck company. They would expect us to cover our position." There was no point. Cane was not a fire officer but an office worker, detailed to one hideout or another his whole time in the job. So it was just "Yes, sir," and "No, sir." He also announced he was not going to eat with the company! But had brought his own gourmet dinner in a "brown bag."

The company had two runs: one, a car fire, and the second, food on stove. These were very easy for the captain to command as a company stayed together for both jobs. The drill was on searching. The captain said that there was no need for firemen to have flashlights; it only encouraged theft. Ducky, Tully, and Smithy had worked with this captain and realized that they were dealing not only with a bean counter, but also with a mental case. So they said nothing. This all would be straightened out as soon as they would go to a real fire.

One of the ladies of the night busted into quarters. She was trying to escape a beating from her man, the pimp. She was spaced-out on drugs and was crying for help. The captain acted indifferently to her predicament and ordered Smithy to escort her out of quarters. As long as the captain was going by the rule book, Smithy, who had been a captain in the Special Forces outfit in the army, knew how to play the game. "With due respect, Captain, I'm not putting my hands on this lady. She's a citizen, and she requested help."

"She's an animal," retorted the captain, "and I want her out of these quarters."

"With due respect, I am prevented from carrying out any unlawful orders against citizens. It's my duty," said Smithy, "to report her request and entrance into quarters in the book and get help for her."

With authority, the pimp entered quarters with a big stick and two more ladies. Tully opened the apparatus door. If there was going to be a fight, they were going to need room. Smithy didn't wait for the officer but picked up the department phone and asked the dispatcher for a police car. Ducky took a pike-head axe from behind the front seat of the truck. Smithy pulled a nightstick from under the desk and slammed it on the desk. This startled the captain and rattled the pimp. The pimp threw up his hands in surrender; he backed off. "Everything cool, man. This ho can do anything she wants. She's back on the street for all I care." He vacated the scene.

Two other girls stepped in and got the girl from behind Smithy and comforted her and told her she was a good girl. And it was OK. The captain stormed upstairs mumbling that the place was a zoo and to read his regulations; without them, he was lost. For his leadership was based on someone else's general rules, not his experience in the field, in the street, or on reason. The girls came back to the firehouse and told Smithy they owed him a favor; the pimp had been persuaded to go easy on his woman as the firemen had witnessed the altercation and that to hurt her was a mistake. They had recorded it in their watch books.

Smithy told them, looking up at the clock, "You can do me a favor later tonight when traffic slows down."

"You name your poison, baby, and you got it," said both girls, rocking their stuff. Smithy told them what he wanted in hushed tones.

The third fire call of the night was a vacant building on Hundred and 123rd Streets. The fire was on the third-floor rear of a five-story tenement, and it was going good; the fire was out into the hallway. To say any fire is easy is a mistake, but with vacant tenements located, the fire is less difficult. There was no forcible entry; all ventilation of windows and doors were already done and off their hinges. The fire did not bank down early. Because the building was open, the first order of business was to find the fire and then confine it, preventing its spread to other parts of the building. There could always be squatters in the building, or it could be a scene of a crime, but in this case, there were no complications. The captain hadn't assigned anyone to the roof. This probably was going to be OK as the roof bulkhead door was open. The covering chief stopped the engine from stretching 1 ½ hose line because it was not regulation when the fire is above the first floor. This had been a bone of contention between uptown and downtown companies for generations. The simple fact was lofts and tenements were different types of fire; the bigger 2 ½ hose was needed in large open floor space of lofts and heavy fire load, while the faster and lighter 1 ½ was in most cases better at tenement fires. The legendary Chief Halligan, inventor of the Halligan tool, was captain of Engine 35 in years past and had worked out a brilliant compromise: attach a 1 ½ hose and a nozzle to the big feeder line, the 2 ½, the advantage potential for double the volume of water should the 1 ½ hose attack fail. Disconnect the 1 ½ from the 2 ½ controlling nozzle; hence, a 250 gpm attack is at hand and the regulation is satisfied. This was never challenged, provided the fire didn't get away. The covering chief was a bean counter but was not in the same class as Captain Cane or Chief Berger. Still he went by the regulation all the way. Avoided any messy new thinking. Ladder 43 responded and took the normal positions, the floor above and the roof.

Ladder 43 reported from the roof that there was fire on two floors. This caused the covering chief to panic and order a second alarm. This caused the deputy chief, the next highest-ranking chief, to respond. When he rolled in, he wanted to know what the hell was going on. He started giving orders to put the fire out with two engines and trucks and sent everyone else back. The deputy chief began an on-scene investigation to what pulled him away from the Mets game. He personally would have to answer to the big chief. What went wrong at this box? Chief of department Mann hated second alarms for vacant buildings. It was a waste of manpower in his book. Ladder 43 reported to the chief that no one had made the roof from Ladder 14 and no one put up the tower ladder to the roof. Ducky reported he was giving orders not to do so or anything else without direct orders from the covering officers. Plus he didn't assign the company positions, and that's why no one got to the roof. The deputy came back to quarters and had the captain give out assignments while he stood there. And he had the senior man, Tully, recite the latitude of each position, and then he took a mark in the book. To the fact, he also asked the captain and the chief their last assignment; both confessed it was Chief Berger's office. He shook his head with an "Oh brother" under his breath and left quarters.

The truck had only one more run of little consequence and then a car fire at 1230. Smithy was talking to the girls in the street as the truck backed into its firehouse bay. Upon returning to quarters, the captain was somewhat subdued and tired from the night's activity. This was the most fire calls he responded to in years; in fact, this was the busiest night of his career, and this was a slow tour so far for Tower 14. All he could think of was hitting the hay. The covering chief was in quarters, and he was in bed already. He was not pleased at how this night had gone, and he planned to retire before he let himself be talked into coming up here again. The captain walked up the three flights of stairs to the third floor.

He took off his fire-drenched officer's shirt and put it over the chair in the dark, kicked off his shoes, and dropped his pants; the last thought in his mind was to lie down. He sat down on the naked girl who had fallen asleep waiting for the birthday-boy surprise party! She squealed and he jumped back in shock and he snapped on the lights. The girl gracefully stretched her beautiful slender body, her arms above her head. When she reached the apex of her stretch, her thighs snapped open like a mechanical sex doll, and she quivered. She had gunfighter's eyes that never left his face. She had a racehorse tattooed above her vaginal area. "Giddy up, girl," she said. "It's time for business." She gave it a gentle slap with her riding cape, and she did a grind and a bump that would knock your hat off. "I know what you want, birthday boy. Discipline and order, and I'm the momma who can give it to you."

The captain stood and gaped in total disbelief. He broke into a cold sweat, in his confused thinking at this point. He was lucky that this den of vipers had not waited for him to sleep and had his throat cut. The logic in this was a review of fifty mortal sins. The severity of what he was witnessing easily outweighed murder. Still there was something strangely appealing about it to him. He shook his head to rid his mind of this idea. It was the strain of command. He must collect himself and rise above it. "You dumb bitch, get your tart clothes on, and get the hell out of here."

"Oh, you want to play games, birthday boy," she said as she gave his backside a crack.

"Now stop that," said the captain, pulling the riding crop away from her.

"Hey, don't get sassy with me," said the girl.

"I told you to get your clothes on and get out of here, and it's not my birthday."

"OK, you have it your way, it's your party. I know what you want," said the girl with real enthusiasm. "You want me to do the boys downstairs while you watch. And then I spank you."

"No no no no, put your clothes on and get completely the hell out of here." The captain did add *please* as an afterthought with a pleading tone.

Ducky had brought the attack duck into quarters at 1:00 AM. After the last run, he had bed down with the werewolf, the company dog, behind the radiator. With all the commotion on the third floor, the dog knew, of course, that the girl had gone upstairs between runs, and she knew the dog and gave him a cookie. Now he wanted to join in the fun. He did so by running around the apparatus baying. The duck was flying after him trying to get a hold of his ear to make him behave if anyone had gone to sleep. That moment was over now. Back on the third floor, the girl was putting back on her red panties.

"You have it your way, big daddy. You're the boss man and love to give orders." She put on her colorful jockey hat and picked up her riding crop and her knapsack and started down the spiral stairs.

"No, no," the captain pleaded, "put your clothes on," as he ran after her with them.

"That's more like it, big daddy!" she laughed.

Smithy had stationed himself on the second floor with his Polaroid camera by the light switch. He hit the switch and turned on all the lights as Captain Cane came down the stairs with the girl. He snapped off a perfect picture of the covering captain's catching the naked girl as she fled for safety. *You hypocrite. You call these brown people animals, and look at yourself, a disgrace to this department.* With this commotion, the chief got out of bed, came out of his office like a warhorse, and caught the captain red-handed with this girl and her laughing like a banshee.

"Cane, what in the hell did you get us into now?" steamed the chief.

Smithy snapped a second picture with the nymph striking a totally classic pose between the covering captain and the chief, both in their Skivvies, and her just in red panties, jockey cap. Smithy was a trained warrior. Plan the ambush, spring the trap, persecute the enemy till neutralized, of which one last step was left. Smithy slid in the pole and waited by the front door. The captain, in a near state of collapse, was red faced but determined to have this nightmare end. He made it to the front door with the girl. But Smithy blocked it and took his last picture. The girl posed for it, with her small breasts, and darted her tongue in the direction of the same. Cane made a lunge for Smithy. But the girl booted him from behind for the ruff handling, which tripped him up. The werewolf executed the coup de grâce, nosed him in the butt, and he went into the apparatus door, ass over teakettle. Tully and Ducky helped to pick him up.

Smithy, who had the killer instinct, started the eulogy. "Drunk and unable to do his duty. But have no fear, Cane, we'll protect you from yourself." Addressing the two probies, he said, "Men, go upstairs and collect the captain's whiskey bottles. "I think there's some good in this man. After all, he is a brother. After he sobers up, we'll have Father Cook come over to hear his confession and bless quarters." He turned to the girl, "Go in peace, my child."

She left half dressed and strolled down the street hoping for a last trick. A police car passed her without comment. The time was 3:45 AM. Their tour was ending. The cops just looked at each other. A naked beach had opened at Rise Park this past summer. So toplessness on 125th Street at three in the morning must be OK for working people. Just one more sin against oneself.

CHAPTER 17

WHEN THE CAT IS AWAY, THE MOUSE WILL PLAY

CHIEF BILL WALSH and Captain Patrick McLaughlin were in the firehouse at 7:30 AM, one hour and a half before the start of this morning tour. They found an empty firehouse. The company dog and the duck were lying down in their bed of hay. The tower and the chief's car were out on a call. There was no relocating company in quarters. The chief had asked the captain to the second floor to have a cup of coffee and called the dispatcher to find out if the companies would need to be relieved at the fire, and he was told no, but if they did, the dispatcher would call back. They talked over the brownstone fire they had on the night tour.

"The fire the other night went as good as can be expected, Pat. What do you think?" said Chief Walsh.

"Well yes, we were shorthanded with only one engine and a truck, so I'll say damn good considering."

"I'm going to write Tully up for his work. I might have let it go with a pat on the back. But his work through the rest of the tour, continuing on duty with a smoke injury and putting up with the covering Captain Cane, merits this command gratitude. If it just amounts to class A award, it's better than a stick in your eye."

"Well yes! No argument with me. I spoke with him on the phone, and we had a long talk on a good number of things." Captain Pat was keeping his comments short to keep away from what had happened with Captain Cane; the lesser said, the better.

"Well, good, let's go on with it," said Chief Walsh. "I have been trying to find the time to talk with you on a few things. Off the record, chief of department Mann and Chief Berger's dislike for each other is starting to spill over into operations."

"Yes," added Captain Mac. "With Berger's control of the personnel, it was only a matter of time until he sent his spies up here."

"I had a conversation with Chief Mann at Chief Cortland's party in Brooklyn," said the chief. "He told me he had big plans to convert many ladder companies over to tower ladders. But if Tower Ladder 14 could be discredited in any way, it might give ammunitions for the tower ladder's opponents."

"Oh, I see. Well, it comes to that, has it?" commented Captain Mac.

"I wanted to let you know that Tully's trouble with Captain Cane may have had something to do with it," added the chief.

The captain knew the chief was a fighter. Someone had to step up and take a beating for the little guy, even if it meant sidetracking his own career. The chief had actually had a fistfight with a deputy chief in Bronx on the fire ground because his men were not being treated fairly. His job was saved by the chief of department Mann, and he was transferred to Harlem Twelfth Battalion. But before he left, he was given a party that would end all parties. He was presented with a new car by his men. He had been dealt many injustice in his life and was a quiet man, but a dangerous one because he would die for a just cause. The captain felt a kinship to him that he felt for few men. The ironic thing was the chief, the captain, and Tully were all cut from the same mold – birds of a feather personalitywise. Captain McLaughlin recognized it. He saw his job was to safeguard him to the best of his abilities. He thought the best plan here was to keep his powder dry and not add fuel to the fire that was already burning in the chief's gut.

"Chief, I will give you my word! I, we will do everything in our power to run our operation in a peerless manner. God willing." The adding of the God equation seemed to help the chief relax. Chief Walsh sat back in his chair. "Another cup of coffee, Cap?" offered the chief.

"Yes, that would be fine." The chief poured from his thermos. "You didn't try any of the coffee cake, Patty."

"Well, to tell you the truth, I've been watching my weight."

"You look in good shape to me." The captain didn't reply. "Captain, do you think there's anything to saying that God's work is done by the average man?"

"I don't think there's any doubt about it, that's why so little is getting done today!" answered the captain. Both men laughed.

"In my talk with Chief Mann, I brought up an operation that Tully had picked off a jumper below the fire."

"Oh yes," Captain Mac nodded, remembering the incident. "It was an order that at the time I thought was right, but Tully said there was a drill on this, dropping off the roof man first was the most good for the greatest number. If possible."

"Yes, we have a drill on this," said the captain. "It's a very close call. What I remember was there was a man holding him from jumping."

"Yes, that's right," said the chief.

"Well, my point is the chief of department knew Tully was a volunteer and called him the messenger. It didn't surprise me that he knew him," said the captain. "I sent him in to talk to the commander at fires where we are especially called to find out where they want us." The captain thought for minute before continuing. "Do you remember the collapse of the eight-story icehouse located on the 125th Street?"

"Oh, I do, I was on the roof, and we were ordered off."

"Well, do you remember there was talk of a miracle radio silence? It was broken by a question, how long is this fire burning?"

"Yes, I do," said the chief.

"It was Tully. I punched him the minute he said it. He had a blank look on his face, and then the chief asked for the message to be repeated. When there was no answer, he ordered everyone out of the building. It was less than fifteen minutes, and she came down! I say, without doubt, thirty men would have been lost. We were in the bucket with Danny Peters, ammonia pipes broke that had been used for refrigeration, and this turned to steam, it put us on our knees. I thought the tower ladder was coming down, it rocked back and forth. But we all got out of it fine. There were some questions, but the chief was happy to let it go as dumb luck."

"Or divine providence," added Chief Walsh.

"Well, that's the rest of the stories," said Captain Mac. "Tully is not what you call a religious man. He didn't really want to talk about it." Both men were quiet for a time.

"How are things going in your life, Patty?"

"Well, it's four years now. Without Maureen. The hardest part is not having someone to meet me when I come home. The lights are out, and as they say in a song, the pots and pans are cold. Maureen was never one to be complacent in her wifely duties. She greeted me after each night tour like I've been away for six months at sea. She'd have steak and eggs, home fries and two fingers of Irish whiskey set out for me, and the pipe and slippers. And she'd be more than agreeable with any other thing else I had on my mind."

"I truly can't think how it would be without Margaret," said the chief.

"In the end, the brotherhood came through for me. Tully's been like a son to me. He helped me out in personal ways more than once. I'm very happy with the rest of my crew, Smithy and Ducky. Romeo and things are going good. There is something I can let you in on." Patty moved closer with his chair. "I have a good feeling about this. Well, I was telling you about the talk I had with Tully. He told me his mother-in-law, the Mrs. McCarthy, was coming out of a most respectable bereavement period." The chief had moved closer not to miss a word. "And with my permission," Patty sat up proudly, "he'll talk to the poor woman. To the possibilities for herself to test the waters of male companionship. The poor thing is but forty-four. With me being fifty-eight, thirteen years difference, I promised to be as gentle as a groom with a maiden filly."

The department phone rang its old-fashioned ring of a rotary phone. Chief Walsh reached for it and answered, "Twelfth Battalion."

"Chief, is the truck officer in quarters?" asked the dispatcher.

"Yes, he's right here, I'll put him on," said the chief, handing the captain the phone. And after a brief conversation, the captain put the phone back in its cradle.

"They had two DOAs at the fire, and the truck will need relief at the scene. The assistant chief is coming up from downtown, and the officer wants to fill me in on the operation."

"Yes, I think I'll take a ride over myself, but before you go, Patty, I'd like to tell you. You're a good man. If I had a daughter or sister the right age for you, I'll highly recommend you make a fine husband in the true sense of the word. And I'll keep my fingers crossed for things to work out with you and Mrs. McCarthy." Patty reached out and shook the chief's hand and then stepped back and gave a Kent Regiment salute.

* * *

The chief looked at the picture on his desk of his two daughters toting fishing poles, holding up a string of fish. They were twelve and fourteen years old. How manageable they were then. That was ten years ago. And now they were proving to be a handful. He wanted all the freedom and equity that this new age could bring them, but what was being lost was impossible for them to completely see. But he could see there was losses already. One of the indirect cost would be the virtue of this type of man. For he was the old-school gentleman that was about to fade from the scene. A dinosaur, as his daughter would call him. But this is the type of man a father would pick for his daughters. These were changing times, and it was taking all his patience to keep peace in his family.

Two years before, after his neighbor's daughter had run away and another became pregnant, he and his wife, Margaret, started a conversation that continued for a month. In the end, they came to the conclusion that what happened to their neighbors could happen to their daughters too; they needed a plan. Part one, the chief would let his wife hear them out. He would stay out of it. Two, she would take them to the doctor and have him write a prescription for the pill. Regardless of what their church said about birth control and sexual relations before marriage, they were not revolutionary. He and his wife. Their views just changed when they saw lives ruined in families just like their own.

But it was easier said than done. There was guilt, and because it was not easy to change yourself after a lifetime of thinking one way, it also opened up a very old wound for the chief. He had been brought up in the New York foundling home, his start in life probably because of a mistake of his mother; he did not know that for sure. He was told she was too young to marry the father. Her name was Walsh. As time went on for the boy, he had lost the ability to smile at the groups of people who came to look them over for adoption. There were many children like Billy Walsh who were aging out of the system. Someone had the idea. "Let's go put them on a train and send them to the Midwest. They could be adopted by farm family." Billy's same problem worked against him on his ride on the orphan train. There were only three children left on the rainy morning in August as the train pulled in to Lincoln, Nebraska. The children had come down with a nasty cold, except Billy and Margaret Ann Connors. Her brother, Joseph, had it the worst. A doctor had come on the train in Chicago to look at them. "They would get over it," he had said, "but it's not going to get better riding and sleeping on the train." The night before, Billy and Margaret slept next to Joseph to keep him warm. Sister had come on them and shook her head and said, "Poor babies," and kept saying the Rosary.

In the morning, Joseph could just about stand up as they filed onto the platform. There was only one couple waiting for them. They picked Margaret first. Sister said, "She has a brother." They looked at Billy because he was standing next to her. He bit his lip to keep from smiling back. *They look like such nice people,* he thought. They looked at Joseph with a sad look. Sister stepped in and said, "He had been seen by a doctor. He has no fever, it's the trip on his system and only a common cold." Billy put his handkerchief to his face and faked a cough and gagged himself and threw up on the platform. "Oh my!" said the perplexed woman. She looked back at Joseph, and he smiled, and she said, "We will take the brother and sister." The nun put her arm around Billy and walked him back to the train. Margaret took the woman's hand and kissed it and ran after the nun and Billy Walsh. Catching up with them, she said, "Someday, Billy, we'll be together forever. And no one will part us, I love you. Thanks for what you did for Joseph, we will never forget you. I love you." She sobbed and kissed him hard on the mouth. Tears were running down Sister's face as she held the children she had cared for from babies. "Go, Margaret. God loves you, child."

* * *

There was a knock on the chief's door. Skitter stepped in. "Chief, are you OK? You didn't pick up the phone. I buzzed you from downstairs. I am driving you today," said Skitter.

"I'm sorry, I was just thinking how lucky I am."

"Chief, how about the day off?"

"Skitter, I said I was lucky. I didn't say anything about you being lucky! But I may buy you coffee and cake. Sit down by the typewriter."

"Oh boy, this doesn't have a good sound to it."

CHAPTER 18

THE FAT CATS

HOWARD PARKER DOUBLE-PARKED the black Buick. The license plate was car 5. He carefully checked the inside of the car for cleanliness before stepping out and locking the car. He checked his watch; it was 9:00 AM. The chief had told him to pick him up a little later this morning than the usual 7:00 AM. He had a political dinner to attend last night and would need more time to get going this morning. The street was showing some activity of morning chores. Bringing in the garbage cans and sweeping the front steps. It was a residential block lined with brownstones on both sides of the street; the houses were well cared for. The front curb was lined with maple trees with cobblestones encompassing them. Ornate flower urns in the shape of a lion head with a brass ring in their nose sat on both sides of the front steps to Chief Mann's house. The ornamental ironwork was in fine order and freshly painted black. This neighborhood was holding up well. Part of its secret was its individually low-density units owned by one family. The tenements on the other hand had sixteen or more apartments. There was more to take care of and more to go wrong. A strong super and a good owner could work together and keep the building up. But an owner who was trying to take every cent out of the building and put nothing back, coupled with tenants late or behind in their rents, was a poor combination for good building and a good neighborhood.

Howard was wearing a blue class-A fireman's uniform. He wore three gold pins on his left sleeve. Awards for class-one rescues. He danced down the three front steps to the ground floor entrance. He had taps on the front and back of his shoes. From time to time, he danced into a room. It always brightened the room with smiles from even the "grinches." The cost was small, and it gave Howard a persona that was priceless. "You know Howard?" "Oh, sure, the dancer." Howard rang the doorbell next to the iron gate under the stairs then opened it and walked in. There was an antique mahogany foyer piece of furniture built into the wall. It had three oval mirrors and a place to sit and change your overshoes and hat and an umbrella rack. The Manns called it a hall tree. John Mann and his wife, Elizabeth Mann, were committed to maintain, restore, and at the same time, modernize where they could without losing the charm of their brownstone. They were also doing all they could for their community. They both belonged to organizations that had muscle and could bring civil powers to bear on violators of building codes and sanitation.

Howard stopped at the hall tree and checked his tie and Afro before walking down the long hallway. There was loud talking coming from the rear sunroom-and-kitchen combination. The morning sun was playing through the rear glass doors. Over the doors were triangle glass panels, which gave the room a cheerful, open airiness. The glass wall overlooked a redbrick walkway and a flower garden of budding roses and hollyhocks. To the left of the yard was a magnolia tree in a sunken garden located next to the building foundation. The tree was out of its recommended region by three hundred miles, surviving by happenstance. The last owner of the house had a black housekeeper and cook, whose son had helped her to bring the young tree to Brooklyn from Charleston, South Carolina, to remind her of the South in spring. They planted the tree, praying it would take hold facing the South with the morning sun and protection from the north wind by the building. But it was the escaping heat from the cellar furnace that kept the ground and the trees' roots from freezing in harder New York winters.

To the joy of all, Susan Mann was standing in front of the glass doors holding a teacup and looking at the tree. She was dressed in a light cotton cover-up. The back lighting silhouetted her slim elegant frame. She had beautiful blond flowing hair, her facial feature small and delicate, her bosom was round and full, her long legs ended in gold slippers with a small heel. Around her ankle, she wore a small gold bracelet.

"Good morning, Miss Susan, Mrs. Mann, and chief," said Howard in deep, pleasing tones. All returned the greeting. They had stopped talking as Howard entered the room.

"Please sit down, Howard," said Mrs. Mann. "What would you like this morning, bacon and eggs or just a sandwich?"

"A sandwich would be fine, Mrs. Mann."

The chief had started to read the *New York Times* that Howard had brought in with him. A fine haze was visible in the rays of the sun from the morning cooking.

"Daddy," said Susan in careful tones, "I still can't see why you can't transfer Terry to the firehouse down at the square. Why does he have to go all the way up to Harlem? He is too tired to take me out or do anything but take me to a movie, and then he goes to sleep on me. It's like going out with an old man."

That got a snicker from the chief from behind his newspaper. Howard couldn't help but chuckle at the chief, but he caught himself. "Miss Susan, I saw Tom Burke the other day, and he said your Terry was just doing fine at 14 Truck," said Howard, wishing he said nothing.

Susan put down her teacup and put her cigarette out in it. "Daddy, you're so stubborn and mean. I believe you're trying to kill that boy on me."

"Susan, is that any way to talk to your father?" said Mrs. Mann.

Susan turned on her heels and did not answer. But before she left the room, she walked over to Howard and bent down, knowingly revealing her breasts and kissing him on the forehead. "Thank you for being concerned for Terry," said Susan. "You have a good heart."

Howard thought of Salome, beautiful daughter of King Herod. Salome's charms and dance was so pleasing to the king that he said he would grant her any wish. Her request was John the Baptist's head. Females were the weaker sex as far as lifting dumbbells goes, but their powers of persuasion should never be underestimated.

"Howard," said the chief, taking him away from his thoughts, "do you still wish you had three daughters instead of three sons?"

"That was idle talk, Chief, idle talk. I believe it's true that there's more tears shed for answered prayers than the unanswered."

"That's so true," said Mrs. Mann, looking at the four gold stars on her husband's collar. "How are things going for you, Howard? Are your boys helping out at home?"

"They're a big help in cleaning out the refrigerator and filling up the wash basket. But that's about it. But as the saying goes, I take one day at a time and a little help from the Lord."

"Howard, you have not said one original thing all morning," said the chief, looking back at the *Times*. Howard looked sheepish.

"Now, John, don't you pick on Howard, he is just being a gentleman."

"Well, to tell you the truth, Chief, when you're invited to a Manns kitchen in the morning, you get in a lot less trouble watching your p's and q's. And staying far away as possible from originality."

"Howard, you're not only a gentleman, but a scholar and one hell of a smoke eater," laughed John Mann, putting down the paper and realizing he was unfair and put in a cranky mode by his daughter. It's amazing that he could command a ten thousand – man department and not handle his own family affairs better. This whole thing with Terry was getting out of hand. He decided to try and get this thing off his mind. He had thought he didn't have a prejudiced bone in this body. He supported all minorities in the job and pointed them to their organizations for help and carefully assigned them where they would have a fair chance to be assimilated into the job. But where it came to his daughter's boyfriend, he had come to realize he was not being fair. But only too late. He could not clearly put his finger on it. That small preference for what was perceive as one's own. And that goes double for a father-and-daughter relationship. A Freudian touch. Or whatever. He decided for now to do nothing, but let it all take its course. He had told Terry Pena all bets were off. That he would not last on the job six months. Ladder 14 was one of the best places to learn the job from good people, and that was the truth.

Mrs. Mann handed Howard his sandwich and smiled. "Now if you want anything else, just ask, dear."

"Howard, you were going to a meeting with Commissioner up in Harlem last night, how'd things go?" asked the chief.

"Oh, just fine, we had a good time. He has so many friends up there. He introduced us to Rex Brown. He was famous to us colored kids as the colored cowboy. Back in the old days, we had cartoons on set with the regular movies and as an extra was a colored-cowboy movie. They were great fun. We would get out of the movies and have shoot-outs all the way home. Well, it turns out that this actor, Rex, had an inspiration. To show us boys and girls a different side of life, only in black face. He was an honest to goodness colored cowboy from Texas and rodeo rider. I can't tell you how happy that made me to hear and meet one of my personal heroes." Both Manns showed interest in what Howard was saying, so he continued, "Well, this here cowboy actor had an interesting life himself. He served in the U.S. Army in France in World War I. The colored boys were assigned to separate units under French officers back then, and this unit was in combat longer than any other unit on the American side."

"I did not know that," said Chief Mann.

"Howard, can I ask you a question? Why do use the term *colored*?" asked Mrs. Mann.

"Yes," said Howard. "Black is in now, but our most important organization is still NAACP, Nation Association for the Advancement of Colored People, and I grow up with the term *colored*, and to tell you the truth, I like it better. And because I think of myself as colored." This got a smile of approval from Mrs. Mann.

"Well, Howard, we better get going!" said the chief, looking at his watch. "We got the chief's meeting at 1000 hours."

"Howard, please make sure John takes his blood pressure medicine," said Mrs. Mann, kissing her husband good-bye and giving her hand to Howard.

CHAPTER 19

TOWER LADDER 14 ON THE AIR

CAPTAIN MAC HAD done his roll call and gave out assignments. Mike Paul had brought the tower back to quarters with some of last night's crew. Captain Mac spoke to Ducky and told him that he was going to use the trip over to last night's fire for driver training if they picked up a call on the air. Tully would get them there, and Ducky would take over at the scene. There was some kidding, as Tully pulled the tower ladder out of quarters, that Ducky was losing his seat, but Ducky went along with the whole thing with good humor. Captain Mac used the phone in the cab to tell the Manhattan dispatcher that they were returning to the scene of third alarm. When Captain Mac broke the news to the chief about Tully's mother-in-law, he realized that he was excited about the idea.

"Tully, I was talking with the master of the boatyard at City Island that I was planning on taking out the *Tigerous* for a shakedown cruise. It had been refitted with a new diesel motor and some of its systems reworked. And he liked that idea. The weather looks good this Saturday. Is that too soon?" asked Captain Mac.

"Cap, what street was last night's fire on?" asked Tully.

"Oh, I'm sorry, Tully, I'm acting like schoolboy about this date. It's 138th Street off Madison Avenue. Well, is it too soon?" asked Captain Mac.

Tully laughed. "It's not too soon for me. I can call Kitty at lunchtime and ask if it's OK with her, and she can call Grace."

"We could sail out to your place at the head of the harbor," Captain Mac said.

"Gee, that sounds like a great idea to me," said Tully.

"Well, that's a long first ride if you don't like the water," said Captain Mac.

"Grace's father was an old-time ship captain, and he had a fishing boat out at Montauk Point. She would go out with him as a girl. She has a picture of herself with a watch cap, T-shirt, and dungarees on. She looked just like Kitty. So she knows the water! It's Kitty," said Tully. "We got to be careful with her skin."

"How's that?" asked Captain Mac.

"Well," said Tully, "she can't show up with a sunburn that's not in her script. She's been trying to get a tan slowly. Look, Cap! Let's not get ahead of ourselves," said Tully. "Let me call Kitty and let the women figure it out. I can't tell you just how happy I am that you're willing to meet Grace," said Tully. "Grace is lonely, and we'll be very happy if this all works out. Very happy indeed," added Tully as he picked his way into 138th Street with the tower ladder. "I forgot these old wooden row frames were here," said Tully.

"That's maybe why the assistant chief may want us to take a look at them," said Cap.

There were three wooden-frame buildings, three stories in height. They had significant degree of fire damage to all three top floors, with the front wall burned away and pulled apart in the overhaul process. One charged hose line was going in the front door of the building on the far left, which was most probably the original fire building. It had the most damage.

"Have you been to many of these fires? Wooden frames?" asked Captain Mac.

"A few multiple alarms in the Bronx like this, and a few in Queens before I transferred here."

"Any opinions?" asked Captain Mac.

Tully knew that the captain was testing him and himself for the assistant chief's possible questions. "Well," started Tully, "they're somewhat like a taxpayer. When the fire gets in cockloft, it extends horizontally in the roof space. That could bring the fire to the next building because of the lack of fire stopping between buildings. It's hard to get water on that type of fire."

"Good! What do we do to put it out?" asked the captain, pulling ceilings and getting up under it.

"With the water, it's a fight that has many fronts, you need many small-task teams to outflank it. You need to get ahead and cut it off, instead of chasing it. If this was a big row of frames or row of taxpayers, I wouldn't rule out disturbers into the roof," added Tully.

"You got it, son," said Captain Mac with a look of satisfaction for his pupil.

The rest of the crew had dismounted the rig and headed over to Engine 36's pumper. Mike had brought the tower ladder back to quarters with three firemen, Lieutenant O'Brien, Leroy P. Jimmy M. had stayed with the lieutenant. They were covered white plaster dust, and their faces were clothed with black film from the smoke they had been working in.

"Well, the amazing Mets dumped another one last night, Ob," said Smithy to the lieutenant, who was a fan.

"Well, you can't win them all, Smithy." The lieutenant looked very tired, or else he would have a comeback for Smithy. Smithy realized his attempt to bring a smile to Ob's face went over like a lead balloon.

"I heard the assistant chief was on the air," said the captain, "so let's go over this quick and have your men sit down before they fall down."

"Well, in a nutshell," started Lieutenant O'Brien, "the fire had considerable headway in the rear. I thought second alarm right away from the smoke in the cockloft. But the chief was right behind us, so it was his call. We got in quick, and Leroy and Jimmy found the two kids in the back room. The fire, it looked like it started in the basement playroom. They had a TV down there that would be just below them."

"But they were gone from the get-go," said Leroy. "It was heavily charged. We got them out and started to work on them – " Leroy stopped talking abruptly, put his finger to the side of his nose, and blew out a six-inch of yellow snot; no one commented.

"Rescue company pulled in," interjected the lieutenant. "And took them to the hospital. Case closed," said the lieutenant.

"Romeo brought his car over, you can go back to quarters," said the captain. "It looks like the chief is detained. I'll go over the fire with him, there's no need for you to be standing around."

"That's fine with me," said Romeo. "I just want to hose them down before they get in my car."

"I think they need a good enema too," said Smithy. This got a laugh from the off-going crew.

"How about we just strip down and ride naked?" said Leroy.

"I see no real problem in that," said Romeo. "Except that when you're nailed by the cops as a crazed, horny hunky in desperate need of poontang, my car will get impounded," added Romeo, frowning.

"Here's the chief!" said Tully. It was the assistant chief's car with 26 Truck in the back of them. The chief's car pulled up in the back of the pumper and out stepped deputy chief of the Fifth Division, Bob Bauer.

"At ease, men, I'm covering for Assistant Chief this morning. They're at a meeting downtown. I already stopped at Ladder 26. I had some business there, and I talked to 26 Officer of the off-going crew, and they said Ladder 14 did a good job, and tower ladder did come in handy."

The captain and the lieutenant of Ladder 14 looked at each other but didn't say anything, like two cardplayers waiting to see who was raising and calling before they committed themselves. Asking Truck 26 how Ladder 14 did at a fire was like asking the Mets how the Yankees were doing as far as they were concerned. Of course, Truck 26 would see it the other way around. They were a premier truck company along with Engine 58 housed in the same quarters. Although they had been on the top of the top 10 list of runs and workers for a number of years, it didn't tell the whole story – occupied buildings, multiple alarms, hours worked. It was undeniably busy and one of the best. But Ladder 14 had produced a number of the fire factories' officers. Ladder 14 was also picked as the second tower ladder in the New York City Fire Department and was now servicing all the boroughs' multiple alarms, plus their own Harlem calls, and was in the top numbers game too.

Trucks 26 members came over to join the group. "Lieutenant," said Chief Bauer, "can I talk to you alone?" and they walked to the fire building. "So what, have your guys become the chief's pets?" asked Smithy. "He stops in for a cup of coffee and a blow job before coming over here?"

"You're just jealous, Smithy, because you're no longer sexually active, you asshole," retaliated Franky from Truck 26. He was small for a truckman, five foot nine. He had transferred from Engine 91, had been awarded the silver star in Num, and had busted up Truck 26's kitchen his first night tour there. But Smithy and Franky were birds of the same feather, and they know each other well and loved to face fight, like two dogs in kennels with chain-link fence between them.

"Your tone indicated guilty as charged, runt. And it looks like some telltale debris on your chin," said Smithy.

"No, he's just trying to grow a goatee," said one of the 26ers.

"I detect disaccord among the troops," said Ducky.

"Oh, now we heard from tower shower driver," said another 26er.

Community affairs had used the tower to give the Harlem kids a ride and spray water last summer. It was a good thing to do. But it was something to poke fun at its misuse. The officers remained on the sideline enjoying the cockfight. This got their men juiced up and was an incentive for training, using one unit against the other.

"You know what dumb thing supertruck did last night?"

"Tully, what you got to say?" asked Moose, one of 26's senior men.

"Nothing really. Same shit, different day."

"Look, you got to admit the tower is slower than shit in getting it up to the roof." All Ladder 26 was smiling now. If they sucked Tully in – he was 14 senior man – if they could bring him down, they would win this skirmish. Tully was famous for not talking.

"Yes and no!" said Tully.

"Well, which is it?" asked Moose.

"Yes, your ladder is faster. But you still have to climb it and carry your tool to the roof."

"So?" said Moose.

"Fourteen can extend with two men and the tools and even start the saw on the way up while they're extending and step on the roof fresh."

"Your ass is fresh," said Moose.

"It's also a peach, and you can kiss it if you like. But both statements are the facts."

The fire radio transmitted, "Box 1422, a phone alarm, 119th Street and Lexington Avenue."

"Here the keys to my car, Jimmy," said Romeo. "Put them in the telegraph key box."

"Sure, Vinny. Thanks," said Jimmy.

Romeo ran to the fire truck. All the troops were already aboard. "You're second due," said the captain from Ladder 26.

"Ten four," answered Captain Mac of Truck 14.

"Tully, how do you remain so calm with those jerks?" asked Terry.

"Terry, I'm glad you can ask a question like that as we're responding to a call, it shows control. I like that! I think we're all breaking chops because of those kids who were lost last night. Those guys are great firemen, they'd walk through fire for you, but somehow are weak when it comes to putting kids in body bags."

Terry didn't reply. He just thought about it. *These guys are deep and twisted. But somehow, I feel at home with them,* thought Terry. His mind drifted to Vietnam, but the department radio rescued him. The radio called out over the sounds of the turbocharged diesel, the wail of siren and the horns. "Additional information for Box 1422. Reported and trapped, a paraplegic male. Reported location, top floor of 124 East, 119th Street. K."

CHAPTER 20

THE NUTS AND BOLTS OF IT ALL

CHIEF MANN INSISTED that there was a fire radio in the meeting room. Even if at times it was a distraction, it was a reminder that "the job was fire." When this is forgotten, the wrong decisions are made by managers. The mission of the fire service is to save lives and property. How this is best done can be argued by reasonable men. The New York City approach at this point was to get there as fast as possible with more trained men than you need and more water than you can use. Budget restraints and increased workload were challenges to their system for the first time in their histories. The fire department was showing wear and, in some places, gaping holes. Productivity and safety were helped by issuing radios to truck companies and gas-powered saws. Apparatus replacement was being step up for the busiest company. The super pumper and satellite units were already in service. And there were two tower ladders in operation. But it was not enough. In 1970 there were 127,249 fires, 263,659 total alarms, 3,508 serious fires, 310 civilian deaths. The meeting room was on the eleventh floor of a newer building in City Hall Park. The room had been painted light green and two shades of green carpet. Firemen called it the puke room. There was a long oak table, which didn't overfill the room; it was in the center of the room with chairs around it.

"Gentlemen, I'd like to call this meeting to order," said Chief Mann. The assistant chiefs were helping themselves to the pastries and coffee that Howard and Mrs. Turner had helped put out. "Gentlemen, you'll find a blue budget book with a list of priority that will be presented to the mayor later today. This is what we believe we need to meet the fire challenge of 1971. Chief Berger has his operating budget, he will present it at another time. I will give you a few minutes to look though the book. You have all seen the list before but not in this order."

The fire radio announced, "Ten seventy-five alarm for Box 1422 by orders of the Twelfth Battalion. Report to follow."

Chief Mann noted that few of the chiefs looked up from their budget book and coffee at the report of a working fire in Harlem. "If any questions come to mind, feel free to ask them," said Chief Mann.

Chief Hopkins spoke first. He was assistant chief of the borough of Queens. He had a good bit of experience as a fire officer, and the mayor was his nephew. "My question is the tower ladders, it looks here that you went and ordered five more, isn't that jumping the gun? I had the impression that we were going to talk about this."

"Yes, that's right," said Chief Berger. "We put the second tower in Ladder 14 for a trial only. And I for one do not think they have passed the test. Just a few nights ago, they dropped the ball by not getting the roof at a vacant building, and the fire went to a second alarm. I tried to tell you that tower will never replace aerial ladders in working companies. It only confuses their mission, especially when they're already confused." Howard passed a folder to Chief Mann and whispered in his ear.

"Yes, I'm so glad you brought this up, Chief Berger," said Chief Mann with a note of confidence. "I have the report here that you assigned a Captain Cane and a chief to work in the Fourteenth and the Twelfth Battalions the same night. And your captain suspended preassignments for the truck and never gave an order to open the roof at that fire. This is the report by the chief of the Fifth Division who investigated the fire." Chief Mann held up the folder for all to see. "I spoke to the commissioner on this subject, and these officers are being reassigned to the training division for retraining."

"They're my people, you had no right to go over my head," said Berger. The phrasing of his words he regretted the moment they were spoken.

"I was going to try and keep this matter private," said Chief Mann. "Charges were discussed. Retraining was considered a moderate first step. You're, of course, free to take it up with the commissioner."

"Yes, of course," replied Berger, "like he's always here and not out of town giving a speech."

"Mrs. Turner, let's go off the record here," Chief Mann said to his black secretary, who was taking the minutes of the meeting. "Commissioner Black is a very important person for this city. He knows the job. And right now he's having a meeting with the mayor. He is a big help to this department. He can say things that I cannot, he can go to places and talk to people that I can't. He is in the fray all the way. If you want to go on the record with your position, Chief Berger, be my guest." There was silence. "OK," said Chief Mann, "then let's get on with the meeting. The success of the tower ladders has been reports from all field commanders. Tower Ladder 14 has been overused, and there's a strain put on its personnel. This is why we need more towers, Tower Ladder 14's average. Many nights, ten or more hours of fire duty in a fifteen-hour tour. Yes, some company are out all night with false alarms, and we plan to address this. By removing the pull box for a talk box and only sending one engine unless the caller speaks into the call box." The chiefs all looked at each other in amazement. They had not heard this before. Chief Mann continued, "That all hands just transmitted was in Harlem, and Fourteen is working as we speak. Yes, we need the five new tower ladders because if there's a multiple alarm in the Bronx or Queens and a tower is needed to save a block, we have to call Tower Ladder 1, and they're downtown here. With five new towers, we can put one in each borough and still have a spare."

CHAPTER 21

RESPONDING

CHIEF WALSH WAS pulling out of quarters at the same time as the original alarm came in. Ladder 14 and 26 with Engine 58 were responding. He could hear them acknowledge on the department fire radio. By the time he rolled in to the fire scene, it was clear to him he wanted a full assignment for this fire. He ordered a ten seventy-five for the box. Ladder 26 had let Engine 58 in the street first. They dropped two lines at the front of the fire building and went for a hydrant. Ladder 14 came from the other direction but stopped to let the engine pull out of the block to find a hydrant. The one in the center of the block was marked Out of Service. Ladder 26 didn't hog the front of the building but only took the space they needed to ladder the roof with their one hundred – foot aerial ladder. The fire building was a five-story old law tenement. The fire was on the left side front, fourth floor. It had a diamond-shape air shaft located midway between the front and the rear of the building. The design produce light and ventilation for the middle of the building, but in a fire, this design could carry the fire from floor to floor.

There was an vacant lot to the right of the fire building. This was the direction that Ladder 14 approached the fire building. Ladder 14's driver, Ducky, and captain both saw the open space to the right that the tower ladder could pull into on an angle. The tower platform could still reach the shaft windows at the side of the building to maybe the fourth floor, the roof, and the front of the building. Ducky only had to glance at Captain Mac for him to nod his approval without any conversation. Ladder 14 was second due position, which was the floor above the fire. Captain

Mac held his inside crew back a minute to help with the setting up the tower ladder jacks. This freed Tully and Smithy to enter the platform bucket as the truck frame was being leveled.

Tully carried a Scott Air-Pack. He was thinking if it was possible to drop down to the top floor from the roof. He might be able to locate the paraplegic who was reported trapped. The mask's face piece could be used as an inhalator for the victim. Tully would not use the mask himself, only to get out as a last resort. The air tank was only good for fifteen minutes under working conditions. To use it, it was believed, gave the wearer a false sense of security. Without the mask, conditions were easy to assess. You proceed from safe to hazardous to dangerous, you vented windows as you searched, letting smoke out and air in, crawling alone on the floor. There was more good air to breathe hopefully there. This was how New York City firemen did this job for more than a hundred years.

Ladder 26's ladder was up and reaching for the roof when Ducky switched the power to the tower ladder bucket. Smithy took the controls, raising, rotating, and extending at the same time. Tully started the saw in the bucket. Ladder 26's roof team was climbing smartly; they were halfway to the top. Smithy thought of John Henry, the steel-driving man, race against the auto spike driving locomotive in their fabled contest. Smithy had to admire the spirit of Ladder 26 to beat Ladder 14 to the roof at all costs. He saw Tully smiling out of the corner of his eye in approval too. Ladder 26's tools hit the roof first. Moose ran to the bulkhead door to open it. He slammed the adze end of his Halligan tool between the door and frame and popped it open. Heavy black-and-brown smoke vented out the door. Smithy set the bucket on the roof parapet. Tully carried the running saw to the rear of the roof and put it down. The fire was blowing out two windows on the fourth floor on his left overlooking the roof. All four top-floor windows were pushing smoke.

Tully keyed his portable radio. "Ladder 14 roof to Ladder 14 officer, K."

"Go ahead, Tully, K."

"Cap, the fire is out two windows on the fourth floor. Ladder 26 has started to open the roof. I'm going to drop down on the top floor. Is there any info on the layout? K."

"Tully, the engine still doesn't have water. These are railroad flats front to rear. The man's sister had to be carried out. She was burned coming down the stairs, she said it's the apartment on the right side of the hall that he's in. Tully, the fire is in the public hall now. The stairs are unusable. Use extreme caution. We're pinned down until they get water, K."

Moose from Ladder 26 was at Tully's side. "I'll go with you," said Moose, hearing Tully's plan on the radio.

"Moose, do something for me," said Tully.

"What?" said Moose.

"Go with Smithy in the bucket and vent the shaft windows," asked Tully. And pointing to the middle of the building facing the lot that Tower Ladder 14 was now in, he added, "I'll work my way to that shaft window. That's halfway to the front, I'll know if I can go on from that point. If not, I'll bail out there."

Moose looked over the side of the roof. Engine 58 still didn't have water on the fire. The radio blasted, "Fifty-eight, can you give us tank water? K."

"No. There's something caught in the impeller of the pump. From this fuckin' hydrant!" said the pump operator. "But Engine 91 has a hydrant, and they're stretching a line to feed your line. K."

"Look, Tully, this is definitely a circle jerk," said Moose. "But I'll do it your way. It's your ass!" Franky was already opening the roof with the saw a few feet from them.

"Moose! Fill Smithy in," said Tully.

As he went over the side of the roof and down the fire escape ladder to the top floor, fire was blowing out the two windows below him. And now to his right, as he now faced the building, the metal fire escape cut the radiant heat in half; still the smoke and heat were intense. To get into the apartment would at first be a relief. He took out the window and its frame; he snapped on his lantern, which hung over his left shoulder and rested on his right side. He was wearing a heavy belt with a D ring. The Halligan bar could go in his belt if an extra hand was needed. The window had a security gate. The gate had a steel frame and was locked from the inside. He put the adze end of the Halligan bar on the hasp's side and forced the bar down; the screws came out of the wood holding the frame with one pull. The gate folded away from the window. That first step in the window is the most precarious. Tully sounded with his six-foot hook; the floor was there, all right. His plan was simple. Stay to the left; the shaft window would be on his left side. A wider search was not going to be possible. The six-foot hook was the key to keep contact with the wall. He went to the floor and turned to look back at the window. He could still see from the floor light and smoke billowing together like fast-moving clouds reaching for the sun. He turned back with his back to the window and entered the darkness moving forward. He tapped the six-foot hook as a blind man would use his cane. He was in the kitchen. He went to his left using his hook to reach over the table and chairs, to tap the wall here and there, to make sense of the room. He found the doorway to the hall. He could hear the saw operating over his head, but in the back of him now. It was hot, about two hundred degrees. It was painful to breathe; it was dry. No water was on this fire yet, he could tell. He needed to find that shaft window for some air fast. He turned to his left, leaned on something metal, and it gave away and rolled over on top of him. By instinct, he pushed it away, but it held on to him. He calmed himself and stopped fighting it. Using his lantern, visibility was only inches. The beast was a wheelchair. His mask's belt was caught in the spokes of the wheel. The smoke was so thick there was little hope of him working it out with this visibility. He reached into his left pocket for his carpet razor blade and cut the belt free. Tully turned on the air tank and put the face piece on and breathed out slowly to try and clear the mask. His head started to spin.

"Ladder 14 outside vent to Tully, K." Tully heard this on his portable radio, the speaker resting on his chin. "This flat is going to light up, Tully! Talk to me, man. Talk to me."

Tully tried to clear his head. Yes, it could be one thousand degrees on the ceiling, and the smoke was protecting him from the superheat above him as the cloud protects us from the sun. But for only so long. What Smithy saw venting out the window was smoke turning into fire when it hits the air. The smoke was superheated fuel that only needed oxygen to burn, like gas in a tank, only the gas was on the ceiling and only needed oxygen. Tully freed himself from the wheelchair. He kept going to his left. He was hitting the wall with the hook, and then he found the opening. *But it can't be the window,* Tully thought. *I cannot see any light at all. It must be a closet.*

"Tully, we see your hook," said the radio. "Get out. Now. We are right below the window. We'll catch you."

Now Tully felt the heat building in his fire coat. It was like bees biting his arms. He started to go out the window, but he was kneeling on something soft. He took off his glove and felt it. It was a person. He was small like a child. Tully tried to lift him to get his head out the window, but he couldn't. He was losing his strength.

* * *

Smithy and Moose looked at each other. Smithy went to the radio. "Mayday! Tully's trapped at the shaft window. We see his hook. We are extending as far as possible, we cannot reach the window to go in and get him. He doesn't answer."

Engine 58 had received water and was advancing into blistering heat. Engine 35 had arrived on the scene and was stretching the second line from Engine 91 up the tenement stairs with the determination to pass the fourth-floor fire and advance to the fifth floor where Tully was trapped.

Tully put his face close to the victim. If he was dead, Tully would leave him and get out. But it was a boy, and his eyes were open. "Don't leave me, fireman. Please don't leave me."

Tully took off the Scot Air-Pack, reducing his upper-body weight by thirty pounds. He grabbed the boy and lifted his head and arms out the window. Tully let himself out the window headfirst, holding on with his right arm. He felt hands on his legs guiding them to the railing of the tower ladder bucket. He balanced himself and snatched the boy from the windowsill. Moose caught him and the boy as they all fell into the floor of the bucket. The bucket warbled; it was fully extended. Smithy retracted it in hopes of stabilizing the rocking boom. For a time, the bucket rocked then stabilized. The window they had just come out of exploded into fire. Then water and steam followed the fire out the window. Engine 35, with the help of Captain Mac, had made the room and pushed the hose line forward.

"Tully! You are one clumsy son of a bitch!" laughed Moose. "Remind me to never get involved with your hair brains again."

The boy had his arm around Tully's neck. He moved his tearstained little black face closer to Tully, and he kissed him.

* * *

The time of the fire, 9:30 AM., had made it perfect for television news crew to get uptown and get something in the can for early evening-news shows and still handle scheduled meetings that were newsworthy, which had been laid out for their day. Jimmy Callahan of the *Daily Mirror*, and Chief Walsh's boyhood friend, had showed up and was talking to the chief and the firemen who were picking up hose, ladders, and tools. Tully was sitting on the tailgate of the chief's car. The boy he had rescued had been taken to Harlem hospital, the same place his sister had been taken to earlier.

"Look, Tully, I don't want any of your lip," said Captain Mac. "I want you to get checked out at the hospital. Rescue 3 will take you. Case closed. And I am going to call Kitty and tell her." Captain was holding up his big hand at the same time to stop Tully's protest. He continued, "This whole thing is going to be on the radio at the top of the hour. Would you rather have Kitty hear it that way and worry all day?"

"No, no," replied Tully, giving in to his captain and looking at his watch. He cleaned its dirty face with spit. "She will be at Grace's soon, they were shooting scenes first thing this morning at the Harlem River on the Queens side. She was going to her mother's for lunch, and I'm going to meet her there after work and go to Long Island tonight. One thing!" Tully added. "If you talk to Mrs. McCarthy, Grace, be very careful. She's an excitable woman on these type of matters."

"Oh, I hadn't thought about calling Mrs. McCarthy," said Captain Mac, trying not to show his concern and awkwardness with the task. Tully sensed this.

"Well, of course, we could just forget about this hospital trip, and there'd be no need to call."

"Oh, you're a clever one, Tully! There's no trap that can hold you. You're too slippery. Like a weasel, you are." Tully laughed and upchucked the coffee that someone had given him.

"That's it, my bucko, you're going to the hospital," said the captain. And he walked away to the rescue rig to get them to take Tully to the hospital.

CHAPTER 22

END TO THE CHIEF'S MEETING

CHIEF MANN HAD conducted the whole meeting with the fire radio, reporting the progress of the fire. He had used this backdrop to wear down his opponents to his budget. The point had been well made. That the tower, even when matched against one hundred - foot aerial ladder, in the hands of a top truck company, the tower could do things that the aerial couldn't. What was also clear was that the tower ladder was not just a toy and its only real use was as a water tower. Chief Hopkins made an interesting point that Engine 58 had one of the last water towers in the job, and it was housed in their old quarters. They were, of course, at the fire. The portable radios the fireman wore had communicated the situation and helped all at the scene to act as a team and to bring a successful outcome to a dangerous situation. The hydrant out of service had turned a bad fire into a near disaster. Pumpers carried small water-booster tanks to supply twenty-five-gallon-per-minute booster line. This was not designed to be used inside fires. But suburban departments without hydrants were now ordering pumpers with five hundred - gallon tanks and larger as attack pumpers. This was being talked about for FDNY as tank water could make up for a delay in finding hydrant. And last was the Scott self-contained air mask in services now. Something lighter with longer duration was needed. Tully owed his life to the mask and the tower ladder. So did the little boy he saved. This fire helped almost all the chiefs to see these needs.

"Gentlemen," said Chief Mann, addressing all from now a standing position, "I need to meet with the mayor in one hour. Anyone who would like to accompany me, you're welcome." All said they had other commitments. "Well, that's fine, let me finish this meeting with this insight. The day I was appointed chief and received this job was the happiest day of my life, and the second happiest day will be the day I get the hell out of it. Until then I need your help to try to make this a better job than we found it. These people need more help. A time will come when it will be asked, how did they do it with so little? It might be mistakenly thought they did not want better masks, radios, or better tools. But they did. I hope it's not said we didn't give it to them. The time for change is now." Chief Mann, followed by Howard, his driver, and Mrs. Robertson, left the room.

* * *

A few of the chiefs held back to have a second cup of coffee and to talk over some of the points of the meeting. Chief Berger moved over to the group with Chief Hopkins.

"Congratulations on standing up to Chief Mann on the tower ladders. I think this is all a mistake. And he's trying to shove this all down our throats, think of the cost!" said Berger.

"Well, yes and no. He has a passion for his ideas, all right," replied Chief Hopkins, "but I'm starting to think he's more right than wrong." The other chiefs held their opinions to themselves. Chief Berger's stock had taken a hit. Chief Hopkins continued, "I'm going out to Chicago next week on a busman's holiday and visit the Chicago Fire Department. They have snorkels, and they're running them as squads. And then I'm going up to see Ladder 14 and talk to them before I make up my mind."

"Chief Hopkins, do you plan to see Commissioner Quinn while you're out there?"

"Yes, he invited me," said Hopkins.

"That's interesting," said Chief Berger, burning inside that he wasn't picked to go. He had sent Captain Cane up to Ladder 14 to put a nail in this tower ladder thing, only, only to have it backfire. A trip to Chicago would have given him position of reporting how the snorkels were a better idea and tower a poor one. "Interesting," said Berger. "Commissioner Quinn and Mayor Daley are related, as are you and our mayor are!"

"Why, yes, I see what you're getting at," said Hopkins. "I wouldn't be truthful if being chief hadn't crossed my mind, but as time goes on, I think of it less and less. Being assistant chief of the borough of Queens is more than enough."

"You were born there?" asked one of the other chiefs.

"Yes, Jackson Heights."

Oh, how Berger hated small talk. *Next he'll be showing pictures of his wife and children,* thought Berger. Berger's wife had left him for a fireman in his company twenty-five years ago. They had no children after seven years of marriage. His wife had become pregnant unexpectedly. She knew at once it was her lover and made plans to leave her husband. Her lover was unmarried. He was a first generation German as was she. They were drawn together as nature designed the mysteries of fertility. They knew they were breaking the rules, but love doesn't always play fair. As luck would have it, her lover had an old uncle who had a farm in a German town in New York who was after him to quit the fire job and run the farm for him. This they did. And this soured Berger Craw for twenty-five years. Chief Berger found himself drifting away from the conversation. This was happening more and more to him. This was important. He needed to stay focused on getting as close to Chief Hopkins as possible as an ally. Chief Hopkins looked at the clock on the wall. He had an appointment for lunch at Shea Stadium with the security people for Shea at 1230. It was now 1130.

"Well, excuse me, gents, I got an appointment I got to get to." They crossed hands and said good-bye.

Chief Berger watched him as he walked out. *He's getting fat in his job,* thought Berger. *The fight has gone out of him. But I need him in my corner. I'll ask him out for lunch when he gets back from Chicago. Some nice Italian place.* Berger hated German food.

CHAPTER 23

KITTY IS TAKEN TO HARLEM TO SEE TULLY

KITTY HAD LEARNED at the location of the morning film shoot that a Harlem fireman had made a dramatic rescue of a paraplegic boy. Both were saved. The firefighter was being treated and expected to be released; the boy was being held overnight for observation. The outdoor film shooting crew were detailed from the news department. They did double duty for the station. They used two crews, and they monitored fire and police scanners. They also had Motorola two-way radios, which worked citywide. One press car responded to the morning fire across the Triboro Bridge. The station traffic helicopter had tipped off the film crew that this was a serious fire.

The show's director, Albert Marshall, had a list of scenes called scene breaks that would be spliced into future shows that would be shot largely in the studio. He had a reputation for taking the viewer to the most interesting places in the city and, when possible, in the world. He had worked his way up from scriptwriter, after breaking in as a jack-of-all-trades in a New York independent film company. He now had been in the soaps for over twenty-five years. His enemies joked he was well preserved and waited from year to year for him to fall on his face. But he had great resiliency. He had been a writer, and that was important. But knowing his audience and what they wanted to see was his gift. He had supplied it now for two decades, season after season. He also had discovered and developed his own stars and was a nurturing father to them. His team included dramatic coaches, trainers, and handlers who were available to help in all parts of his casts' needs. His people were all family.

Kitty was no exception. He had seen her at a cowboy bar in the Hampton's. She gave him a wonderful idea for a new character, but he did not realize at the time her theatrical experience or her ability to play the role on national television. So he didn't consider her. The owner of the bar was a go-between who got Kitty an interview at Albert Marshall's head of the Harbor, Long Island, home. And she won the role. And a summerhouse with a dock and an inground swimming pool, all located just below Albert Marshall's place. The film's news crew didn't return from the Harlem fire but called back when they found out that the fireman involved with the rescue was Tully and that he was taken to the hospital. The director, Albert Marshall, called Kitty over to his side. Everything was all right, he said, but he wanted to send her up to Harlem to see her husband in his chauffeured limousine. The chauffeur was an ex-cop, and he would help her with her needs. The car was hers for the day. It had a phone, and he said, "Call me if you need anything, just use your code word, Pink Lady, to get through."

For some reason, this made Kitty blush for the first time in years. She caught his eye and remembered their card game of long ago. Everyone was being so nice it started to unnerve Kitty. Was Tully hurt more seriously than they were telling her? She was helped into the backseat of the big car. From the minute the limo pulled away from the curb, she wanted to get out. She was having a panic attack. She looked down at her too short red dress with plunging neckline with no bra, which had become her trademark. She had on five different outfits this morning's shoot, including workout pants and sweater. Now she had to have on this outfit, and she had forgotten her sweater. She looked ridiculous, she said out loud. *I got to get a hold of myself.*

The driver had just pulled onto the Triboro Bridge, and he looked in the rearview mirror with concern. "Is everything all right, Kitty?"

"Yes, yes, I'm just being silly," said Kitty. "Marty, do you have the ABC News jacket?"

"Yes, right here." He passed it back to her. It was used to get crew members through police lines.

"Thanks, Marty." It was extra large, and Kitty swam in it. But it felt warm and comfortable. She sat back and started to practice yoga breathing.

It was clear to her what was happening. It was a flashback to her brother's funeral and the limo and their ride to the cemetery. Tully was in the car with them in his uniform with his marine medals. She was sixteen. She made a pledge that day that her brother, Michael, would not miss anything in this life because she would do it all twice once for him. He would always be with her. She remembered the passion, too, she had for Tully that day. She was longing for him. But he didn't want her the way she wanted him. She was a little skinny girl with too long legs. But inside she knew she was a woman, and one day he would know this side of her too. She started to cry as she did that day, only that day she had Tully to put his strong arms around her. But now she was alone. He was hurt and could have been killed. She loved him so; he was her rock, her safe place.

"Ms. McCarthy," interrupted the driver. "There's a compartment to your left, open it and you'll find Kleenex, a mirror, sample makeup cover girl, etc." Marty continued in a gentle tone, "You had yourself a good cry. Now buck up, girl, and get cleaned up. We'll be there in a few minutes." This stopped Kitty from crying. But a new emotion was swelling in her breast – anger. Marty didn't give it a chance to vent. "Kitty, you know, I was cop up here, and I got shot in a stakeout. I got hit in the left shoulder. The bullet went through and missed artery and bone. I was medicated comfortably, and I know I was lucky. Up comes my old lady, and she has to be admitted for severe nerves condition. I mean a real basket case, a totally crazy woman." Kitty was laughing and sobbing at the same time. "Now mind you. I understand this is all because she loved me, but it wasn't helpful. Secondly, you don't want to be admitted up here, Miss Kitty. They're all diaper heads. They'll get a load of you, they'll have all your clothes off, and they will be examining all of your openings and fondling your protrude means. Of course, all in the interest of science."

Kitty caught her breath and exhaled and felt the tightness in her chest relax. She started to repair her makeup. "Thank you, Marty. Humor is a tool my father used when I was a little girl. To stop me from crying. He used ethnic humor too."

"Shame on you."

"His favorites were Pat and Mike. The two dumb micks to ever walk the face of the earth. I really thought then that they worked with him on the Long Island Rail Road. Thank you, Mr. Rosalie, you're a real gentleman," said Kitty.

"And you're a real special lady too, Ms. McCarthy." He pulled the car in front of Tower Ladders 14's quarters on 125th Street. The front doors were open, and there were street people just hanging out on both sides of the doors. "I'm going to check inside to see if your husband is back from the hospital before I take you over there. I'm going to lock the doors. So sit tight, I'll be right back."

Kitty was back in control. Smithy came out of quarters with Marty. His blond hair was wet and combed straight back. He still had a young man's face after all he's went through in Vietnam. It was obvious he had just come out of the showers. Marty opened the door and then stepped back to let Smithy enter the backseat with Kitty.

"Kitty! Tully is fine," said Smithy. "He just went to the see the doc to get checked out." Kitty took his hand and kissed him. "Chief Walsh just went on air, and he's bringing Tully back," said Smithy. "Captain Mac is upstairs talking to your mom."

"Really," said Kitty.

"Why, yes! Tully said that's where to reach you. He didn't want them to call you at your work." Kitty's just listening like a good fireman's wife, happy the news was all sounding good. As they were talking, the chief's car pulled up and backed into quarters. "Kitty, don't get out of the car. I'll get him for you," said Smithy.

"Smithy, I want to ask you and Carol out for a barbecue before the summer is over."

"That would be great," said Smithy.

"Great."

He exited the car. Tully, Smithy, and Marty exchanged hellos and what fors, and Tully got in the back with Kitty. *He looks awful,* thought Kitty. His eyes were red. His face was streaked with black. His hair matted. Kitty moved to kiss him.

"Please, Kitty, I don't want to get any of this crud on you. You look so beautiful," said Tully.

"Tully, I'm not a gun drop that's going to melt from a little dirt."

"Kitty, thank you for coming. But I feel very uncomfortable with you being up here and all. Let me go and take a fast shower and knock off the heavy stuff."

"Why didn't they clean you up at the hospital?" asked Kitty.

"We're at the Knife and Gun Club," cracked Tully.

Kitty remembered Marty coaching, and she decided to leave it alone. She just held his hand and waited for him to explain what he wanted.

"The department doctor gave me off for the weekend. Come into the kitchen, have a cup of tea, and Smithy will sit with you while I'm getting cleaned up."

"Yes, dear, but I'm going to rip your clothes off when I get you home to check you out."

"Likewise, I'm sure," said Tully.

* * *

Tully cleaned up in record time, filled Captain Mac in on what the doctor had said. The captain walked downstairs with him and talked briefly with Kitty. Kitty thanked Marty and sent the car back. They would use their own car to get home. They didn't talk until they were half across the Triboro Bridge.

"How do you feel, Tully?"

"I got a small headache, and my throat feels like I just smoked four packages of cigarettes."

Kitty was determined not to ask a lot of question. She was happy to have him sitting beside her. She touched his leg and looked at the side of his face. He was handsome in a bad-boy way, with sweetness in his eyes that gave away his soul. He was her do-gooder for better or worse, and she still loved him as she did as a teenager. She thought of how sweet Albert Marshall had been to send her over with Marty. And then Albert's words, Pink Lady, crossed her mind. Kitty decided she was going to tell Tully about their card game between her and Albert long ago where she won her role.

"Kitty," said Tully, "traffic is moving so well, why don't we go straight out to Long Island? It makes sense. And to tell the truth, I'm beat. I'll stop at the Netute

Diner and get us a cup of coffee and butter roll, and you can call Grace and tell her the plan, she will understand."

She gave him a long look. Her mother was looking forward to cooking for them and having a nice visit. She saw more of Tully than she did with him sleeping over between night tours. She really wanted to see her mother, but today her husband had to come first. "Under one condition," said Kitty. "That you let me drive."

"Gladly," exclaimed Tully.

In about ten minutes' time, Tully had a hot bag of buttered rolls and two cups of coffee for the road. Kitty had made her call to her mother, and they were back on the Grand Central Parkway heading east.

"Kitty, I think it's best if you get over in the right lane if you're going to get on the Long Island Expressway."

"Yes, I know," said Kitty, but she didn't make a move to change lanes.

"Sweetheart, should I put on a crash helmet, or is it you're not going to try to cross three lanes of traffic to enter expressway, which is fast approaching?"

"Tully, you said I could drive."

"Yes, but I didn't say I want to die," said Tully.

"Tully, I'm not getting on the expressway, I hate the trucks and their smell."

"Oh, I didn't know that," said Tully. Tully was starting to relax. After all, she was a good driver, was not drinking beer out of a can and cursing the Congress and their wives, as some of his car pool buddies did. "Love, do you have any clothes on under that baggy news jacket? Did you notice the eyes you were getting at the diner? I thought we were going to have to fight our way out of that place." Kitty opened the jacket and flashed her short red dress. "Oh, that's a nice part of a dress," said Tully.

"See what you miss by not looking at our show," said Kitty.

"I'll hear about it from your fans at the firehouse." She gave Tully a fast look to see if he was serious or only kidding. She couldn't not tell which. "No, sweetheart," said Tully, looking back at her. "It doesn't bother me. At a party a long time ago, your friend Albert Marshall talked to me. He had a story he told me about Marilyn Monroe. He was young in the business. He had a location job with a New York film company. Shooting scenes for the film, some like it hot."

"I'm intrigued," said Kitty. "Go on, Tully!"

He sat a cup of coffee next to Kitty. She took a sip. "Well, what he said was Marilyn was born a showgirl, what you saw is what you got, she was totally open to the camera."

"She didn't hold back. She lived to be seen."

Tully took a bit of the roll and a slug of coffee. "Well, they were shooting this scene where she had to stand on the metal grate over the subway tunnel. As the train moves, it pushes air through these grates, it helps to vent the tunnel. Albert said he had the idea for the scene, and it's why he was able to sell the location to the producer. As the train pushed through, the air blew up Marilyn's thin white dress, and the crowd went wild. The producer knew he had what he wanted on the first take. But he took take after take. Joe D. was there that night."

"Joe DiMaggio, her husband?" asked Kitty.

"Right," said Tully. "He walked away at some point in the night shoot never to return to her life. After her untimely death, it was learned he never missed a day that he did not send flowers to her grave."

"Yes, it was sad, and I've heard part of this story before," said Kitty. "But what was Albert's point in telling it to you?"

There was a pause, and Tully took another sip of hot coffee, which hurt his throat before he answered, "Albert said you were the same type. A good girl who just happens to be a showgirl. And he asked me, 'Tully, promise me you'll never walk away.'"

Tears started to run down Kitty's cheeks; she reached in the pocket of the jacket for the Kleenex she had stuffed there. They didn't talk for about a few miles. When she could trust her voice again, she said, "That was sweet of Albert to arrange the car and all today. He is like a big brother to me."

"Yep, I do appreciate it too," said Tully. "I may even dance with him next time he asks me at a party." His eyes were getting heavy. He yawned and slid down in the seat and closed his eyes.

"Tully, do you remember the night that we went out to Albert's for a reading?"

"Yes, of course, I was there."

"Yes," said Kitty, "but not the whole time, you went to see a fireman friend at the firehouse in Storyville. And we were just living together at the time."

"Kitty, I went to the hospital today to get some oxygen, not to have a lobotomy. You told me all about it before."

"Not all of it," said Kitty.

"What, you're going to tell me Albert is not gay?"

"No, he's gay, all right. But there was a little more to it."

"OK," said Tully. "But first I want to ask you one question. Why did you cry when I told you what Albert had said?" Kitty moved to the far-right slow lane.

"Well," Kitty started thoughtfully. "First, it was sweet that he was thinking about us as a couple, but partly because it hurts me to think what I do could hurt you."

"Yes. And, Kitty, it hurts me, really hurts me to think what I do for a living could hurt you too. But we are both doing what we want to do. Right?"

"Right," said Kitty.

"Sounds crazy after a day like today, but you're an actress, I'm a firefighter. I love you, Kitty, really love you. And you don't have to tell me anything. That happened a long time ago." Traffic opened back up at Woodburry, and Kitty moved back to the fast lane.

CHAPTER 24

GRACE AND CAPTAIN MAC

"DAMN DAMN DAMN," said Grace out loud. What had she done to spoil the wonderful relationship she had with Tully? And now her foolish actions had the potential to sour even her own daughter against her. Kitty called off their dinner invitation with, "Mother, my husband comes first. He needs me to take care of him. And that is what I'm going to do." *That cut me to the bone. Who is to care for me? Did it signal Tully might have said something about the other day?*

Now sweat was running down her face. *Oh no, hot flashes. What next? Is there no end to my torment?* She took off her sweater and slacks and threw them on the floor. She had on no bra, only panty and sandals. She opened the refrigerator and took out a bottle of tonic water that was chilled. She opened a tin of aspirin and placed two on her tongue, poured a glass of tonic, and drank down the medicine. From the cabinet, she took a fifth of gin and poured three finger in with the tonic water and drank it all down. She put the cold tonic bottle to her forehead and her breasts as she walked to the bathroom and shower, turned on the cold water, and stepped in. This is why she was the way she was, not herself, because of her hormones that were in full retreat. They were deserting her – the bastard – just when she needed them. Her remedy was working this time.

She looked down at her figure. She still was great for a woman of her age. Except, of course, she was losing her mind. She still had on panties and her sandal. *Oh well, why sweat the small stuff.* Grace took off her wet things and placed them on the edge of the tub to dry before putting them in the hamper. She didn't bother to put on any clothes except a pair of shorts, and she started to pick things up. She had already turned off the tray of lasagna she had cooking in the oven. Nothing would spoil. She could freeze it with the sauces and the Italian sausages and meatballs. The garlic bread wasn't put in until the last minute, all could be frozen.

She clicked on her small black-and-white TV in the kitchen. The early news was on a report on a fire in Harlem. The reporter was interviewing the sister to the boy who was rescued. The black woman was saying it was a miracle that fire had not gotten to the boy. "I'd prayed to God. Please, God, save him. And that fireman put his own self in that fire to get to the boy, praise the Lord!" The on-the-scene reporter turned to face her camera. "This is ABC exclusive. Firefighter James Tully of Tower Ladder 14 is released from the hospital. He is being recommended for the highest award for his heroic actions at this fire. This is Kelly Dewer reporting."

Grace sat down and started to cry. *I'm totally missing the point. This is my family. Everyone is doing the right thing but me.* The next scene was of Captain McLaughlin and fireman Smithy answering questions out in front of the firehouse with the nose of the tower ladder pulled out onto the apron. They were talking firemannese, their terminology; no one could understand them. The floor above! Take a feed! Stretch a line, hit it and knock it down, catch a job! No wonder they never get the money they deserve. No one knows what in hell they're talking about. There was a close-up on Smithy's face. "What did that little boy say when you got him and fireman Tully outside?" Smithy stopped and answered, "He didn't talk really. He just put his arm around Tully's neck and kissed him." The scene was cut away to the boy being put in the ambulance and a fireman giving oxygen to what looked like Tully. But Grace couldn't tell.

Grace went to the hall closet and found a designer silk scarf. She tied it around her neck and put on high heels and went to the hall phone, picked it up, and dialed the firehouse number.

"Ladder 14, fireman McKone."

"Could I speak to Captain McLaughlin?"

"One minute please."

"Captain Mac here."

"Captain Mac, this is Mrs. McCarthy, we talked earlier today."

"Yes, of course."

"I just had an idea, I hope you don't think me too forward, but Kitty and Tully were supposed to come to dinner tonight and all, I have all this food. But because of the fire and all today, they went straight out to Long Island. Kitty was going to drive."

"Oh, I am so happy to hear that Mrs. McCarthy and that nothing else is wrong."

"No, no," said Grace. "My idea is why don't you, if you have no other plans of course, join me for dinner. Here." There was silence on the other end. "Oh, Mac, I am so embarrassed. Please forget it. You have other plans, of course."

"No, no, Mrs. McCarthy, please, I . . . I . . . was looking for a pen and paper to write direction down. The directions, I don't know how to get there."

After he received the directions, he asked, "Could I bring something?"

"No," said Grace, "just yourself will be fine."

CHAPTER 25

KITTY AND TULLY'S DRIVE ENDS

KITTY AND TULLY had stopped at a deli at Smith Town to pick up eggs, milk, bread, and sliced ham and cheese for a snack and breakfast tomorrow. Tully had slept most of the trip and was sleeping again. Kitty thought of their talk on this ride, and she felt peacefully in love with her man. How different he was from any man she had known or the other husbands of the girls connected with the show. Kitty believed that it was his job that had a great deal to do with it. It kept him focusing on today. Firefighting was piece work. He had said, "We didn't cause the fire, we respond to a call for help, we do the best we can. You're relieved, and someone else takes the watch. Your job is over till the next time." It was this mind-set that kept their love life on an even keel and moving ahead. The small issues of love that really don't amount to anything seem to spoil the sweetness of love, the accounting of who got what and when. The bean counting of it all robs the magic. For love is only in the heart. To try and weigh it like a pound of fish only cheapens it. Tully excepted her love like a baby, like mother's milk without a thought. It was his, it was good, period. No need to analyze it. Kitty turned left onto Storyville Road, the last mile of their trip. Tully was very tired. She'd put him to bed tonight, he being her baby, and she'd kiss him and hold him ever so tight.

CHAPTER 26

CAPTAIN MAC'S DRIVE TO ASTORIA

AS SOON AS Captain Mac paid the toll for the Triboro Bridge and crossed into the borough of Queens, he started to take stock of the situation. *Was this all a good idea taking this step to get involved with Mrs. McCarthy?* There was little doubt that without Tully, he wouldn't consider meeting the woman; his needs – what there were – were fairly well being met as far as the ladies went. He had always been an underachiever in that department. Never a ladies' man.

His life in general was in order; he was happy at Ladder 14. He had a small side job at a boatyard in City Island where he helped to restore boats to seaworthiness. It was his first trade, which he learned in Ireland from his father and uncle before enlisting in the British army. He didn't need the money; he did the work because he liked it. His first wife was the only woman friend he had ever had. Oh yes, he had known women before. But none could be called a friend as his wife, Maureen, was. He knew it was his fault as much of any of the women in his past. He just didn't know how to talk to them, find a common ground, a place to relate to each other.

Maureen made it easy for him. She had been a nurse in the U.S. Army in World War II. Her unit had landed on Normandy on D-day. Their task was to stabilize the wounded before they were transported back to the hospital ship in what was called the golden first hour. If care didn't start for the seriously wounded within it, it was learned their chances of recovery were greatly reduced. Her duty after the start of the war found her caring for United Kingdom troops and German soldiers. After the war, her experience got her a job in the emergency room at Bellview Hospital where her skills were held in high esteem by the hospital staff and coworkers. Patrick McLaughlin and Maureen O'Brien met at a wedding party by coincidence, for a fireman and a nurse, in a downtown bar called O'Tools. Maureen had a love affair with a young doctor. When it became serious and known to his family that she was a Protestant, they were strongly against it. Maureen was hurt but, in time, got over it. Any man that was so strongly controlled by his family was not the type of man she really wanted. She did understand how some differences were hard to overcome, such was the nature of prejudice. Her own family would have been against her pairing up with a papalist, as they would have said it, had they had their chance. But both had passed away peacefully during the war. Patrick didn't consider himself a ladies' man, but as a young man, he had turned the head of many a lass, as he did that day with Maureen O'Brien. Patrick caught her eye; she turned away. Something caused her to look back at a very striking man. The way he carried himself and moved produced an energy that seemed to cause her to undress the man; she wanted to see him naked. Maureen asked a friend in her party if they knew him. He was a greenhorn, she was told, just appointed to city fire department, with no family in this country. The friend offered to introduce them; she said no and walked up to him directly and introduced herself as a past U.S. Army nurse who served in the European Theater and asked about his service. They went together like bacon and eggs. And strawberries and shortcakes. If it would be left to Patrick, they would have been engaged and married in about three years. Maureen took him to bed for a month and told him she loved him, and there be no more sex until they were married. They were married in six months. Their life was a happy one. She remained a nurse, and he went up the ladder in the fire department. They never had children. Not because they didn't try, as Patty would say. They had medical advice, but it didn't happen. After twenty years of marriage, Maureen got sick; she had cancer. She passed away after two years of treatments. For Patrick, the loss was like losing an arm or a leg. He was not who he was before, and the loss was not going to be replaced. But you could go on. It was his job, which was helping other people who needed help, and his crew at the firehouse – they were his family – that got him through it.

    Mac made a right turn to leave the Triboro Bridge onto Astoria Boulevard. He had crossed his bridge of no return. He decided he was ready to move ahead. He followed the el onto Ditmars Boulevard to a bakeshop that Mike Paul had told him he could pick up a coffee ring, and next store was a flower shop where he purchased a spring bouquet. Mike was the cook on the incoming crew and the chauffeur. He was one of the best storytellers. Captain Mac found a parking spot in front of Grace's H-type apartment building; he noted it was the correct side of the street for tomorrow, not that it would affect him. He took the elevator to the third floor – it was a well-cared-for building – and found her apartment and rang the bell. Grace opened the door. She had changed to a light flower-patterned summer dress with a sweetheart neckline. She might have picked something more formal, but with the hot flashes, she needed all the air she could get.

"Oh, thank you," said Grace, taking the flowers and the cake. "I can't imagine the type of day you've had, it exhausts me just thinking about it," said Grace, following it with, "Whatever's wrong with me, please come in. The flowers are beautiful."

"I thought they were too, until you put them in your arms and they paled," said Mac.

"Uh-oh," said Grace. "My heart just did something."

A brush of pink came to Mac's cheeks. He was truly taken aback by Mrs. McCarthy's beauty. This was the first time he saw her, and though he was told that her daughter didn't fall far from the tree, she looked and smelled beautiful. Grace led Mac into the living room off the hallway. The dining room and kitchen lay beyond.

"The dinner is warming and only has to be put out on the table. Why don't we sit down for a minute and have a drink. Please take the lounge chair, and do put your legs up. What will you have to drink, Pat?"

"Well, I don't know if I trust myself. Us being unchaperoned and all."

"You're right of course, Pat, but I promise to control myself. Is it all right that I call you Pat?"

"Yes, of course."

"So what are you drinking, beer or highball?"

"Well, I'm trying to keep my drinks to two per night." Grace kept herself from rolling her eyes.

"After the day you've had, I think a drink would be a tonic. How about two fingers of Irish whiskey and a beer chaser. That's two drinks!"

"Yes, you're right," said Pat. "That'd be fine!"

Grace came back into the living room with a serving tray with the drinks. She put two coasters for Pat's drinks on the mahogany table next to him. She sat in the chair half facing him, crossed her long legs, and leaned forward with her drink in her hand. She had long amber hair pinned up to the top of her head. There was a white streak running down the center. It was becoming like an artist blending the white into a beautiful color. She had Mediterranean complexion, but with green eyes, a coloring he had never seen before. He wanted to be attentive but didn't want to stare. His eyes were being drawn to her plump breasts and back to her shapely legs. Grace had the television on with the Mets and Braves game with no sound. Pat was able to look away at the game at the right moment. So it was Mrs. McCarthy's breasts, then her legs, a sip of his drink, a peak at the ball game, and then back to Mrs. McCarthy's breasts.

"Mrs. McCarthy, that's a beautiful set of televisions you have, I mean color television you have," said Pat. Grace half laughed but went on seamlessly not to embarrass Pat.

"Yes, Kitty and Tully gave them to me for Christmas." And they both laughed. "Would you like me to turn the sound up?"

"No, thanks. It's lovely the way it is. With them running about in the green grass and all."

"I turned it down so I could hear you ring the bell."

"My wife was a baseball fan too, you know. I would take her to the old polar grounds. She told me it brought the sweetest memories of her dear dad back to her. He had taken her to the games as a little girl."

"You know, Pat, it's funny you said that. It does remind me of my dad. And you remind me of him too. I was always in love with him. He was a tugboat captain of the *Helen Dawn*. Captain Jack. He brought me up alone, and he'd taken me to the games and prizefights too. He had my hair cut short and dressed me up like a sailor boy. I asked the ship's cook one day who was in charge of me when the ship was under way, why Dad always cut my hair short and dressed me like a boy. He said, 'One, this is no place for a girl. And two, you may remind him of your mother who was an entertainer of sorts and who left us one morning at Twenty-second Street pier and never to return.' That's all I know about her. Dad would never talk about it. He said, 'If you can't say something nice, it's best to say nothing at all.' I did not go to regular school until I was thirteen. Dad made arrangements to place me in a convent so I could finish my schooling. He had read me the Bible, Shakespeare, Emerson, and Mark Twain, and he had *Encyclopedia Britannica*. For my questions, I asked, 'What more could I learn, Daddy?' He said, 'To be a lady, and you're not going to learn that here with the likes of us. Now no more of your questions.' It's the most hurtful thing I've ever had to do. But it's the right thing to do. When he had said it was time to go, he cried, and it was up to me to be brave. I did not show my tears, but I cried myself to sleep every night in the convent. That wasn't the worst of it. I was getting my mouth washed out daily, and I was losing weight, and I was built like a little string bean at that time. I was told that I cussed like a brewery driver. One day two of them were washing out my mouth, and I threw up. And I the screamed at the top of my lungs fuck you' ten times with the puke and soap bubbles coming out of my nose. – . They threw themselves on their knees, started to pray. They were convinced they were in the presence of the devil.

"Sister Superior turned me over to Sister Margaret. She took me by the hand, made me a cup of tea and toast, and she sat me in a rocking chair facing a lovely window and sat beside me. 'No one will hurt you anymore, dear. I stopped this by calling Sister Superior. I told her I would go to the cardinal if I had to.' We looked out the window, and she told me her story. 'I was not a pretty girl like you,' she started. She had been brought up in the foundling home with her brother, Joseph. They had been put on the orphan train destined for the West. They would be taken off at each stop for prospective parents to look them over. They reached Lincoln, Nebraska, and there was only three of them left, her brother who was sick with a cold. 'They picked me,' said Sister Margaret. 'When the people were told I had a brother, they looked at the handsome boy standing beside me who had lost his smile long ago. His name was Billy. I loved Billy,' Sister said, 'but what he did that day, I adored him. He put his hand to his mouth and gagged himself, looking away from them, so they would think he was sick and they would take Joseph and not him. I never forgot him. When I got old enough, I wrote to the foundling home asking about Billy. But they told me it was against the rules to give out that information.' She looked every way possible to find him. With no success, she saved her pennies and came to New York and visited the foundling home to ask about Billy's whereabouts. It was at this point that day that Sister Margaret stopped her story and looked at me. I will never forget it. She said, 'Sometimes things look hopeless, but with God's help, we would find our way. And for now, we have each other." I ran to her, cried and cried in her lap with her arms around me. We were kindred spirits, lost lambs in life's storm, and we found each other. Two motherless deers. She was going to take care of me, and I her. We were safe. Now look at me," said Grace, wiping a tear from the corner of her eye. "Patrick, I haven't opened my heart to anyone like this in years. This must be so boring."

"Far from it, Mrs. McCarthy – "

"Grace! Please call me Grace," she interrupted.

"I was fascinated with many parts of the story. You being brought up around the water and ships, so was I. And I would love to hear the rest of your story. Especially Sister Margaret and Billy."

"Yes, there is more. How about after dinner? The end is not sad, but I would like you to enjoy your meal, you poor man. You must be starved," Grace said, standing up. "Would you help me put out the dinner?"

"Yes! That would be fine, Grace." He gave her his arm. She squeezed it to her breasts, and they walked arm in arm into the kitchen.

*   *   *

Grace served shrimp salad as an appetizer and white wine. The room had good lighting, but because the sun was going down, she had the tiffany flower light over the mahogany dinner table on. This room had parquet floors, and all the molding around the windows and doors were wood-stained. The room was painted light yellow with wildlife border at the top of the wall and around the room. There was a painting of Grace and Kitty at about fifteen.

"I see you're admiring the painting that was done by my son, Michael," Grace said. "He was Mr. McCarthy's son from his first wife who passed away before my daddy introduced us. I babysat for him and fell in love with Michael before I fell in love with the father! Mr. McCarthy was not that much older than me! But at my tender age of nineteen, his thirty-nine was like fifty years. To be married to an older man has its good and bad side. He treated me like his daughter in many ways and spoiled me. I never had a lustful love affair that I think every girl needs," Grace paused. "Times are different now. I was ashamed to tell him my fantasy for fear he'd lose confidence in himself and worry about me straying. I wanted the safety of his arms, but girls like to daydream." Grace stopped and realized she was going somewhere that was best left for another day. "Well, excuse me for getting off the subject again, I don't know where my mind is going." Pat just smiled, determined to be a good listener. "Our son, Michael, loved to paint. He did that painting before he went into the service. We lost him in Korea. He and Tully were together, did you know?"

"No, I'm so sorry, Grace. I didn't know that."

They sat down, and Grace served him. They started to eat. Both had a glass of wine. "Please go ahead and serve yourself some more."

"Well, I think I will. Everything is so good."

Grace added on hot tomato sauce to his helping of lasagna. She was surprising herself in how she was enjoying this meal like she was the guest. This helped Pat to relax after he finished his second plate and had a second glass of wine. Grace said, "Before I tell any more of my story, I'd like to hear about your wife. It sounds like you had wonderful communication. That baseball father story was what got me going."

"To tell the truth, Grace, I had no skill conversing with Irish or American ladies at the time. When I met Maureen, she had been a soldier, a captain, matter of fact. She was a straight talker. No blarney. She'd say, 'Out with it, Patty.' There was no doubt it saved us untold time. I can hear her now, 'Patty would get directly into the bush and flush the bird if there's one to flush.' The bird, of course, was my point. I never took offense at her directness because it was in all areas. You never missed out on anything with Maureen."

"She sounds like a dream."

"Yes, she was!"

"Still wear my rings too, Pat, as I see you do too," said Grace. "How long has it been for you since you lost her?"

"Four years," answered Pat.

"Four for me too," said Grace. Pat thought it might be best to change the topic from his wife and her husband; if she wanted to tell him more about her husband, she would.

"Grace, I have a point in asking this. Do you know what happened to Sister Margaret and Billy?"

"No, not exactly," answered Grace. "But they did find each other. Sister entered the order of nuns at the foundling home but didn't take her vows. Somehow she got a hold of Billy's file. She found he returned on the train and was adopted by people in Brooklyn. He attended Our Lady of Sorrows grade school. The family that adopted him had a fairly common name, which I forgot now. But they had moved too with no forwarding address. Sister Margaret went to the school Billy attended and was lucky to find an older sister who had Billy in school. She felt obliged to help after she heard the whole story. After three weeks, I received a letter from this Sister Rita that he had been in the navy and then went in the fire department, and she was on the case and would contact her when he was located. But my life was also about to change. Without me around, Daddy had time to meet a very nice lady. They were married. I was able to leave the convent, and we all moved to Long Island. Daddy retired from New York Harbor to become a fishing boat captain. So this all was so much for a young girl. I did not write Sister Margaret until Christmas. The card came back forwarding address unknown. Dad finally found out for me that she left the convent for her Billy. But I was never able to locate them," said Grace.

"Oh, that's a wonderful story," said Pat.

"Yes, it is. But if only I could see her again and see them together."

"I'm not going to say a lot about this, only I'll look into it for you," said Pat. "This all could be a coincidence, only that I do know a Bill Walsh. He was in the navy and went to Our Lady of Sorrows in Brooklyn and married a Margaret. He is a fire chief. In fact, he met you at your husband's funeral."

"Oh, Lord in heaven," said Grace.

"I would call him now, but they just went on a short holiday. He will be back in three days."

"This is all turning out to be too wonderful for words," said Grace. She was wiping tears from her eyes and was thinking she had to stop this crying. She wouldn't drink any more tonight; she wanted to respond if they made love. No, she had to get a handle on herself. This would scare him. His wife was a woman of the world, no telling what that girl saw in her experiences in World War II. But she couldn't take any chances in moving too fast with him. This might scare him off.

Pat was becoming concerned he should have kept this coincidence to himself until he could check it all out. He had promised Tully he would be as gentle as possible with Mrs. McCarthy and treat her as a maiden filly. But he was starting to feel that Tully and his inexperience had not taken full measure of this lass. She was a barracouta and had been without a man for four years. If he was right, anything could set her off. If he was wrong, he'd spoil the whole thing, which he didn't want to do. Yes, she would take a commitment of work, care, and a lot of love for things to work out, but it would be well worth it, for she was without question a fine woman, who had more than her share of heartaches.

"Mrs. McCarthy, Grace, maybe I best be going."

"But, Pat, you didn't even have coffee and cake, you didn't like my dinner?"

"Oh no, Grace, I loved the dinner and being with you. It's been a wonderful evening." She looked like she was going to start to cry again. Pat needed to do something more to reassure Grace he wished more contact and only was thinking of her delicate nature. He got up from his chair and started to walk to her side of the table. She was up and met him. He took her hands and looked into her eyes. "Grace, I can see the pain in your eyes. Your smile is saying one thing, but your eyes another. You are a very beautiful person. I had a wonderful evening, and I would like very much to see you again."

"Pat, can I be frank?"

"Yes, of course."

"What you see is longing to feel like a woman again. They tell us, to lust with our eyes is the same sin as doing it. Pat, if we're going to burn for our desires, let's burn in each other's arms."

She brought both hands to his face and kissed him with wild passion and longing. He kissed her back and left all reason behind. She had taken him to her room. He did not remember how they got there. It was also natural there was no time to think. In fact, there was no thinking; it was all instinctive. They had been bridled and restrained so long that this part of them once released took total control. He melted into her, and she into him. They fell asleep in each other's arms as only lovers could manage to do.

She woke at 4:00 AM, reached for the clock to take a closer look. This was the first night in a month she hadn't been drenched in sweat when she woke. She was cool and had a mild headache, but outside of that, she felt the best she had in months.

"Patty dear." He sat straight up and turned his legs to his side of the bed. "Patty, it's OK. You're not in the firehouse, relax, dear. It's OK." Pat lay back down like an obedient zombie. "Patty dear, I forgot to ask you. Do you have to go to work today?"

"No, no, lass. I thought this whole thing was a dream, a wonderful dream."

"It's not a dream, Pat. You took me to bed, you were so strong. You know how to sweep a girl off her feet. You can go back to sleep now, you need your rest, dear."

She turned away and pushed her naked form into him. He placed his hand on her hip and kissed the back of her neck. She could feel his excitement coming to life. She would have to be gentle with him and not cripple the poor man on the first night. She pulled the covers up to her chin and fell asleep with a smile on her face.

CHAPTER 27

HOME SWEET HOME

T ULLY WOKE AT 5:00 AM. He had a headache, and his throat felt like he was coming down with something. His eyes had crusted over. He felt like he had the flu. But he knew the symptoms of what was called in the job as taking a feed (smoke inhalation) the day after. A fireman's ability to take smoke could be compared with the first time you try a cigarette. Your lungs say no thanks. But with a little persistence, you build yourself up to high levels of tolerance for toxin. One other factor that was in play here for a fireman was the body also adjusted over time to use less oxygen and function with higher carbon monoxide in the bloodstream. Kitty turned over in bed; she was naked too. He pulled up the covers over her gently, not to wake her, and got up quietly.

He went to the back of the house, which was a new addition. It was a combination room with a kitchen and a dining room with a room for a pool table; the walls were paneled in knotted pine. He looked out the back glass sliding door; there was an assortment of wildlife, squirrels and birds running around the railing of the deck. There was an inground pool in the middle of it. There were seagulls flying about, and bobwhite quail were calling to the left of the house in a stand of pines, feeding on a blanket of teaberries, and a hillside of mountain laurels for escape cover above them. This was a natural and man-made setting separating Albert's main house and their beach cottage down on the beach. Only a small woodland trail connected the two houses. Their unit had been a guest summer cottage before Albert gave it to them for their use. He turned on the gas under the teapot. He went into the bath utility room, which was built in the back of the kitchen using all the same water-in and water-out connections. There was a washer and drier and a back stairs with a trapdoor that led to a small porch with a shower to wash off sand and salt after a swim. He used the bathroom, washed his hands and face, and brushed his teeth and coughed up congestion. He had a bottle of cough medicine he took a swig of. This would help bring up debris he inhaled at yesterday's fire. He had his cup of tea. He could go back in and go to bed, which he felt like. But it would be best for his system to go out on the water and let the salt water and fresh air work its healing powers and check out his lobster traps.

He looked in on Kitty. She was still rolled up in a ball. He had put on swim trunks and sweatshirt and New York Mets baseball cap. The first breath of sea air started him to coughing. The smell of the sea air was invigorating. He knew it was good for him; the beach and sand had a morning sky above it. He was alone on their beach, except for sand crabs waddling along, doing the important work they had been assigned. A washed-up horseshoe crab lay in the sand, testimony to the ongoing turnover in the world. He carried his oars and his ditty bag with stuffs like hardtack, a can of tuna, a compass, water. He didn't plan to be out long enough to eat. It was his military training, which was his creed, to be prepared. He didn't see Albert Chesapeake's retriever, which was just as well. He didn't have the heart not to take the dog in the boat, but the dog was too bossy. He thought it was his job to discipline the lobsters even if meant him losing an ear. Tully had even been knocked overboard in one of those battles. The fight ended when the dog dove in to save him. He threw his gear on board and pushed his boat into the water. He set his oars in their locks, and he set course for his traps. He pointed the bow to the east of the inlet's entrance. The stern to their pier. The first trap was sixty degrees off that line, which was Albert's right corner of the main house. The pots were marked with plastic bleach bottles visible at low tide, which coincided with the fact that large boats could not come in the inlet because of clearance at that time and see the traps.

The inhabitants of the inlet respected each other's uses. One of the owners had horses and bird dogs. They did not shoot birds on the beach, but they hunted with their dogs in braces; the setter would find and point the coveys of quail. This fascinated Tully, as he had an Irish setter as a boy. He hunted and fished in the salt marsh off LaGuardia Airport. His dog would find a pheasant once in a great while. When he told his father he found a pheasant, he told him that all the pheasant were gone, that it was a seagull. Tully took this information in the same manner as when the people told him Irish setters were not bird dogs. Tully had a fantasy that if they lived there all year long, he would get a bird dog, but he had to remember for now there were only guests on the beach. Tully found his first trap. He was careful in what he harvested in number and size, keeping only what was for his table. The first trap had two lobsters. He let the smaller of the two go and put the second in a boil lap bag and tied it over the side of the boat. Tully looked at his watch and had to laugh to himself; the face of the watch was still black with soot from the fire.

The watch had a leather band with a large guide, which ran under the metal case. He had lost his last watch when the plastic band melted sometime during a fire. He put his red bandanna in the seawater and cleaned off the glass. The tide must be coming in by now; he thought he needed to row to the farthest trap. And he could fish some there. His return would have the help of the tide to carry him in. The last bleach bottle was still visible. He had one good-sized lobster – he anchored – and fish with bait rig, which had four hooks. If the flounders were running in a school, you could, with luck, snag a fish by just having them swim into it. All in all, and he was starting to feel good, he'd broken out in a sweat in this last row, and everything was working fine. He caught six fish in fifteen minutes and started to head back in. He checked his other traps, which were empty. He thought about the pool party that Kitty was planning; it was a week off. He checked his traps the next two days and saved his catch. He most likely wouldn't have enough for the party. He would have to pick up lobsters at the fish market. But it wasn't just to save the money. It was a great feeling of well-being to be able to harvest your own food from the sea. As a boy, his dad would tell him how Queens was when he was a boy. It was a story he hated to hear, to think it was all over and he would never see it. Now he realized how lucky he was to have his chance here, but would it be lost to the next generation? He hoped not. What we'd leave the next group that followed us tells the most about us.

Three-fourths of the way in, he could make out Kitty; she was watering a mix of vegetable and flower planters. She had on a large sun hat and red swim trunks and no top. She was a show. She wasn't always on as everyone suspected, but he took a wild guess that this was showtime. Kitty had explained her craft early on, that it was necessary to get into character each day. Most people thought that Kitty was only playing herself, but she really wasn't. She worked out things as she learned her lines. She was always playacting the last few years; Kitty had played the same character. She had said that the character was now starting to tell her what to do. Her director, Albert, liked this and trusted her. The character Kitty was playing was Jennifer Hutton, a Western showgirl turned news reporter using her charms to gain advantage in all areas of life. The daytime soaps were not all that risqué as the movies had become, but they were always pushing the envelope. Kitty rehearsed her character beyond what the role called for before the cameras; this helped to give her energy to play the part. The rehearsal she played off Tully was a little more fun for both of them – sometimes. Tully had maintained a resistance to be included in her playing-acting, as he called it. She told him that was OK. In a way, it helped. If she could get it done at home without an actor playing to her words, then the for-real shot was a lot easier. But at times, it tried her patience when he threw curveballs after curveballs to gum up what she was trying to do. But in the end, it was all working out. For after all, stage people also did the same thing. When one of the stagehands walked across the set naked except with sneakers and brown sox and a baseball hat, Kitty's reaction was, "Nice sox," and kept going with her lines.

After Tully reach shore, he beached his boat, stored his catch. He went into the downstairs shower entrance to wash off his feet. He heard the washer going into the spin cycle. He remembered he promised to level it two weeks ago. He darted up the stair to find Kitty riding the washer.

"Don't worry, Tully, I got it under control, easy boy!" she said, like she was riding a bull.

Tully pretended all was normal. He only said, "Nice hat," paying no attention to her toplessness and the rocking of the machine.

"The games had began." He washed his hands, looked in the mirror; his color was better.

"Tully, you're so cruel to me, you never kissed me good-bye. And you went off on that silly little boat. And now you know I'm incredibly seductive in this position, and I'm trying my hardest to spin my nipples in one direction. And you pay no attention!"

"Oh, are they doing something?" said Tully, poker-faced.

"And why didn't you take a shower before coming up here? You know I want you fresh."

"Well, I forgot to tell you. The doctor said I was not to service any of my women for five days."

"Did he really say that?" asked Kitty.

"No," said Tully, "but I thought it was a good line for your show."

Kitty dipped her sun hat to hide her smile. She came right back with, "Oh, did I tell you they are talking of moving me for real to the news department?"

Tully didn't bite. "Oh, that's nice."

"And I also filed to take the new fireman's test. There's opening for red-blooded women." Kitty flexed her chest muscles.

"Kitty, do you want a spanking?"

"Yes, Tully. Please, if only I could have a spanking, it would be so purifying. My sins would be absolved with each delicate slap. Please, could you?" asked Kitty.

"No," said Tully.

"Why not pray. Tell!"

"Well, I want it to be my idea! I think," said Tully, "maybe later if you're very good." The washer stopped. Kitty dismounted the washer.

"You know, with a few adjustments, this could be a woman's dream come true," said Kitty, patting the washer. "Would you like a nice little breakfast, Scrooge?" she asked, crossing in front of him with her bare chest protruding.

"What do we have?" asked Tully.

"Poison apples," answered Kitty.

"Good, I'll have three over easy."

"Tully, I must compliment you. You've crafted a great role for yourself."

"And what was that?" asked Tully.

"A big prick. In fact, you should come in and give acting lessons."

"Do you really think I was that good?" asked Tully.

"Oh yes! A real German helmet, all the way."

Tully walked across the room in his thoughts and looked out off the deck window. The tomato plants looked good. They'd have tomatoes soon. There was a copy of Oscar Wilde plays lying on the corner table. Tully thought of picking it up and reading from any page. It would probably be better than anything he could think up in an hour or longer.

"I'm glad you're feeling better, James Z, and you can take some kidding. I love you," cooed Kitty.

"I love you too, cupcakes!" said Tully, sitting down to eat. "I didn't kiss you because I didn't want to wake you. And I knew I couldn't only kiss you once."

"Oh, you're only saying that because it's true. Tully, how do you like this top?" Kitty had put on a colorful cutoff T-shirt before she had began to cook the eggs. "This is the latest in fire island fashion. I was thinking of getting them for the girls for the pool party."

"Kitty, you have better judgment in what the girls will or will not wear."

"Tully, you know I'm not a slave to fashion. It's about what works, and this is fun, a girl is never too old to learn new tricks."

"Kitty, did you eat?"

"Yes, while you were fishing," continued Kitty. "Tully, do you know the legend of Scheherazade showgirls' patron?"

"No, I didn't know that they had a patron. Tell me."

"Well, she was in the harem of a young Arabian prince. The girls were part of palaces, as were the flowers and pools. But each night, one would be plucked for the prince. After a night of pleasure, she would be put to death."

"Genghis Khan did some crazy stuff like that?" asked Tully, still eating.

"Yes," she answered and continued her story. "She realizes that they had been taught all the arts of lovemaking, but this hadn't saved the other girls. So she spent months in working out a plan. She invented a musical tale. She would sing and accompany herself on the harp. Finally, her night came. The handmaidens had perfumed her body and hair, softening her with precious oils. She was afraid but brave. She wore seven veils, each very fine that you could see through clearly, but with the seventh, one needed their imagination. They had embroidery at the ends with gold thread to help them swing when she would dance. The horns sounded for her. All the girls danced out into the throne room. Scheherazade was carried in the center, high in the air, symbolizing an offering. She was put down in front of the prince. As soon as her toes touched the floor, she broke into a wide circle of dance no one had ever seen. Her energy was so high that she could have easily escaped out a window. The guards were alarmed and looked for orders to stop her. But the prince held his hand up to let her continue. She was a thing of beauty. Her spirit was like that of a highbred Arabian mare, to stop her would be a sin. She lost all of her veils but two, as she planned. Her dance ended as she came back in front of the prince and fell on a pillow at the prince's feet. He was enthralled with her charm, grace, and beauty and was speechless. She sat up without being told, which shocked everyone. This was a performance that would be remembered for a lifetime and retold to each generation for a thousand years. She strummed her harp from upright kneeling positions, and so started the tale of a thousand nights. She won her life by her imagination and skills that night, and she became the teacher of all the girls and the mother of four of the prince's sons. The girls she schooled she gave this riddle: Conquest is short but sweet, but mystery will lead to long life."

"Kitty, how long have you known that story?"

"From a little girl."

"Who told it to you?" asked Tully.

"Grace," answered Kitty as she exited the room and flashed her eyelashes over her shoulder and went out on the deck.

As Tully stepped out on the rear deck, he scented the aroma of sea air; it was a trigger to inhale deeply. Perhaps this was why the seashore was always recommended for those with lung ailments. It turned an involuntary reflex to a compulsive one. He felt like he had a mild cold now from yesterday's fire. But he felt better. Tully could see the tide had come in. Small waves were now hitting the beach and running inland with each beat, the pulse of the sea breathing new life into the inlet. Kitty had a veil on and was dancing around her plants, singing to them. She had put ankle bracelets on that had bells on them. The vegetables and flowers were blooming. She had four types of lettuces, tomato, onions, and peppers, with herbs and hanging flower plants. Tully took the time to walk around and look at everything. He could hear the quail communicating with each other with little chirps at the corner and below the deck. But he could not see them. Kitty had help with her gardening from Albert's mother, who was at the harbor most of the week in the summer. He looked out on the water. There are no boats or people on the beach, which had no public access. He was happy to just lie down on the cushion and close his eyes. The sun felt good.

Kitty came over and lay down with him. She had on a very serious face when she spoke. "Tully, I did the little ones on the washing machine, are you very angry?"

Tully opened one eye and, imitating a mad man, said, "Yes, very angry," with the one eye peering at her.

"Tully, I need to do the big ones. Very badly. You're going to have to do that special thing again."

"Oh no, not again."

"Yes, you must. Tully, I know you've been making love to Maria, the Harlem ice girl. I could tell when I took her to the Edwards' agency. Just the way she talked about you. You're such a cad, Tully."

"Yes! That's me, the cad."

"They like her very much, you know, and may give her a contract."

"Really, Kitty? That was a nice thing to do, you're a good person to try and help her."

"Tully, I know you're going to leave me for her."

"No, no, I thought we could all do it together with her German shepherd!"

"Tully, don't ask me to do it with dogs, you dirt slob. I hate doing it with dogs, they always try to get their balls in."

"Kitty, now you're going to get it." Kitty sprang on top of him with all force, snorting and sniffing like a dog and putting her tongue in his ear. He was spanking her and laughing.

"Tully, what breed of dog am I?"

"A foxy foxhound."

"Right, and what do they do when they strike a rabbit trail?"

"They bay!" he said, still laughing.

"No. Two words."

"Give tongue."

"Right!" said Kitty. "Now get to work, baby." Tully lay on his back and hung his tongue out as a dog would do.

"Tully, now's my chance to suffocate you with love."

"There can't be a better way to go," said Tully.

"No! I will spare you this time, lover puss." She pulled down his trunks. "Oh, this is what is the matter!" she exclaimed. As she held up one divine finger in the air, she said, "Mr. Happy is all purple and puffy, this must have given you a very bad headache. Poor dear." Tully strained to see as she handled his member in her hand. "You weren't clamming with this baby again, were you?"

"Maybe just a little," Tully said in a sheepish way. "Just for a bushel or two."

"Mother knows what to do here. It's just as well. We can't get into any missionary work today. I had to come off the pill."

"What?" exclaimed Tully.

"Yes, Albert said my breasts were getting too big."

"Kitty, will you please stop!"

"I am telling you the truth."

"So what do you have to do, take them out and show them to him each morning at work?"

"Tully, yesterday you said you loved me and I didn't have to tell you anything if I didn't want to."

"I said that?" asked Tully.

"Yes, yesterday," answered Kitty.

"I had to be delirious. This shows what smoke can do to a person's brain. Was I unconscious at the time?"

"Well, that's hard to say as you're always half unconscious around me," answered Kitty. "Excuse me, mother has work to do," said Kitty, licking her lips. Sensually, a robin landed in the carrot patch and flashed her red breasts. She pulled the worm out of the earth, it was big and fat and juicy, and she held it in her mouth. She looked in both directions with no expression. She was in no hurry. She held her prey in her jaws; the worm was stretched to its full length. The worm could battle, but it would lose. He was put on earth for one reason, and that was to be consumed. She gobbled the creature in small increments slowly but steadily, and then she spit him out and then slowly swallowed him again in a sporting fashion. Finally, he began to quiver and give up the battle and surrender to his destiny; she left a small part of him behind. He fell into his hiding place. And she was gone.

"Tully," Kitty said to his close-eyed expression.

"Yes."

"Thanks you for loving me the way I am!" she said, hugging him.

"That's not hard, sweet cakes."

"Tully, you know I never wanted to play Alice. That was too easy. I wanted to be the Mad Hatter."

"That's understandable," said Tully.

"Who did you want to be, Tully?"

"I wanted to be the little dirty boy who pulled Alice's pants down."

"Oh yes, that was the film version, wasn't it?" Tully kissed her. "You know, Tully, I can be very disruptive on the set."

"Yes, I can imagine," he said, playing with her nipple. She punched him. "They call me Lady Jonathan Winters."

"Well, you do love to joke around, Kitty. But I see you more as Lucille Ball, Lucy."

"Oh yes, I loved Lucy. My mother and I watched her every afternoon after school. With cookies and milk. Those were wonderful days – Daddy and Michael were still with us."

"I loved them too, sweetheart," said Tully.

"I know you did, dear," said Kitty, looking out to the sea.

Then she turned and crawled back on top of him. Their lips touched but didn't kiss. Breathing a breath of passion, they looked into each other's eyes, and they saw love. The world was shut out; it was only them in the universe. Their bodies fit together. There was no hunger, or longing. They belonged to each other in the sweet rhythm of life. She was him, and he was her. Theirs was one ship docked in love's obit; they looked back on earth. They knew they must return or miss their life, but neither cared. Kitty was the first to pull out.

"Tully, how much do you love me?"

"I'd die for you, Kitty."

Her chin and lips contracted, and her face turned red, and she started to cry. Tears were running down her face. "Don't die for me, baby. Live for me, James Z, live for me."

He kissed her salty tears. And the quail began to sing.

CHAPTER 28

SLOW TOUR, BUT ALWAYS SOMETHING TO LEARN

TULLY WAS CLEARED for fire duty by the medical office, and he returned for the night tour. All the calls of this night would be forgotten in a week's time except for two. One was an MVA on the East River Drive. There were three cars involved. Only one had entrapment. The make of the car was a black 1950 Chrysler New Yorker, which had been in mint condition before the front end got creamed. Both side doors pounced in, adding insult to injury. The inhabitants were a Puerto Rican family, mother, father, and grandmother, with three children. From a quick examination, no one was seriously injured. But the captain told the ambulance to continue in any way. On the dashboard, the family had all known saints and the Holy Family. The front tires were already flat, so the car was not rolling anywhere. The air was let out of both back tires to stabilize it. The engine company washed down the roadway with the booster line. The foam inductor was made up on a pumper outlet in case it was needed.

Though almost all car accidents in the movies end up on fire, this was not the case in real life. But if it could happen – it well could – it's best to be ready. One side of this car had a lot more damage than the other. The partner saw was fitted with a steel cutting blade and was started on the other side of the car. Lieutenant Sanchez spoke to the family in Spanish and told them what was going to be done. There would be a lot of noise and sparks. There was a new tool on the horizon, the

Hurst tool. Tully had already seen it in Long Island. It had been made for the air force, and it was a powerhouse. But New York City didn't have it yet. All was fine until the saw started to cut the center post. A blanket had been put inside the car to protect the occupants from the sparks. But the noise was too much, and the woman began to scream. Who could blame her? If there was one reason to replace the saw with the Hurst tool, it was to prevent a secondary fire. But the noise the saw made was not helpful. In time, the people were all removed safely. And maybe the Holy Family had something to do with it.

The second incident of note was the fire in a mattress on the third floor of a fire escape. Sleeping on the fire escape was not uncommon in the heat waves of July and August, but fires were unusual. It was only when people started to bring more of their life out on the fire escape, like candles and their smoking materials, that the probability of fire increased. The tower ladder and the engine had found ways to work together on operations that were out of their reach, like train-elevator platforms. Getting the water to the red stuff was half the battle in almost all fires. This was not a department operation. But it had been helpful in the past, so it was continued. The tower took up Lieutenant Sanchez and Skitter from the engine and their booster hose line strapped to the outside of the bucket. Captain Mac and Smithy operated the controls. Tully, Romeo, and Terry climbed the fire escape and carried up hand tools up to the fire. The engine wet down the mattress and then shut down. Tully in the past had shown Terry how to tie the mattress with the hose strap they carried; it had a number of uses for ladder men. Terry did a good job of wrapping the foam mattress and managed to get it over the railing and let it go. But it got caught on the fire escape one floor down. The mattress flopped open and lit up like it was dipped in gasoline. The draft carried the fire up to the curtains and window shades of the floor below. The tenants who had come out on the fire escape to give direction and berate the couple who were careless with a candle that had caused this inconvenience were now diving back into their apartments to get away from the smoke and fire and were cursing the fire department for their incompetence. They were going to burn down their tenement. "*Bombero mucho loco* and also assholes." As luck would have it, the strap held for just so long and dropped to the street in a flaming form. Just as the chief's car turned into the street, a scream added drama to its fall.

Tom Burke, driving the chief, exclaimed, "Oh my god!" and reached for the phone.

"Hold it, Tom," said Chief Walsh. "I don't think it's what it looks like. They only reported a mattress fire."

There were three windows of fire on two floors and a good bit of smoke as the engine was hitting the fire with fog not to drive the fire in back to the apartments. The mattress fell between two parked cars and was now out of sight. Was it a person? Tully, Terry, and Romeo each took a different window and quickly had the fire out and overhauled, being hit with fog stream at the same time. Captain Mac saw the chief's car and radioed.

"Ladder 14 to Twelfth Battalion."

"Go ahead, Cap."

"We got it, Chief. And we'll be careful to checking it out before we take up. K."

"Ten four, cap," answered the chief. To his driver, he had this observation. "You know, Tom, they almost always get it right. But sometimes, it's ugly."

CHAPTER 29

MAKING CALLS AND REMEMBERING

KITTY WAS SITTING on what they called the lifeguard chair. It overlooked their view of the inlet and the pool. It was located at the far corner of the pool. Tully had been a lifeguard at Rockaway Beach and had built this as a look-alike, only it was constructed of treated lumber. It had an umbrella and a police street box with a real phone. She had just made her last phone call and finally reached the new man, Terry. He was the only one of the firemen she hadn't met. Tully had said he was working out after a rocky start. He sounded nice. Kitty was excited about the pool party; it had been her idea. There had been company picnics, and they had been fun. But a small party with the crew that Tully worked with, especially after the rescue Tully and Smithy had been in, there needed to be a payback in some way. Kitty had called all the wives and girlfriends. It looked like only Smithy and Carole, Skitter and Barbara Ann, and Terry and his girlfriend were the only ones that could come. But this was the size of the party Kitty was hoping for. They had never gone out with any of the couples before. Kitty knew Smithy and Skitter from a trip or two in the car pool when she need to catch a ride into the city with them. This would be interesting because these were three very different couples from each other with only one common bond, the fire department. Kitty had promised herself that she wasn't going to do a character study on anyone for acting quirks she might copy and imitate later but just be a good hostess and have a good time.

Albert Marshall had just left. He had loaned her a big punch bowl. He had suggested a caterer to Kitty. It was true she had been to one hundred parties or more, but she never ran one, and maybe she was having a little stage fright at this point. But she pulled it off. Albert's dropping in had reminded Kitty of their card game and the night she got her role in his show. It was all innocent enough. Albert at the time had told her agent she was too much the girl-next-door type. This, of course, was correct, but after all, he had gotten the idea from the part she played at a cowboy Western bar in the Hamptons, where a hometown girl would top all the local heifers in a wet T-shirt contest with style and grace, ride the mechanical bull, and pull off her wet T-shirt at the end. The lights were dimmed, and she ran off backstage with two bodyguards. Kitty had no billing and would come on out of the bar. No pictures were allowed of the contestant to encourage real locals to participate. All were winners and got a free dinner on the house and free drinks the night of the show. Many a boyfriends would talk it up to their girl to enter. And some husbands too. Kitty was an actress doing what many do to find work between stage roles that could lead to a role on the stage.

This was all before Tully and Kitty became a couple. She told Tully most of it. The only part that Tully didn't know about she had made up her mind to tell him on their ride home the other night. But he had stopped her, feeling guilty about what he put her through, a day as an injured fireman's wife. And it was a terrible day for her, bringing back all the memory of her brother's casket coming home with Tully from Korea. Her riding in that big black Cadillac to Harlem had brought it all back. It was a trade-off for both of them. And Kitty, of course, didn't know about the pressure her mother had put on him, which was on his mind too. She would not try to tell him again that she had played the role of the reckless cowgirl Albert was looking for in their strip poker game. Kitty made sure she lost that night at Albert's. Kitty stood up and stretched in front of the beautiful Sound. She ran her hand up her T-shirt, revealing her high breasts, and said, "But that was all yesterday, and this is today. Eat your heart out, boys. It's all Tully's now."

CHAPTER 30

A MIX-UP WITH A PUNCH

CAPTAIN MAC AND Grace were out on the his boat and would be returning in just a minute. Kitty had never remembered seeing her mother so happy. She was aglow from head to toe with her new beau. Grace had helped with finger sandwiches, lobster salad, and baked clams. There would be corn and potato steamed with clams and clams on the half shell. Kitty only had to make the punch. She added four packets of frozen fruit juices, water, cutup fruit, and two half-gallon bottles of gin, which filled the bowl to the top. *Just right,* she thought. Grace and Mac came back upstairs from changing their bathing suits laughing like kids.

"You can sample tonight's party dishes."

"Let me know what you think. There's a ton of food," said Kitty.

"Where's Tully?"

"He went to the Storyville Fire Department and will be picking up some things for me."

"Is he really a member?" asked Mac, biting into a sandwich.

"Yes, I guess," said Kitty. "When we first got this house, there was a fire in town. A small boy lost his life. Tully went down to the firehouse to see if he could help out, and they needed help, so he volunteered."

"Well, there's a department order out against city firemen belonging to volunteer departments," said Mac.

"My position," said Kitty, "this is not a bad thing. And he wants to help, so it's OK with me. Lord knows my job could be a distraction for him, but he has not said a thing to me about it." Grace was going to say something but held her tongue. Her newfound love had calmed her discontentment, and Tully had brought Mac into her life. She was not going to start trouble tonight. "Mom, do you have anything for a headache? I never get one, so I don't have anything to take."

"Yes, Valium! I will leave the bottle here." But she failed to say, "Take only one."

"When are you going?" asked Kitty.

"Well, we're going to see the guests and help serve, but then we thought we'd get out of your hair and go back on the boat for the night. If anyone wants to stay, there'd be the extra room."

* * *

Skitter and Barbara Ann and Smithy and Carole got turned around, and Tully found them by chance and led them to the house. As they all came in the back sliding door, Skitter and Barbara Ann had some type of dispute over the babysitting arrangements and the new house dog, a Brittany spaniel, and this kept going on as they were all saying their hellos. Kitty put out the punch bowl from the fridge and filled a glass for her guests. Kitty had taken two Valiums and now a tall drink of the punch. Grace was introduced by Captain Mac to his crew. Terry and Susan let themselves in.

"Hi, we went to the wrong house on the hill. His was very nice and said he was your director. Kitty, I never knew you were in the theater." Susan was wearing a low square-necklined white sunsuit. Terry was dark and handsome with an open white shirt and white slacks. "I think he liked Terry better than me," she said and laughed. Kitty hugged her and kissed Terry for some reason and had another drink. The food was set up in the big back extension.

"You can change into your swimwear downstairs," said Tully, who already had his trunks on and a golf shirt.

The guests were drinking merrily. Grace came over to Kitty. "Dear, I just tested your punch, and I think that's a half of gin to the mix or more. I would guess that may be a bit too strong. Kitty, that's like three shots per glass, some of those girls have had three drinks or more already." Kitty had lost track of how many drinks she had. "Do you want me to help you dilute it?"

"Yes, I guess so," said Kitty, perplex. Grace started to dilute the punch with orange juice. Everyone had stripped down to their swimsuits. They were sitting around the patio table, eating and drinking and having a good time. Kitty's punch was a hit. Carole asked Susan if she knew what she was getting herself into with a fireman as a boyfriend.

"Well, I hope so! My father is Chief Mann, the chief of the department."

Smithy spit out his drink. "You got to be kidding," he blabbed out.

"I kid you not!" replied Susan. Terry put his hand up to cover his face.

"You guys didn't know this?" Susan said to no one in particular.

"I did," said Captain Mac. "Terry told me himself. And, Susan, I had the privilege of meeting you about twelve years ago."

"Oh my god, Patty McLaughlin?"

"Yes."

Susan reached for his hand. "You took us out on your boat waterskiing and you sat me on your lap and let me steer the boat." Patty blushed. "Of course, I was ten years old and had negative A cups at the time." She squeezed his hand. "I never put it together. I would never have worried so if I had known my Terry was with you."

"I am surprised your father didn't tell you."

"Well, to tell you the truth, I've been very hard on him lately. But that's a long story. What a beautiful spot you have here. How did you find it?" asked Susan.

"It found us," said Kitty.

"Well, I was going to enjoy it and not just talk about it," said Barbara Ann. And she got up and dove into the pool. Mac and Grace got up and said their good-byes and left.

Tully came over to Kitty. "Are you OK? You seem to be a bit out of it." Without waiting for a reply, he asked, "What did you put in that punch?" Tully was slurring some of his words.

"Tully, I made a mess of things. We already diluted the punch, but the damage is done, my head is spinning. I put in the big bottles of gin."

"The two half gals?" asked Tully.

"Yes."

"Oh boy, don't look now." Barbara Ann just pulled off her top. "Kitty, get some coffee and towels." Tully went over to Smithy. "Man, we got a problem here. We might have to put in a second alarm." Carole stepped out of her suit and jumped in.

"Don't worry, man. This is my meat." He pulled off his suit and dove in.

"Smithy, no no," said Tully.

Kitty came out of the house with towels with a very shaky gait. Terry had jumped in with no suit, and Susan was walking naked on the diving board like a runway queen.

"Kitty, it's our responsibility to halt all fraternization between unmarrieds. That's the COD daughter."

"Yes, sir," said Kitty with her eyes crossed, and she ran to the end of the pool, pulled down her suit, and jumped in between Terry and Susan. She embraced Terry and said, "Don't worry, Susan honey, I save you, dear."

"Kitty, this is the best party!" said Susan. "Do you do this all the time?" said Susan, floating on her back.

"Oh yes!" said Kitty, as she bobbed up and down in the water with Terry.

"And to think I was thinking of not coming. This is the greatest. How far do you go with this?"

"Oh, all the way," said Kitty, still bobbing up and down and hyperventilating. Kitty disappeared under the water.

"Terry, what did you do to her?"

"I did nothing! I think she smashed."

"What are you going to do?" Terry took a deep breath and dove to the bottom. Kitty was at the bottom, floating like in a dream. He squatted, took Kitty under her arms, pushed off for the surface of the pool.

Susan was crying now for help. "Something's wrong! Help us!"

Tully was trying to clear his head. He had run to the lifeguard chair and had a flotation device and a rope. He knew the rules of water rescue: let one person make the grab, be in position to assist. The light were on in the pool, and Tully could see Terry had Kitty, and he was bringing her to the top. Tully pulled her out. But something was happening to him; he was flashing back to Korea. He was cold, and he was dragging Michael, Kitty's brother. He was wet with his own blood. Tully started mouth-to-mouth breathing. "Michael, breathe," he was saying.

Smithy knelt at Kitty's other side. "Tully." He back-turned her on her side, and she threw up. Barbara Ann was giving out the towels and put on the shirts Kitty had given all the girls earlier. "Let's get her in the house."

They put Kitty on the couch inside the glass doors. Kitty started crying. "I made a fool of myself and spoiled our party."

Carole was holding her. She said, "Kitty, look at the shirts you gave us." Hand-painted across the front was, "Friends never have to say you're sorry." And Kitty laughed.

Tully went in the downstairs bathroom and puked. He was in cold sweat he looked in the mirror and said, "What the hell happened to me?" He put water on his face and came upstairs and put his arm around Kitty and kissed her and said, "I couldn't save him, Kitty, I am sorry."

"I know you couldn't, James Z, no one could have."

"I am sorry," said Tully.

Carole looked at Tully. "Are you with us, guy?" said the army lieutenant and now Veterans department nurse.

"Yes," said Tully.

"We all need some of that coffee," said Carole.

People started to use the bathroom. Barbara Ann picked up Kitty's guitar and started to fingerpick a Beatles tunes. All started to gather around the candle's light, and the music got all to mellow out.

Kitty was recovering now that she got up the content of her stomach. Susan and Terry got ready to go, and she came over to Kitty. "We got a long drive home back to Brooklyn, Kitty, so I think we're going to leave. Thank you."

"No, thank you, Susan, for coming." Kitty started to say more, but Susan stopped her.

"Kitty dear, I know this was not the party you planned. But you have a friend for life. You all have totally changed my view. I forgot how firemen and their family love each other, and I couldn't be happier that Terry have friends like you. And I hope you'll all come to our wedding. I love you," she said and kissed Kitty. Both were crying.

* * *

All had left but Carole and Smithy. Kitty was having toast and tea, everyone else coffee and cake.

"Carole! Would you like to stay tonight?" asked Kitty.

"Well, I don't know," said Carole.

"We have an extra bedroom. Mother and Mac have been staying on the boat at night."

"How romantic," said Carole.

"You could help us eat some of this food tomorrow."

"Not having to drive home tonight would be nice," said Smithy.

"OK," said Carole.

"More coffee?" asked Kitty as she got up to check out their room for the night.

"No, I'm floating now," said Carole, looking at Tully. "Tully, how are you doing?"

"OK, I guess," he said, drinking the last of his coffee.

Smithy walked out to the pool. Knowing what was coming by the question Carole had asked him after the pool scene was stabilized. "Have you ever seen Tully like that before?" No was his answer.

"Tully, I hope you take this as a shoptalk from a friend, but I just went to a conference for nurses in combat. It was on the golden hour, as it's now known, what we do in that first hour of emergency will determine the outcome of recovery or demise of the wounded and the strain that this put on us all to carry it around after the incident. It's natural to have something that triggers our memory to the event. But when we relive it – this is a flashback – this is not good."

"I've talked to VA doctors about it before," said Tully. "They screen for stuff like this. I was told to cry, my answer was, 'If I start to cry now, I'm afraid I'll never stop crying.' Besides, Carole, this was an extreme situation involving a loved one and the punch."

"The punch?"

"Carole, are you kidding you didn't notice people's behavior was a little unguarded? Like removing swimming suits."

"That was the punch?"

"You tell me, Carole."

"Tully, you're a master at changing the subject."

Smithy came back in. He had been listening from the door. And Kitty, who had changed her clothes, was back too.

"Anyway, Tully," Carole continued, "there is going to be another conference. Would you like to go? It's open to all combat vets."

"Well yes," said Tully. "But let me think on it."

"Well, we all best get into bed," said Kitty. "I mean into our own beds." All laugh. "It's funny we were all naked earlier, and now it's like it never happened."

"That's right! Is that all there is to a naked pool party?" said Carole "What a dull bunch!"

"Come!" said Kitty. "I'll show you your room. We share the same bathroom, so if you sleep naked like I do, we have to remember to be decent when you come in the bathroom."

"Oh my god," said Tully. "Here we go again. Let's just go to bed."

* * *

The next day, the unplanned turned out surprisingly perfect. Grace and Captain Mac were back from their night on the water and helped to make breakfast for everyone and supplied good humor over coffee and fruit. On the swimming pool deck, there were two conversations going at the same time, male and female. Male, it was the Mets and Yanks and fishing. Female, it was love and the braless trend. The males were keeping an ear open for invitations to the girls' conversation but were locked in to their chat when it turned to firefighting and volunteers. Tully was responding to the question, how good are they?

"Well, with very little training or experience, some are still very good at engine work."

"Well, what are you trying to do?" asked Mac.

"Well, I don't think I am going to last long enough for anyone to learn anything from me. And teaching is new to me."

"Not totally," said Smithy. "You add a lot at training discussion. Plus look at the work you do with new men."

"Thanks," said Tully. "But it is a daunting task. With this department, we're not starting with a lot of combat experience at any level. In FDNY, you get ten weeks of training to put a handle on it. Then you join a twenty-five or more experienced men. With four officers. All try and put a mark on you, plus we have fires. Here there's 10 to 12 fires per year. With Ladder 14, we have 4,000 runs and 1,500 fires, with special call tower ladder and other 250 real fires," Tully said, looking at Captain Mac.

"That's about it," he said. "The numbers game don't tell the whole story. I think we have a little overkill these days. Each man brings something to start with. If you've been in the military, it's helpful. What type of work experience you have. But you do need about ten to twenty meaningful fires too, as they used to say, bloodied in the military and hardened off. Your red badge of courage is a fine book on this point and the civil war," said Captain Mac.

"Well yes," said Tully. "I always took longer to learn anything. I would say that every fire I have been to here have been meaningful a few weeks ago. There was a daytime fire. We're making an attack in the front door with the first engine in and using 1 ½ preconnected line. The fire was in the rear kitchen. We were moving in and planned to push it out the rear window. 'Good, cut off the fire to the rest of the house,' said Captain Mac. Next thing we're getting killed with heat and fire. They put a big line in the back window, and we lost water pressure. I got us back out. I went around to the back, and here was the chief from the next town with one of our chief with the line in the back window. When I called him out on it, he said, 'Well, you weren't going anywhere. Not except to the hospital.' A week later, they did the same thing at a night fire, only I called them assholes this time. This is, of course, no way to make friends or to teach either. The trouble is not with the firemen – they would like to learn – but with the chiefs who don't want you to steal their fire. I do have a following of people from the new end of the town. And I do like them. There are well educated. And they're new to the town like me. If I can only train one group and not get anyone hurt, put out a few fire from the inside, then we'd have something to build on, then there would be a clear choice to stay outside and burn it to the ground. Or vent, go in, get the people out, put the water on the fire, and nine out of ten times we'd put it out if the fire's not in the walls or roof. That is, of course, the second part, truck work, which will come later. If I last that long."

"I can see that this could help you when you become an officer on our job," said Captain Mac.

"To tell you the truth, we were taken by the hand to learn this job. And with a fire, every tour's to screw up until we learn it."

"You're right, Tully. Fires are the most expensive fire school in the world. It's a lot like the battlefield. If you don't get killed out the gate, you get a chance of learning something."

"I'd like to go down and see their firehouse," said Mac and Smithy.

"Well, the chief may be there, and he's the only one that got a brain."

"Is he paid?" asked Mac.

"No, no," said Tully.

"Well, let's go."

"Girls, we're going down to town to visit the firehouse. Do you want anything?"

"No, we have our own adventure, we're going for a braless walk."

"On the beach?" asked Mac.

"Oh no, in town."

"What do you think, girls?" said Grace.

"Let's do it."

"Loverly," said Mac. "Loverly."

CHAPTER 31

BUSS MAN HOLIDAY
BOY, THEY GOT GOOD STUFF

THE FIREHOUSE HAD been the area high school before the new school district, so it was a well-constructed building with a bus garage to the rear and below. Their first-line pumper was a 1968 Hune 1,000 gpm pumper with a five hundred – gallon water tank and a preconnected 1 ½ line, a Mack truck, a city service truck with full complement of ladders, and a '58 Mac, 750 gpm pump used as a hydrant truck. Tully waved to the volley sitting in the radio dayroom as they entered the firehouse. The first thing Tully wanted to show them was the Scott Air-Packs mounted in the jump seats with a new one-piece glass face mask with speakers built in.

"Boy, I'm impressed," said Smithy. "We're still carrying our old-style World War II face piece in the suitcases locked away. That's one reason they're never used."

"Gentlemen," said Barry, "I'm the chief here. Can I sign you boys up?"

"Hi, Barry," said Tully. "These guys are my coworkers from Ladder 14. Out for a visit!"

"Well, glad to meet you. If the fire horn goes off, you're more than welcome to respond. We have complete turnouts on all three of the trucks."

"Well, I don't know if we'd be any help," said Captain Mac.

"Believe me, you would be a big help, we're shorthanded in the daytime. Tully just about put a house fire out by himself a few weeks back. We're still talking about it."

"I had two men helping me stretch in, and one to vent the rear window. It was the kitchen fire," explained Tully, looking at Mac and Smithy.

"And he stopped the second engine from putting their line in the rear window," said the chief. "I was out of town at the time. But I got to admit, it's hard to break old habits. That's how we were instructed! The indirect attack, Mr. Layman."

"Oh yes," said Captain Mac. "Shipboard firefighting, but not for house fires."

"Oh yes, that's what we were told. We are trying to change now with the help of Tully." There was a big commotion in the dayroom. "What's going on?" asked the chief.

"You've got to come to see this. There're three beautiful women walking down the sidewalk, broad daylight braless. In little T-shirts."

"Oh well, we got to be going," said Tully. The chief seemed intent on witnessing the sighting.

"Do you think it's them?" asked Smithy.

"Don't want to find out," said Tully.

"Thank heavens, we parked in the rear," said Captain Mac.

* * *

Their afternoon was relaxing, which included checking Tully's lobster traps, lunch and good conversation, and Bobby Dylan's song "Times Are a-Changing." No mention was made of the girls and their downtown mission and their celebration of equal rights, by golly. After lunch, Carole and Smithy said good-bye, and everyone took a nap.

CHAPTER 32

OH, WHAT A BEAUTIFUL MORNING

IT'S 5:30 AM. Captain Mac and Tully were having a cup of coffee on the back deck looking at the Long Island Sound. It was Tully's suggestion before starting off to work.

"You know, laddie, things are working out so good it's scary."

"Know what you mean," said Tully. "I have this nightmare it's all going to come to a screeching halt. In fact, this is why I start my day off like this and say thank you."

"That's a fine way to start the day," said Captain Mac. The tide was going out, and the quail were calling in the mountain laurels off to the right, in front of Mr. Marshall's house, playing in his landscape. "You've done a lot with this place, Tully."

"No, not really. It was all here when we were invited to use it for the summer five years ago, and that's what worries me because we can't afford to buy anything like this on what I make."

"Oh yes, I see what you mean, Tully. I tell you the Lord's truth. There's one part of our job that's forever reminding us to ask, 'What if this happens?' It's what has saved our lives a time or two to be sure, but it also sure as hell takes the fun out of life at times."

"So what you're saying, Cap, is what's saving my life is also killing me?"

Captain Mac started to laugh. "Tully, my boy, that is the same question, 'To be or not to be?'" Tully had a look like he wasn't getting it. "Tully, let me say it another way. The worst thing you can do when you're making love is to think of its cost or what can go wrong. It's the moment that we've been given. To ask about tomorrow is to be ungrateful for today."

"I have to remember that," said Tully.

"Try and live by it," said Captain Mac. "It works for me."

"Well, back to the reality of worry," said Tully. "We better get it on the road and get to work before the city burns down. But first we need to look in on the girls. That they have their covers on before we go."

"Tully, you're a good man," said Mac.

* * *

It was a peaceful drive out of Storyville Harbor, lined with tall oaks and dogwoods and mountain laurels. They took Twenty-fifth Avenue to Smith Town and made a right to Northern State Parkway. They didn't turn the car radio on. They got off at Kings Park to pick up Smithy. Smithy and Carole came out of the house holding hands, and she kissed him and waved to the car. He jumped in the backseat of the car.

"Looks like you have things well in hand," said Captain Mac.

"It was the party, and the day after. That sounds crazy, but it did a lot for us."

"That's great," said Tully.

"You know who was a big surprise?" asked Smithy.

"Terry and Susan?" asked Tully.

"Yes," said Smithy. "And the fact that Susan is Chief Mann's daughter."

"I was holding off for the right time," said Captain Mac, "to tell the crew. But I though it needed to wait. After the episode with the covering Captain Cane and there was not any leaks of the story, I think that showed he wasn't a tattletale with an open line to the Chief Mann."

"Yes," said Tully. "That's true."

It was only a short drive to Skitter's development in Deer Park off Long Island Expressway; traffic was starting to build up. Tully steered the six-cylinder 1966 Mustang around bicycles and baseball bats into their driveway. Tully tapped the horn, and Skitter exploded out the front door with Barbara Ann in close pursuit. He tripped on a roller skate and took a header. Barbara Ann in a nightie took aim at Skitter's butt. In football kickoff fashion. Skitter's military training enabled him to stop, drop, and roll out of harm's way. Barbara Ann missent her bottoms up onto the lawn.

Skitter darted for the car, shouting, "Back it out, man, back it out!" as he leaped into the backseat of the moving car. "Floor it, man! Burn rubber!" yelled Skitter. Tully left the street like they just done a bank heist.

"God, oh my!" exclaimed Captain Mac. "Is everything all right?"

"Oh yes," said Skitter with his head tugged below the rear window. "It's only a small family altercation."

"Man, what did you do to her?" asked Smithy.

"Man, why does it always have to be me? This woman's lethal. She pulled a gun on me."

"OK, that's a bad sign," admitted Smithy. "Where did this all happen, over the breakfast table?"

"It's all because of the party," said Skitter.

"The party?" said Tully.

"Well, in a way, yes."

"How?" asked Tully.

"Well, you remember the dog?"

"Yes, the Brittany spaniel. Bruser."

"Yes. Well, I got him a good collar and a nice chain and secured him on the upstairs landing when we went to the party."

"All this is because he chewed some stuff," said Smithy, ready to grant dispensation.

"Well, no," said Skitter. "He's dead!"

"Dead?"

"Yes, dead. He jumped over the railing and hanged himself."

"Oh, this is bad!" exclaimed Smithy, like he heard a hundred stories like this every day.

"Yes, but that's only the half of it," said Skitter.

"Half," said Smithy.

"Yes. Well" – here the scene was explained by Skitter in action news style – "we came home after picking up the kids. They thought they should have been taken to McDonald's for a late supper after they only half killed the babysitter. But anyway, here's the semi-happy family apron entering said home shocked that the dog's hanging in the stairwell."

"Oh god, this is bad."

"It gets worse, er . . . the dog did his final bowel movement, so as I'm trying to secure the scene, I'm getting pelted by the bystanders," said Skitter.

"You're family," said Smithy.

"Yes, we are family."

He started to sing the song "We Are Family."

"Smithy," said Tully, "go easy on him. He loved that dog. Yes, we were getting ready to train it for bird hunting. It's true he was a little excitable," finished Tully.

"I'm sorry, Skitter. You know I love you, man," said Smithy.

"Go ahead, what else happened?" said Smithy.

"Well," continued Skitter, "it took about three hours of slamming doors before the house settled down and the kids went to bed. She was putting the swimsuits in the washer, and I started to get that old feeling. I said, 'Maybe it would do us both some good to end the night with a little love.' Well, this was a big mistake. She tells me I'm cut off and she will have to go to confession because of all the dirty, filthy things I made her do in the pool and we're never doing them again, never."

"Skitter, you made her do dirty things in the pool?" asked Smithy.

"I don't remember," said Skitter.

"Don't look now, here comes your wife in the yellow Impala, and she's gaining on us," said Tully.

"Man, it's all over now. We can't outrun her. She's got three hundred horses under the hood with two four-barrel carburetor. Her old man is a used-car salesman, he gave it to her. He hates me that's why he gave her the gun."

"I don't think she had time to get the gun, she still got on her nightie," said Tully, looking in the rearview mirror.

"Tully, just pull off the next exit coming up and I'll take the beating," said Skitter.

"OK, man, it's up to you." Tully signaled and put his flashers on, pulled off the exit and onto the grass.

The Chev came skidding past him, almost hitting them, and tearing up the grass before stopping three car lengths ahead sideways. Skitter got out of the car and stood as Barbara Ann ran at him with rage in her eyes, no weapons visible. Skitter opened his arms and said, "I love you, Barbara Ann. Why do you treat me so bad?" She hit him as hard as she could. He stood his ground. "I love you, Barbara Ann." Blood trickled down Skitter's face. She started to cry and put her arms around him and kissed his face. The traffic that was pulling by were shouting, "Get a room!"

Smithy was out of the car now. He put his jacket on Barbara Ann, and Captain Mac said, "Skitter, I'll put you on sick leave. Take the girl home."

"I loved that dog too," said Barbara Ann, crying to Skitter, "I loved him," and he walked her to the car.

They pulled back on the express, which traffic was now standing still. All were quiet for a time.

"You know, man, what's the difference between war and fire department is," said Smithy in a philosophical way, "in war, you don't get a chance to go home at night, but that's OK because that's why there're wars. So our families are safe at home. But here, you get a bit mixed up. Because you do go home and you go a little overboard with the celebration that you're alive and we got to keep up with the Joneses. We are being told some things are a must, like living in a good neighborhood, having a good house, having a second car, and then kids start coming. Is this all a wonderful dream come true, or is this start of a nightmare, and will it be our undoing, like a bridge too far?"

"Man, that was deep and dark," said Tully.

"Yes, but it's an honest question," said Captain Mac, "because we're going places we have not been and doing new things. The new plastic money, credit cards, is a way to stay up. But will it pull us all down in the end?"

"Skitter got a lot more on his plate than we do," said Smithy. "Our wives are working and helping out. He has three kids."

"Yes, that's true," said Tully.

"Not being born in this country." said Captain Mac, "and having a poor upbringing, my thinking and ways are old, but I can say we are all moving at one hundred miles an hour now from the end of the war, 1945.

"I can see what you're saying," said Tully. "I grew up in a tenement house and never knew the difference. But now, how do you slow down when we're all in free fall? We love the fall, but fear the landing."

CHAPTER 33

WORRY AND TROUBLE ARE MY MIDDLE NAME

FROM THE START of the tour, things started to go wrong. Captain Mac was detailed to the Sixteenth Battalion as chief. The tower ladder had been to fires in the Bronx and Queens last night, and the truck needed a major cleanup. With all equipment put in order, the tower ladder also needed to go to the department shop for repair to the bucket. The infamous Captain Cane was detailed to Tower Ladder 14 to take Captain Mac's place. And then there was a small fire at the Crescent Moon, which was a dive on Park Avenue. After the fire was out, Captain Cane ordered an unbelievable amount of violations and gave a lecture on fire safety. This drove the owner to rip up the violations. Captain called the chief to respond. There was a small pushing match. Cane was a hothead, which was now becoming clear. The owner, who was called Breed, was trouble and no saint. He got decked. He called the police. The cops are called bulls not because of their genteel behavior. They're not unlike baseball umpires. They only take so much lip and you're out of the game. They closed him down. After they found a gun and a knife on his person, they slapped the cuffs on him. This all took close to two and a half hours for one small fire with Captain Cane. The crew decided on subs for lunch. They got them almost made, and there was a call to a vacant-building fire, a small fire on 123rd Street building on the top floor front. They made fast work of it and mopped up and went back and got the subs and took them back to quarters. The captain went upstairs to do paperwork, and it was decided to eat fast before anything else happened. There was no one at the front desk but the assistant chief Hopkins, whom Tully remembered as a onetime chief in the Sixteenth Battalion. He had a nickname, "All-Hand Hopkins," because he never put in a second alarm for a tenement fire. He entered the kitchen. Tully jumped up and saluted.

"Chief, do you want me to call the chief and have the men to line up?"

"No, relax. I've come to visit the men. The dispatcher told me Captain McLaughlin was detailed, so I called him. He said this crew working here was the best to talk to about the tower ladder."

"Chief, would you join us? We have an extra ham and cheese, the covering captain is not eating with us."

"Why, yes. His loss will be my gain," said the chief. "Let me get right to the point. It's Tully, right?"

"Yes," answered Tully.

"You were at the meatpacking house fire on 125th Street."

"Yes." Tully reached out his hand and introduced the crew.

"I've seen how well the tower ladder can perform on apartment house fire a couple of times, but in Queens, the fires now seem to be mostly in taxpayers' mercantile establishments, like last night's fire the tower responded to. I was out to Chicago, and I saw what they were doing with snorkels, articulating booms that can bend over the roof of a building fire. This seems to be safest and more effective. Missing power lines and trees." Tully looked around the room, and it looked like he was going to be it.

"Chief, if I had my pick, I'd take the tower ladder because the overall length is shorter and the ladder faster. Its ladder is only an escape ladder, but the snorkel has no way out of the basket when it's ninety feet in the air."

"Have you seen them in operation?" asked the chief.

"Yes," said Tully. "At a few fires and also at Nassau County training center."

The chief took a good bite of his sandwich. "I can see having one or two snorkels may be good as rescue truck," said Tully.

"Yes," said the chief. "Chicago's using them like that as squad units. I'm from the old school, I believe in talking to the men. Someone has a good idea to start with, and pride keeps them from changing any part of it. The truth is we all learn from trying something new."

"Chief, can I ask you a question on this point?" asked Tully.

"Yes, of course."

"A few years ago, we were called to a third alarm you were in charge of. When we got there, there was steam coming out of the cornice of the two-story taxpayer. We went to the roof, and it was easy to see it had been a bad cockloft fire. I asked the officer on the roof how they put it out. He said, 'Distributors in the roof! It was the chief's idea.'"

Captain Cane walked into the kitchen, and he looked flabbergasted that the assistant chief was sitting at the table with the men. He saluted.

"Men, outside and line up for inspection."

"Hold it, Captain," said the chief. "I wanted to talk to the ladder men about the tower ladder. They have done everything right. So at ease, please. I was just asked a very astute question by this fireman."

"Who, Tully?" questioned the captain.

"Yes, Tully, who handled things very well, and I'm going to ask you to answer it You're the chief at a taxpayer fire. The fire's located in the center of the street. The building have all the same height, one story. This looks to be a fast-moving fire. What do you do?"

Captain Cane answered without hesitation, "Put in a second and third alarm."

"Captain, were you a lieutenant?" asked the chief.

"I was detailed to headquarters."

"Oh yes," said the chief. "OK, Tully, you're the truck officer, what do you do?"

"I'd divide the company in four task units of at least two men."

"That's eight men," noted the chief, enjoying his game.

"Chief, you didn't tell me I couldn't use both trucks."

"OK, so what are you going to do with them?"

"One team finds the fire, and other team vents the roof, that's the inside team and roof team. The other two teams pull ceilings to each side of the main fire building."

"OK, good!" said the chief. "But now your task units find fire in the ceilings to both sides of the main fire."

"Well, Captain Cane already put in a third alarm."

The chief laughed and slapped Tully on the back. "Tully, you're as good as Captain Mac said you were. Here's the answer to your first question. The cockloft fire is a fast-moving fire. Once you learned of it, you need to address it almost like any exposure fire because it is a separate fire and it can travel the length of the block in a short time, it's unprotected roof beams of wood and dried out in most cases.

"In the old days without any mask at all, it was natural to think of using distributors and cellar pipes for cockloft fires. There were drills on their use and an evolution for how to do it. We also vented the roof over the main fire and try to get to both sides of the vent hole with distributors. This, of course, is not an everyday fire. Not like a bread-and-butter tenement fire for you guys. We went in the front door as you do now. But over time, once the evolution was deleted from the training regulation, its use disappeared. I once met a chief from Syracuse. He told me his father, who had been chief, had invented a most outstanding roof-distributor tool for the roof that had a fifty-foot hose with six hollow stainless spikes that could be driven in the roof. This was a help in stopping horizontal fire spread. He drew this on the blackboard used for drills. Well, anyway, back to the Syracuse fire department story, he took me to the engine company who had carried this tool, and guess what, it was no longer on the truck. They had taken it off because not one remembered what it was for. What a shame, but it's very easy to see how this can happen because it is not a one-man operation. It calls for teamwork between the engine and truck company to get it done, so the chief has to call for it. By the way, the names of the distributors are named after the chiefs who commissioned them. It must be a chief's call because no one can be under this roof when this operation starts because it can blow down ceilings."

"By the weight of the water?" asked Smithy.

"That, of course, is a factor," answered the chief, "but steam explosion. The expanding of the water to steam. When you hit the fire, it can be explosive."

"Box 1439 Lenox and 121st Street," was transmitted.

"Turn out, men," said Ducky.

"Thanks, men," said the chief as the crew left the kitchen.

The fire call turned out to be an MFA. A second box across town was transmitted, Lenox Avenue and 125th Street.

"If the next box is at the end of our district," said Tully, "we're being set up, they're going to hit our quarters."

"That's the end of our district," said Tully. "We are being set up – by someone."

"They're going to hit our quarters?" quested Smithy.

"That or paranoia is setting in," answered Tully. The third box was also a mickey. Truck 14 headed back to quarters – without incident. And back in, the crew began checking out quarters. Their new color TV and then their personal stuff all seemed in order. No one said anything about Tully being wrong. It was just forgotten.

Tully started on the committee work. He was assigned to making beds. This was a job that they paid a matron to do, a fireman's widow, but as times changed and the neighborhood became too dangerous, she was told to stay home and her small check was mailed to her.

This morning drive now seemed like one hundred years ago. The talk about worrying, and it's taking the sweetness out of life; it was a hard habit to break. Tully thought about the three boxes leading them out of their respondent district; it was a case in point. It was paranoia. Dad was forever telling him, "Don't do that or you will knock your eyeball out." That was probably the start of it all. Times were so different in the '40s in the city. He was let out and played by himself in the city streets when the school-age children went to school. And he saw many things he could never tell as he was not supposed to cross the street. One day he saw a large crowd outside the tailor shop. He crossed the road, but he was too small to see over the crowd. One older boy picked him up so he could see the tailor had hanged himself. He had not thought of that scene in thirty years. And then there was the time he was staying at his aunt's house and he was playing in a back lot. He thought he saw a man jump off the roof. He looked again, and there was a man lying in the courtyard. When he told his aunt, he was punished for making up stories again. "If someone jumped off the roof, I would know about it," she had said. In a few days, she came to him and said she heard about the man. It was terrible. It had occurred to him at the time bad things were happening all the time. More than he knew of. His father was right. Look out or you'd get your eyeball knocked out. Tully started to laugh to himself. *I'm starting to lose my marbles for sure. No, not really. When I start laughing wildly like the phantom of the opera, then it's time to worry.* There was the worry thing again. I can't get away from it.

There were three rings on the phone. Tully slid the pole. "What we got?" asked Tully, putting on his gear.

Smithy had the phone to his ear. It was the dispatcher. "He thinks it's a rekindle at the vacant we had before, top floor. The captain is on the phone telling him it's all our fault." They could hear him now sliding the pole.

"Man, he's a nut job."

"Well, you've done it again, Fourteen. Fuckups," the captain said as he got in the front seat of the cab, talking to himself.

"You know, I'm really learning to love this man. He's just so much fun," said Smithy as he and Tully took their spots on the truck as it was rolling out into harm's way.

It was the same building all right, and it was the top floor. But something didn't look right to Tully. He couldn't put his finger on it. The time sequence for one thing. The fire had not gone anywhere but looked to be in the same place as the last fire. Rekindles are usually above in some spot that was not overhauled and wet downright. Tully helped Engine 35 with their line. It was black rubber 1 ½ hose fed by 2 ½ hose line with 2 ½ controlling nozzle connecting the two different-sized hose together, and it was going in the front door with no problem. Tully had outside-vent position. He headed to the rear of the building. He thought he saw a guy scale the backyard fence. The rear fire-escape ladder was in a down position. He climbed the ladder overlooking the rear. On the second floor, there was a door blocking the window from the inside. Tully passed it and continued up. It looked almost OK on the third and fourth and fifth, but instead of going in and meeting up with his company members, he went back down to the second floor and slowly pushed the door out of the way.

There was light smoke and the smell of kerosene. In one room, there was a hole in the ceiling with series of small fires with newspaper-trailer materials leading to Clorox bottles hanging from the wall in four different places in the room. A gas bottles trap! This could go at any time. The thought raced through Tully's mind. By removing the door, he had added air, and the trails were burning. He could make it back to the fire escape and save himself, but he walked gingerly to the front apartment door. It was off its hinges and would fall back into the apartment as the booby-trapped fire exploded. As soon as he replaced the door, he tried to remain calm as he transmitted, "Mayday! Mayday! Get out of the building. It's booby-trapped." Tully ran to the 2 ½ line in the hallway and shut it down, breaking the line, removing the 1 ½ hose, and pulling the line with the big controlling nozzle down the stair. He turned and pointed the nozzle at the door of the booby-trapped apartment. There had been a repeat message. Tully just reached for his mike and said, "Get out, get out now!" They were coming down the stairs now in a stampede. As they passed him, he just kept saying, "Get out!"

Captain Cane was the last one down the stairs. He shone his light in Tully's face in a belligerent manner. "What is the meaning of this outrage!" he shouted.

Tully could see the fire flash behind the crack in the door. "Get down! Get down!" he shouted, opening the nozzle. The captain was blown over him, taking the full blast of the fireball, and blown down the stairs. Tully was lying on the stair foxhole style, operating the nozzle into the apartment doorway.

The marshal later found gasoline was used on the third floor. The second floor was a wick, which helped the fire to travel through the ceiling to the gasoline on the third. When it lit up, the explosion rocked the building, and the whole hallway lit up above him. That would have trapped the companies on the top floor. Smithy had come back in and was alongside Tully.

"Are you all right, man?"

"I don't know, I'm afraid to move to find out. Is the captain OK?" asked Tully.

"He's burned bad on the back and may have broken something. He was talking crazy, he said an angel with fire gear told him to get down, then carried him down the stairs, and then went back in to get you. He told me to look for you, Tully. You were right about being set up. It must have been done by the Crescent Moon sweethearts."

"Whoever did it know what they were doing," said Tully. "This was not their first rodeo."

"When the third floor kicked in, it blew right up the hallway and out the front windows," said Smithy.

Acting chief Mac rolled in and put in a second alarm. Engine 35 relieved them on the line. Tully got four weeks off with burns on his ears and neck and wrists. Tully wanted to see Captain Cane in the hospital. He had to lie on his stomach and didn't make any sense to Tully. But he was a changed man. The anger in him was gone. Father Cook had visited him, and he made peace with everyone. As Tully hit the street, he started to sing to himself, "It takes a worry man to sing worried song, and if you're worrier, it can save your butt in this man's job."

CHAPTER 34

WHAT A DIFFERENCE A DAY MAKES

ON THE WAY to work, Tully picked up Smithy. "Hey, Tully, I want to bring this up before I forget it. Do you still want to go to the Eighty-sixth Street tomorrow between tours? The new movie *Deep Throat* has opened up."

"OK, that's a good move for me, instead of going to Grace's."

"Is everything OK there?" asked Smithy.

"Fine. It could not be better," said Tully.

"Well, that's good. How's the burns?"

"Like a bad sunburn. I was using Foille ointment. It helped, fireman's first aid cream. I'm on the mend."

When they got to Skitter's house, both came out to the car, and Barbara Ann was as sweet as she could be, and she said she was sorry about the last time and thanked both Tully and Smithy for being so kind. She was looking forward to another pool party before she started showing. Skitter got in the car, and they pulled away. Skitter had a big beaming smile.

"Skitter, did I hear right? Barbara Ann is expecting?"

"Yes! She's always in love with me when she's that way."

"You're not going to believe this," said Smithy. "I was not going to say anything, but Carole took a prego test, and she's pregnant too. She said it was the pool party and all that male sperm floating around in the pool. It made it a fertility bath."

"Get the hell out of here!" said Tully. "Kitty is not pregnant. At least, I don't think so."

"You better check that woman out, man. Carole said there's science that proves that women who ingest sperm will induce favorable conditions for pregnancy. In the same way as women who come into heat in dorms, and they all come into heat."

"Man, you lose so much credibility when you say stuff like that," said Tully. "You're telling the truth, Carole's pregnant?"

"Yes," answered Smithy.

"Then where're the cigars?" asked Tully.

"They're in the mail," said Smithy.

Tully got off the expressway to pick up Tom Burke at the city line. "Put a lid on these conversations when we pick up Tom. I don't want him to get the wrong idea about the party. I did ask him and his wife, but they couldn't come."

"Well, he probably will not want to come to the next one with three fat heifers floating around in the pool," said Smithy. All were laughing, and it got embarrassingly quiet when Tom got in the car.

"Man, you guys were just telling black people jokes before I got in this car. I can tell! OK, tell me it now!"

"Man! What is the matter with you saying something like that?" said Skitter. "We don't even think of you as black, more like a caramel. Let me kiss you right on the lips to prove I love you," said Skitter.

"Skitter, keep away from me or I'll deck you."

"OK, you guys," said Tully. "You're making it hard to steer the car. Can't you just be a man, Tom, and just let Skitter kiss you. Once."

Trying to change the subject, Tom said, "Tully, did you know the chief and me went over to take a statement from Captain Cane, and he wants to write you up?"

"What did I do now!" said Tully.

"He's recommending you for a class 1 for saving both companies at the booby-trapped fire. There's only one thing. I don't think it's going to fly because he insists there was an angel there with you, backing you up on the line, and he wants it in the report."

"I am not surprised," said Tully. "This has happened to me before, and I'm starting to believe it my own self."

* * *

The night tour went well with ten runs, only one fire. It was a special call to a second alarm in the Bronx. Early on, the tower was being called to vacant building fires, but fire chief Mann had put a stop to this. This was a taxpayer fire. Captain Mac used Tully to talk to the chief to find out what he had in mind. This was also helpful to request supply lines and the pressure that was need to supply a good fire stream with the authority of the chief, a rule of thumb. The motor-pump operator started off with one hundred pounds per square inch for a hand line as an open tip only needs forty per square inch at the tip for a good stream. The tower need one hundred per square inch plus at the tip and thirty-five pounds of head pressure and friction loss of six lengths of 2 ½ hose. When Tully told the MPO he wanted two hundred per square inch, the MPO put up a fuss. Tully laid it out for him, plus "this was the orders of the chief of the fire." Tully returned to the tower and went to the roof to help the truck companies in opening the roof. The operation took two hours before they returned to quarters.

There was a visit from the fire marshals with two detectives from the Twenty-fifth Precinct. There was clear evidence that the fire the other day was arson, but no leads as to who set the fires. The owner of the Crescent Moon, Breed, had a witness of his whereabouts at the time. The police came into the case partly because they were at the Crescent Moon that day of the fire and had taken him to the police station but released him, with time for him to do the job or plan it. The police said it was an explosion and attempted at murder. They wanted in on this investigation even though the marshals would take the lead. There also was some type of gang war going on in Harlem, but the cops didn't think this fire had anything to do with it.

The incoming crew heard of last night's fire operations or lack of them from the off-going tour. It was the ritual of storytelling that helped pass on useful information and produced some comparisons. "Can you top this story?" With only a few fires to talk about from last night, the talk was that Ladder 14 was the only company not being on a relief list with a downtown company when they had a heavy workload the night before. Ladder 14 was excluded because there were only two tower ladders in Manhattan now. One truck responding to a Brooklyn fire was not going to be on a night rest as they had their hands full with tower ladder calls too. Ducky cooked up eggs and bacon with pancakes on the side. And, of course, there was plenty of hot coffee to wash it all down.

The crew for the trip to Eighty-sixth Street and the movie *Deep Throat* were Captain Mac, Tully, Smithy, Skitter, and Ducky because the show was not until twelve forty-five. Smithy had been talking of taking in the museum of art exhibit, Harlem Renaissance. Smithy went on about being in touch with the history of the community they worked in so they might be more sensitive to its background. While this was an enlightened view, in the back of Smithy's notion was eyeballing the young chippies who were always in generous supply at the museum. He even carried a drawing pad to capture the fine lines of the ladies' figures, discovering long ago that women love to be immortalized in pen and ink as they contemplated art. He had met Carole, his wife, just in this same way. He was only a looker now. But then again, is that not why we go to museums, to look in the hope of inspiration?

This seemed to be one of those go-along days. It was the pleasure of each other's company that would carry the day, such as the sailors on the town, out to capture the big town's magic. It was the experience of being together and bonding that made hard times easier to take. Loss of a member would always drive home the brotherhood that was just below the wise guy's remarks or prank. Geo Edgar was a case in point. He had come home from Vietnam and came on the job to continue his service, to do the right thing, only to lose his life to smoke inhalation after a fifth alarm packinghouse fire. He once asked Tully to speak to one of other chiefs he worked with, who was on his case because he had long hair, which Tully did. The chief told Tully it wasn't his place to speak for him, but if you can't speak for a brother, who can you speak for? Geo was killed a short time later. That chief and Tully never talked about it. They didn't have to. Both wished they could have done more for a brother.

CHAPTER 35

DAY ON THE TOWN

THE 125TH STREET station was an express stop on the Lexington Avenue subway line. Going downtown, Eighty-sixth Street is the next stop. The subway had only a small amount of riders after the morning rush hour until it would pick back up again after 3:00 PM. Skitter joined the culture group as they all headed downtown, getting off at Eighty-sixth Street and walking across to Central Park where the museum was located. There was not a great difference in the architecture from Harlem to Yorkville and Eighty-sixth Street. They had brownstone town houses and tenements in the streets, but the buildings facing the Fifth Avenue and off the park were in a class of their own, being of a grander design of the school of Gothic design by Mead and White and Hastings. Some of these buildings were grand town houses at the time of constructions for well-to-do families, later becoming public buildings, as the home of Felix Warburg was now the Jewish Museum. Some of the willing designs are New York Public Library, grand central terminal, and the Metropolitan Museum of Art, today's destination. The multiple dwellings of the affluent were indeed grand but, in some cases, more dangerous in a fire. For example, the duplexed apartment. The fire, instead of being compartmentalized on one floor, would spread to the second floor of the duplex – up the open stairways to bedrooms – and cut off escape. It was natural for firemen to think of the building in terms of fire. Captain Mac pointed some of these facts out as they walked through the streets along with other points of interest. There was more commercialization of the brownstones too. They were converted to inviting restaurants and pubs built into the basements and parlor floor. The cars were also newer than uptown, and there was a busyness of the people going somewhere and doing things.

Smithy was taking note of the pubs that had free food incentives for drinkers for the trip back to Eighty-sixth Street and the movie theater. There would be a need for refreshments before the movie. This was the first time that Smithy had joined them for this between-tours activities. Captain Mac and Tully had done this a few times before. If it had been a heavy-fire duty night, Tully would take the short trip to Astoria to Grace's. He would help out if it was needed. He had painted the apartment over a few month's time and sanded the floors and would wash the windows and, of course, catch some rest before going back to work. The museum had wide stairs leading up to the main entrance, which people sat and talked on, eating a hot dog and having a drink. People would break the New York City rules of not talking to each other there. The museum was the place if you wanted to talk about art. There was a better than even chance that you'd get a conversation.

"Excuse me, sir, how was the exhibition?" asked Smithy to artists type.

"Man. It was happening. Really."

"What's that mean?" asked Ducky of Smithy.

"The gentleman was conveying it was timely. Indeed, timely."

"Whatever," said Ducky.

The show was free and had impressive displays of the places and people of uptown Harlem. Duke Ellington, Billy Holiday – called the Angel of Harlem – the Cotton Club, and Josephine Baker, who had took Paris by storm in the 1920s, which opened the door for other black artists there. Most displays had a sound track. Jazz was king uptown. "Take the A Train" was playing in the background. They also took a walk through the main hall trying not to devour the nudes who stood tirelessly in their frames. Was it possible to mix culture and X-rated movie all in one day? It did cross Smithy's mind what Tully had said that Ducky might go off the deep end. Smithy looked up at a painting just for a second. He saw a dead boy's face and then the sparks from the saw at a car MVA with the woman screaming. He looked up, and he was looking at the painting *The Scream*. And he got a chill. A beautiful young woman took his arm.

"Excuse me! But I saw your face, and it had such sensitivity to it. Are you all right?"

"Yes, for a second I thought I saw something in the painting. Were you a soldier?"

"Why, yes. So was my husband before I lost him. When I looked at this painting, I often see myself. But excuse me, sir. I'm interrupting your visit." And she turned and walked away. Smithy wanted to go after her, but he didn't.

Ducky came over to Smithy. "Are you OK?"

"Yes, thanks, Ducky!"

"Who was that you were talking to?"

"I don't know, just a lonely lady, I guess."

"You know, sometimes you think you had an easy night, and you realize how much debris you're carrying around with you."

* * *

Tully found himself separated from the rest of the crew. The Harlem exhibition had an effect on him that he liked to digest alone. Nothing truly monumental, but little things he started to string together. He had a better understanding of some of the things he thought he knew about Harlem history and some of the missing parts to the puzzle. The enclave that the Negro moved to after the Civil War draft conscription riots of July 1861. Tully had read some on this before; the cause of riots was the draft and the fact that the well-to-do could buy their way out of it. The war in turn was blamed unjustly on the blacks, of course. But they were easier to identify than the rich. The violence that ensued was blamed on the Irish, but the record seemed to indicate that the rioters were the ones who had the most to be mad about. Young working people who could not buy their way out the draft, who put the riot down, were the fighting Sixty-nine regiment, who were largely Irish. The place the victims moved to was a small enclave at approximately north of 125th Street to about 140th Street, Eighth Avenue on the west and the Harlem River on the east. The Pennsylvania Railroad bought later on thirteen large apartment houses on 135th Street near Lenox Avenue for their black workers. This caused other buildings to become available to the growing black population.

Tully didn't know that W.C. Handy and Scott Joplin had come to New York City to promote their music and polish their craft, as writers of the Word had done in the 1920s by moving to Paris. Because of them and others, Harlem did become a mecca for minstrel performers and their music, only they didn't need to paint their faces black! They were the real deal. The patrons who wanted to see the real thing went to Harlem and brought their money. This, in time, created an interesting community of color, and its base were working people – from the railroad and trades, store keepers and musical trades – and the people who came from all over the city and the world to see them in Harlem. It was almost impossible, thought Tully, to keep talent down by just imitating it. He had lived through a similar period in music in the '50s as a listener who heard the blues of the South in the services, later to be called rock and roll. New York stations were not playing the hit music out of the South on small labels. Fats Domino and Penguins and their "Earth Angel" were covered by white singers like Pat Boone and others doing black hit songs. This indirectly led to the scandal called payola. Record companies were tipping disc jockeys to play their labels on radio. This caused laws to be passed against this practice, but in the end, talent and originality won.

Tully's memory returned to one of the first times his father had taken him to Central Park Zoo. And they walked through the museum of art he was now in. He had been told what he would see three or four times. He was daydreaming about it on the way there, riding the train from Jackson Heights to Manhattan on the flushing line. Just before the train went into a long curve just before Long Island City station, a tall figure entered their car from the car in front of the moving train. He was dressed in dark brown sack of a monk with a rope braided around his middle, he had a long beard and wild hair, he carried a long staff. Tully looked around; no one was paying any attention to the strange man. He proclaimed in a loud voice, "Wheoooooooooo to all you sinners! The world as we know it will come to an end before we reach the next station." The train banked into a hard turn. The steel wheels of the train screeched in protest. The prophet now shouted above the horrifying noise, "Repent, get down on your knees before it's too late. Only the ones that do will cross the River Jordan and enter the Promised Land. The rest will be cast into the abyss." James Tully, aged five, felt his heart would burst in his chest. He now looked around quickly; no one was heeding this profound message. This was not totally unusual for James. Adults seemed to live in a different world where they didn't see or hear all that James heard. They needed good light or their glasses to really get in touch. His daddy was an old daddy, so part of James's job was to remind him of things. But he was now reading the newspaper, and he didn't like to lose his place. He would gladly get on his knees and pray for them both. But he had on short pants, and his mother had told him not to disgrace his father by getting dirty. Maybe he could signal to the holy man that he wanted to be saved. He tried to catch his eye, but it was to no avail. James was caught in between the devil and the deep blue sea, as Grandma would say, disgracing his father and mother by breaking their vow. Incapacitated by the choices he was confronted with, he settled on inaction. Just as the world started to close and go black, the monk sat down in total disgust and pulled out the daily racing form from his holy pouch and blew his nose in a dirty handkerchief, making a study of its contents with great interest, like a Gypsy woman of the storefront on his block, reading tea leaves in a teacup of future events, whatever the buggers foretold. The monk got up and got off at the next station. James's father looked up at the station as the doors opened.

"Daddy, did you see the priest who was telling us about the end of the world?"

"Oh! He's not a priest, James. I've seen him before. Someone told me he lives in Woodside and was a handicapper at the racetrack before turning to monkism, and the track banned him."

"What's a handicapper and monkism, Daddy?"

"Well, that is complicated, James. All you really need to know is stick to what your mother and I tell you, and you wouldn't go too far wrong. With people outside the family, never judge until you hear from both sides. If your hear something that sounds wrong, tell us about it before you act."

"I think I did right, Daddy, by not doing anything."

"Yes, James, that's right. You're a good boy."

The rest of the day went well. He loved seeing the seals swim and jump out of the water in the zoo and the polar bears. But his favorite was the monkey house. It smelled bad, but he went right in. Other children ran out because it smelled so bad. The day ended at the art museum. James saw ladies painted without clothes on for the first time. This seemed like a natural good idea; this way you never could get in trouble for getting your clothing dirty. Later at home, he told his mother about his day, and his new view on clothes. His mother told him he was a foolish boy. But his daddy had told him he was a good boy, and that's what counted the most for five-year-old James Tully.

* * *

Without any real plan, the group one by one were checking their watches and started back to the entrance to regroup, in somewhat the same fashion as they would have done at a fire. Training makes us creatures of habit. The time it took to deplete an air tank was part of their built-in time clock. They were all back inside, three minutes of each other. They started back in the direction of Eighty-sixth Street and Third Avenue about two blocks into the walk. Skitter remarked in a loud voice, "Man, I can't believe the culture we got from that art museum" – this was loud even for him – just as they were approaching a young sporting woman walking five dogs on five leads. She had blond hair tugged up and under her black leather jockey's cap. She wore blue cotton work shirt and jeans with a black leather vest and riding boots. She wore no makeup except a tan. She smiled at Captain Mac, and he and Ducky tipped their hats. Smithy and Skitter looked long and hard at her going way view. She had her five charges well under control. There wasn't a better picture in the museum that could match this one for a vibrant energetic woman of any time period.

"Well, boys, there's a bar and grill just up ahead. It used to be operated by a fireman who is an old friend of mine. They serve good food," said Captain Mac.

"I'd like to take a bite out of that dolly's butt," said Skitter.

"Well, so much for all dat art and culture," said Smithy. "It sounds fine with me," he continued.

"Me too," said Tully. Ducky and Skitter nodded in agreement.

"Now we're talking about the eatery, right?" asked Captain Mac.

"Well, if had my pick, I'd say I'd take the dolly, but the bar and grill looks like a sure thing," said Smithy. All laughed.

They walked down the steps of the converted brownstone town house, which had a menu in the window hung with a boarder frame. Today's special is Ruben's. A small swiss bell was activated by the movement of the door opening. There was a long dark mahogany bar with a brass foot rail running around its bottom. Red leather barstools, glass mirrors, and six tiffany shades were hanging behind the bar. There were firehouse memorabilia hanging on the walls, fire axes and fire hooks, and pictures of Ahrens-Fox pumpers, Christie front-drive tractor pulling old wooden

Seagrave aerial ladders lined the walls from a door located behind the bar in the center of the bar. Out stepped the barkeep from the kitchen with two bowls of pretzel and a plate of cheese crackers.

"What will it be, gents?" Without a second breath, he recognized Captain Mac. "As I live and breathe, Patty McLaughlin! You old warhorse, how's it been? I haven't seen you in a dog's age."

"Yes, it's been too long, old friend. I just made a promise to myself before stepping in. If you were still here, I would not lose contact again."

"That makes the two of us, Patty," replied his old friend Marty, extending a warm handshake.

"Are you still a firehouser?"

"Yes, still at the old smoke game," said Captain Mac. "And this fine bunch of young men are my crew from Ladder 14."

"Well, they got the look of smoke eaters or cops, that they do," said Marty. "What can I get you? How about a Turkey coffee, give you a little gobble in the morning."

"That'd be fine for me," said Captain Mac. "But I'll let the boys order for themselves."

"What exactly is it?" asked Smithy.

"It's a shot of wild turkey, which is Kentucky Bourbon whiskey in a cup of coffee with cream on top. It's good for what's ailing you," continued Marty. "You know, firemen called themselves Jakes in Boston."

"Why's that?" asked Smithy.

"Well, being a buff in Boston before coming on the job here in New York, the best answer I ever heard was a male turkey is a jake and has a beard, as most old-time firemen had. Turkeys were plentiful in New England in the old days and held in high regard. Hence, a good jake was and is a good fireman."

"Well, I'll drink to that," said Smithy, "and I'll have the special, the Ruben," followed by "Me too" from the rest of the crew.

From the center doors came a nice-looking woman in her fifties. She had on a white diner shirt and a black tie. "Why, Patty dear!" she said. "I heard your voice in the kitchen and I knew I know you. But I couldn't place it until I see your lovable mug." She came around the bar and kissed him. "How's Maureen?" she asked.

"The poor girl passed away, dear."

"Oh, I am so sorry," Mary said as she hugged him. The doorbell jingled, and in walked the blonde dog walker. She walked straight to where Captain Mac and her mother was standing. "Jerry," said Mary, "I'd like you to meet an old friend of ours, Pat McLaughlin. Do you remember him?"

"Yes, I think I do. You were the fireman with the boat."

"Right!" said Captain Mac.

"You were the nice man who helped a little girl who was a little sick up on your lap to drive the boat and get some air."

"You know, Cap, for a guy who is not supposed to be a ladies' man, that's the second tale we heard of some little tomato on your lap."

"That's right," said Skitter. "Terry's Susan." All laughed. The captain had no comeback, only a blush.

"Patty, lost his dear wife, Jerry."

"Oh, I'm sorry. She was a nice lady. I wished I was a little older. I'd ask you out."

"Jerry, that's not nice," said her mother.

"Oh yes, it is, Mary," said Captain Mac. This had the rest of the boys whooping and hooting.

"I just love firemen," she said, sticking out her chest, which was ample, and kept the whooping going. She looked over the whole group.

"I'm sorry, lass, they're all married but one. Ducky here."

"He's the one for me. He tipped his hat. The rest were looking at my butt," said Jerry with a smirk. Ducky had a red face.

"Now, Mac, you didn't," said Mary with a smile. "Of course, the child is used to handling wild animals."

"It wasn't me, Mary, the saints be my witness," said Mac, standing with his chin in the air. This pose had everyone breaking up. "And I can vouch for Ducky here to be a fine gentleman besides being a skillful operator of the tower ladder and a dandy cook," finished Captain Mac.

Marty reached across the bar to take his hand. Ducky had a thick forearm with a tattoo USS *Saratoga* on it. He had red wavy hair and a baby face and a nice smile.

"Ducky, is it a fact that you're the firehouse cook?" asked Marty.

"That's right, sir," answered Ducky.

"How about coming into the kitchen and helping me out. I have a party of twelve women from the board of education coming for lunch, and my man didn't show up. Your lunch is on the house, one way or the other." Ducky looked at Mac.

"Go ahead, son." said Captain Mac. "It's OK with us." Jerry sold the deal by taking his arm and leading him into the kitchen.

"You realize," said Skitter, "that she's using Ducky to get to me."

"Sure, I pick up on that," said Smithy. "Too bad you wore your dick down to just a stub."

"Have no fear," said Skitter. "I still could gum her to death."

"You know," said Captain Mac in a reflective moment, "funny things like this do happen."

"Cap, don't scare me, tell me you're not talking about gumming some poor tomato to death," said Tully.

"No, no. It's just about how I met my dear departed wife, Maureen," said Captain Mac from another world.

"How was that?" asked Tully.

"Well, that's the funny thing. Marty and Mary here were getting married in a pub downtown just like this. Maureen walked up to me, introduced herself, took my arm, and that was that."

"Cap, you're not saying that this dolly is really interested in Ducky. He's a complete mess," said Skitter.

"You'll never know. Some women can work miracles with men. They take them into tow, gentle them along. Get a sweet bit in their mouth, next the harness, and before you know it, they're pulling the wagon, happy as can be with their ears a-flapping."

"Captain, you left out the part," said Skitter, "when they strap on the spurs and start cracking the bullwhip on your ass."

"Skitter, you got one tortured personality, dude," said Smithy, taking a bite out of his sandwich.

"You're a fine one to talk, Smithy, you pussy-whipped sap. You had to call Carole to ask if it was OK to come out with the boys today."

"Get the hell out of here. That call was to my bookie. I was playing the daily double 8 and 6 at Belmont," said Smithy.

"Do you always tell your bookie that you love them just to place a bet?"

"Captain! I hope this outrage of wiretapping on personal phone calls will be dealt with swiftly."

Mary came through the door from the kitchen. "I'm sorry for leaving you alone, boys. Would you like something more to drink or eat?"

"No, that was fine. Just some club soda for me," said Mac. "How's Ducky making out in the kitchen?"

"Oh, he truly saved the day, and he's so funny too, the way he gives orders, he has Jerry swooning over him."

Smithy's and Skitter's jaws dropped, and they rolled their eyes. The front door jingled.

"Good afternoon, ladies. Your dinner will be ready in just a minute," said Mary.

Jerry and her father came out of the kitchen with two trays of food with Ducky behind them; he had lipstick marks on both cheeks.

"Ducky, did you get anything to eat?" asked Captain Mac.

"Oh, plenty," said Ducky, taking his place at the bar.

Marty came back from the table and put his arm around Ducky. "Hey, this guy is more than just a firehouse cook. This man's a chef. He went to school for it."

"Well," said Captain Mac, "I don't think we know that, but we definitely knew he's more than just chicken-gum baw cook."

"We're going to try and work something out. I could use his help, and he said his mother may want to help too, and she's here in Yorkville. I hope he takes my offer."

Mary came out with the check. "You sure there's nothing else we can get you?"

"No, Mary. It was great to see you."

"Please don't be strangers, all of you." And she looked right at Ducky.

They all started out, and Jerry came from the kitchen and took Ducky's arm and pulled him aside. They all filed out and waited on the street for him. When he came out, Smithy came over to him and said, "So, Ducky, how did you make out? She looks like a really nice girl."

"Yes, she is."

"So what's up?" asked Smithy.

Ducky only looked at his watch and said, "Men, if we're going to make the show and get some popcorn and candy and be seated by showtime, we need to move out pronto." He stepped off in a smart military pace in the direction of Eighty-sixth Street.

Skitter said in questing way to Smithy, "Why is it that morons always make out the best?"

"God help that poor girl," answered Smithy.

* * *

In the theater on Eighty-sixth Street, Ducky was first up to the candy counter. He ordered a large butter popcorn, a jumbo box of Good & Plenty, and an orange drink. There was a strong blend of nostalgia for the group, akin to days of old with boyhood chums on their Saturday morning adventure to the local movie house to see two main features and thirteen cartoons and the bicycle race contest, where if your numbered bicycle rider survived the mishaps – which were many – and came in first, you won a box of candy. There was also the movie tone news and the coming attractions, all for thirteen cents. A latter-day adventure with the boys was the military pass to the village to fraternize with the local women, hopefully only visiting approved cathouses with girls with recent health cards, for social intercourse and other amusements. A short time was two dollars, and for a bunch of boys, it was indeed a short time, but memorable.

It was hard to believe that a movie could be put in this same category as Flaubert's *Madame Bovary* and Henry Miller's *Tropic of Cancer*. It was all said before and revealed before but on the printed page. What was different about *Deep Throat* was it was all in living color on the large screen and for view in public without fear of criminal charges. The courts had ruled that movies of this type with this contents could have social-redeeming value. The only catch was the local fathers had to go along without protest. And they did in Yorkville. The movie *Deep Throat* was a taboo subject about a mixed-up chick whose clitoris was where her tonsils should have been. The story line was uncomplicated. If you got an itch, scratch it, no matter where it is. The movie's title became famous for the tipper who gave the *Washington Post* information on the break-in by the Nixon White House at the Watergate complex and the Democratic Party offices in Washington DC. His code name was Deep Throat. Linda Lovelace, the star of the movie, never had another hit but had her fifteen minutes of fame.

The house lights were on in the theater, so the crew selected a row midway between the front and the back. Ducky led the way. He carried a small hand flashlight, checking the seating and floor. Smithy, who was next in the back of him, looked to Tully and laughed. "What's he up to?"

"I don't know," said Tully. "Ask him."

"Ducky, what are you looking for?" asked Smithy.

"Just to be safe, I'm checking for dick dirt."

"Dick dirt!" Smithy said to Tully. "He must have been here before."

Finally, all checked out, and they were seated and started to work on the popcorn and candy. And they were getting quite comfy when an older gray-haired woman carrying a shopping bag looked them over and seated herself down in front of Ladder 14's finest. This dropped Ducky's jaw, and he turned to Smithy. "This poor old woman can't know the content of this movie. This will totally derange her mind."

"Look," said Smithy to Ducky, "she's a big girl."

Ducky sunk down in his seat with a look of an impending doom. Ducky started to rock in his seat; he couldn't contain himself. Finally, he tapped the woman on the shoulder. She turned and, in a foreign accent, said, "Yes?"

"Madam, do you know the name of this movie?"

"Oh yes," said the woman – *cough, cough* – "*Deep Throat.*"

"Oh, thank you. That's a big help," said Ducky.

The movie opened with the poor girl going from doctor to doctor trying to find the cure for her sexual dysfunction. Medicine triumphs! This condition called for Dr. Louis's hot beef injection to the area of affliction. Luckily, she found Dr. Louis, and her day is saved. With this, the old lady in front jumped up and bellowed out like Ethel Merman's fashion, "Good for you, girlie! Give it to him!" There was an arousing applause from the patrons for her generous encouragement, and Smithy gave a high five to the old lady. The movie was far from a disappointment, and there was even a fireworks scene to celebrate Linda happily joining the normal world, as we come to know from this informative movie.

As the group was leaving the theater, there was skin star in the lobby giving out naked pictures of herself and fliers on her upcoming flick, *Love under the Big Top*. Ducky got a picture autographed, and they headed out in the street.

"Well, boys, I don't think there's any need for us to take the train. We can just as well pole-vault uptown." They had a good laugh and were relieved that they had not been struck blind when they hit the outside light. They were sure their eyes had been challenged and almost popped from their sockets by the performance.

"Don't forget we're going to my mother's for late lunch," said Ducky.

"Are you sure?" asked Captain Mac.

"Oh yes, she will be very disappointed if we don't go. She made pierogies and sausage," said Ducky.

"Really," said Tully. "She's not Irish?"

"No, my father was."

"Well, it sounds fine with me," said Captain Mac.

"And me too," said Smithy. "My only concern is where I am going to put it all, we have done nothing but eat all day."

"Well, the walk will help make room," said Mac.

"How far is it, Ducky?"

"Only a few blocks. Eighty-second Street off Second Avenue." Ducky broke off at a hot pace, with the group bringing up the rear.

"So, Skitter, what did you think of the flick?" asked Smithy as they were walking.

"It would make a great training film," said Skitter.

"You got a good point there."

The walk didn't take long. The apartment of Ducky's mother was in a corner tenement with stores on the first floor, one of them being a bar and grill. They filed into the hallway, and Ducky rang the bell located just below the mailboxes that were polished brass. The front door buzzed, and Ducky opened it. Each floor had a different ethnic-aroma cooking of sausages and spices, as many families' cooks would leave a pot over the gas pilot light to simmer all day. The food would be ready when they returned from work. On the third floor, Mrs. O'Shaughnessy was out on the landing to greet them. She met everyone with open arms. "You're welcome, come in please."

There were quick introductions, and everyone was hugged again and then led into the dining room, which had two large windows overlooking Eighty-second Street. The table was set, and Ducky started to serve beer. Mrs. O'Shaughnessy brought in a tray of fresh-baked pretzels, and there was cheese fondue on the table with its own candle. She put on a Polish poker record as a finishing touch.

"Ducky, Mrs. Krazinski is coming. Do you remember her? She took care of you as a little boy. She called you her little Weenie. She was a Polish singer and worked nights on Eighty-sixth Street and took care of you when we went to work in the daytime. After the war, she went back to Poland. It was a shame all her family had been killed."

"Yes, I think I do," said Ducky. His mother was bringing in a platter of pierogies pasta shells filled with whipped potatoes and cheddar cheese.

"Eat, boys."

"The bratwursts are almost ready." The downstairs bell rang. "This must be Mrs. Krazinski now."

Skitter was now dancing around the room like a fool and had everyone clapping and laughing. Mrs. O'Shaughnessy left the room to let her friend in, and two women carried in the trays of knockwurst sausages and hot rolls.

Mrs. Krazinski had a booming voice. "Biggest wursts, get them while they're hot." It was a familiar voice, and when she walked in the room, everyone remembered at the same time Mrs. K. This was the bag lady from the movie house. She now had her coat off and was wearing a white sweater with a V-neck and size 48 double-F magnums. Mrs. O'Shaughnessy was the only one in the dark. Why, everyone was silent. Skitter, like a knight on a white charger, polkaed up to Mrs. K and danced her around the room. And then Tully, Smithy, and Mac all did likewise. Mrs. K laughed the whole time, but when the music ended, she sat down and started to cry. "Hiddy, Hiddy," said Mrs. O'Shaughnessy, putting her arm around her. "What's the matter, dear?"

"I don't know, I guess I'm just a foolish old woman." Captain Mac poured her a glass of beer and gave it to her.

"When you get our age, Hiddy, you're entitled to be a little foolish now and then. But let me tell you something, you are a beautiful dancer, Frau [woman]." This kindness got a big smile and a kiss. Sometimes our best moments are those when we rescue someone, and in the process, we save our own souls.

CHAPTER 36

THE LONGEST NIGHT

THE BEGINNING OF the tour gave no hint to what the night would bring. The weather was clear and wind out of the north at fifteen miles per hour. Ducky planned a Yankee pot roast; he made it with a good bit of potatoes, carrots, onions, and tomatoes with extra sauces. This was one of the most practical meal for the firehouse because in case of a fire call, a slice of meat was slapped on a piece of bread and eaten like a sandwich while responding; the rest of the food was put on simmer, and there was something hot to eat when they returned. The captain and Skitter had walked back to the firehouse from the train station at 125th Street. Skitter was to drive the chief, the aide relieved early. Tully, Smithy, and Ducky had walked to the A&P food store. They would have been safer in uniform, but at this time of day, still daylight, they'd be OK. Spanish Harlem, the *la barrio*, was open to firemen. But Whitey, in general, had no business here; they had been told. Prejudice is just as ugly in black face as it is in white. Ducky went alone to the back of the store to pick out the meat. Tully and Smithy toured the store for the rest of the meal. They split up, and Tully went to get the bread and ice cream and Smithy the vegetables. Out of the corner of his eye, he saw four Spanish boys fourteen to sixteen approach him fast. Smithy used the shopping cart and his back to the produce to keep them at arm's length and his back covered.

"Hey, Whitey. You don't belong here," said the youngest and smallest.

187

The trace of alcohol was still in Smithy's system and produced a street response to the tip of his tongue: "Maybe I shoulda sent your momma." Instead he said, "Oh, really."

Tully showed back up, put his stuff in the cart. "What's up?" he asked.

"These gentleman said we don't belong here," answered Smithy.

"Oh, Mr. Lopez, the boss man, is not going to like that!" said Tully.

The boys looked at each other. "Who are you, man?" said the biggest boy.

"Bomberos," said Tully.

"See, *bombaos*. Firemen," said the biggest kid.

"I know you," said Tully. "You're from St. Mary's."

"No way, St. Theresa," said the smaller boy.

"Then you're off your turf," said Tully.

"No way, man," he said back.

"OK, look, man," said Tully. "We came to spend our money in the neighborhood store. We're not looking for trouble."

"Right, you're cool, man," said the biggest kid and started to back his comrades away.

"Man, you working tonight?" said one of the kids who spoke for the first time.

"Right," said Tully.

"Man, something's going down tonight. There may be fire." He kissed up his cross and held it up. "Watch your back," he said, and they were gone.

Ducky came from the back of the store, and they all headed to the check-out counter. "You handled that good, Tully," said Smithy. "Everything up here is manhood. That kid made his move, you have to let him save face or it's a fight."

"Yes, but we'd probably win. Probably," said Tully. "I can see the headlines now. 'Black belt fireman kills a fourteen-year-old in his food store while his mother waited at home for some choche Fridos.'"

"Like I said, Tully, you did good."

"I need a cup of black coffee, two aspirins, and enema, and I'll be fine."

"What do you make of that warning for tonight?" asked Smithy.

"I say it's for real. They were off their turf, this is the Bloods grounds. A show of force very often hurts an innocent third party."

The walk back to the firehouse was uneventful. Ducky wasted no time in getting the meal under way, browning the roast and adding veggies before changing into uniform. It was 5:30 PM. There was talk of today's fire at Bathgate and 179th Street in the Bronx. It took four alarms to handle a row of wooden frames. Smithy was trying to tell about the day on Eighty-sixth Street as Renaissance day of art, food, and debaucheries.

The off-going crew was telling him he was full of it. "Tell the truth, Smithy. You spent the day sucking on a beer can and dining on pizza and rat cheese."

Smithy could see he wasn't getting anywhere, so he changed the topic to the fire at Bathgate as he sipped his second cup of coffee. "I hope you didn't disgrace us at the fourth alarm," he said.

"No way, numb nuts. Probably we'll get a unit citation for the brave deeds we performed," was their reply.

"Get out of here, shit for brains," said Smithy. "Something smells fishy here," he said as Box 1468 was sounded.

"Seventh Avenue and 125th Street, get out, chief and truck," said Romeo on watch.

Ducky started the Mack up as the doors slid open. Tully and Smithy were in the jump seats, and the junior men had stopped traffic. The captain was in the officer's seat. Ladder 14 pulled into traffic and responded west on 125th Street. The chief's car had been on the ramp and was already responding. The department radio sounded, "Report of many calls for Box 1468."

"Twelfth Battalion to Manhattan."

"Go ahead, Twelve," Chief Walsh answered.

"Heavy smoke showing from Woolworth, transmit a second alarm."

They were greeted by black billowing smoke, which was rolling across 125th Street. "Battalion 12 to Ladder 14."

"Go ahead, Chief."

"Ladder 14, Woolworth on 125th Street. Ladder 30 and Engine 59 will attack the fire from 124th Street.

"Ten four, Chief," answered Captain Mac. "Laddie, put up the thirty-five-foot ladder for the roof. We're not going to set up the tower until we see where the fire is going."

A four-man team pulled the ladder off the back of the truck, carried it to the building, and raised it. The street was awash with people, and it was reaching riot excitement as people were running wildly into stores and coming out with pocketbooks and shoes from Miles shoe store, which was next to the closed Woolworth for renovation. The crowd wasn't mean but in a holiday mood, laughing and happy, playing grab ass with grab bags. Smithy saw the four boys from the A&P store earlier, running with what looked like a money bag from Miles store. Firemen at times have been known to help stop a crime. But not this time. Smithy had the roof saw secured with nylon strap over his shoulder and was getting ready to climb the portable ladder to the roof. Tully had already reached it with a six-foot Halligan hook. His axe and Halligan were strapped together for climbing the ladder. It was ironic to Tully that the roof of the fire building felt safer than the street, at least for the time being. The street was in full riot now. The cops had their cars on the sidewalk, sirens wailing, two abreast, slowly herding the crowd off the sidewalks and away from the storefronts like cowboys with cows, forcing them to a safe place. There were cops walking in the back of the cars with nightsticks. They were not taking names, but ready if need be to use their nightstick. The shoplifter had every chance to scram and get away with their stuff or stay and get slammed. The plan was simple: to break the riot, which had no cause, only opportunity, because of the fire. The fire had the earmark of a delayed alarm. There was too much fire for this time of day. The building was being renovated and had a watchman, which was good if he or she turned in the alarm of fire and then tried to put out the fire, but it was almost always done the other way around. Tully estimated that this was going to be a third alarm or more if they did not cut off this fire fast. But from the look of things, the fire was already in the cockloft and through the roof over the 124th Street entrance. Smithy had started to cut an inspection hole in the roof, about 150 feet from the main fire, which was already vented. They removed a four-by-four piece of the roof deck. There was black smoke in the hole. Tully could make out a sprinkler pipe and heads not flowing. The volume of fire out the other vent hole was reaching forty feet above the roof and was menacing the hotel. Tully hit his transmitting button on his portable radio. "Ladder 14 roof to Twelfth Battalion."

"Go ahead, Fourteen, K."

"Chief, heavy fire is venting from the roof. It is exposing itself to the hotel. We opened an inspection hole at the 125th Street side. There is a sprinkler in the roof not flowing, K."

"Ten four, Ladder 14," answered the chief. "Attention, all units. Supply all Siamese connections on both 125th and 124th streets by order of Twelfth Battalion."

"Twelfth Battalion to Manhattan."

"Go ahead, Twelve."

"Transmitted third alarm for this box. Report to follow."

Chief Walsh had already put to work a full-alarm assignment three engines and two trucks on front and the backstreet to the fire. With second-alarm units just reporting in, the ten-story hotel would consume the whole third alarm's manpower just to check it out. Skitter came up to Bill Walsh, who had a worried look on his face and was now standing in the middle of the street trying to get the best perspective of how serious a threat this fire was to the hotel. Castro and his people were in the hotel. Could it be the CIA set this fire to get them out of their rooms to spy on them? The Russians had been suspected of this in Moscow in a fire in the American ambassadorial offices. Whatever is the cause of this fire, Bill knew he needed to stay focused on his men and the fire and let the cause and origin teamwork it all out over coffee and donuts later. *For now, let's put it out without anyone getting hurt.*

"Chief," said Skitter, interrupting the chief's thoughts, "Engine 59 had hook to the sprinkler connection as one of their first things. And the watchman said that the welders were working on it. Just before the fire started, the system was disconnected."

"Welders," said the chief. "Were they burning?"

"Yes, I guess. That's what welders do."

"That shoot the CIA thing down."

"The CIA?" asked Skitter.

"Disregard, Skitter. Good job. We'll let the engines hook up anyway. All the water could come out over fire somewhere. If we have any luck."

"Twelfth Battalion to Manhattan, K."

"Go ahead, Twelve."

"Following is first report at Box 1468. Exposure 1 is 124th Street. Two, one-story brick, sixty by two hundred. Three is 125th Street. Four is a ten-story hotel, sixty by two hundred. The fire building is a sixty-by-two-hundred brick being renovated. There is heavy fire condition involving 40 percent of the structure and the cockloft. A full second alarm engaged. Third alarm to be used on the hotel. The fire is doubtful at this time, K."

"Ten four," replied the Manhattan dispatcher.

On the roof, Tully and Smithy were in the process of cutting a trench cut from the front to the rear of the fire building. Rescue 3 has joined them with two saws and were making fast work of the job. Fire in the cockloft was an auto exposure once a fire gets a foothold. Only getting water directly into it will be successful in extinguishing it. Venting lets the heat out, which is imperative for firemen to work below. The steam that is generated below will not enter the cockloft in sufficient volume unless ceilings are pulled down with plaster hooks by firefighters standing in smoke superheat to accomplish it. In a building sixty by two hundred, you have your work cut out for you. The trench was cut open and now complete and fire issued from it. Tully and Smithy made their way to the 124th Street side of the fire by the adjoining roof to the west of the fire building. Tully shone his lenten, which had seal beam that coon hunters were using at the time. On the front parapet, the tar had pulled away with the heat. The fire was still venting from where it vented itself earlier. Charging the sprinkler system had not worked. The roof deck was now resting its weight on the roof beams, which were on fire. They were designed to pull out of the bearing wall and not pull the wall down in a collapse. The Fifth Division had taken command of the fire and struck a fourth alarm, but Tully was sure that Chief Walsh would still be commanding the attack from the 124th Street side.

"Ladder 14 roof to Twelfth Battalion, K."

"Go ahead, Fourteen, K."

"Chief, still heavy fire in the cockloft. The tar have pulled away from the front wall on 124th side. The deck has dropped six inches. The roof have buckled in its center, twenty-five feet from the front wall, K."

"Twelfth Battalion to all units operating on the 124th Street side. Back out and stand down. I repeat, back out, now."

Units reluctantly dragged their hose lines out of the building in tactical retreat. It took ten minutes to get it clear off the building just before the roof collapsed. Chief Mann rolled in at this point and made it a fifth alarm. At this point, the fire became an outside operation. Tully and Smithy and rescue had been taking off the roof by the tower ladder bucket on 125th Street side. The fire radio transmitted, "Box 1341, Harlem box." The relocating companies ordered a second alarm.

On arrival, Smithy said, "Oh boy, I'm glad those guys got a job, I was beginning to worry that they be tempted to wolf down our pot roast."

"Who said they ain't eatin' it already?" groused Terry.

"They might be taking it with them to eat on the way, gnaw off chunks right now, and blame it on the relocating, relocating company," said Romeo.

"I hope they remember to put coal on the fire so we can take showers when we get back," said Terry.

"Fat chance of that," said Romeo. "We are the only godforsaken company in Manhattan with a coal furnace. No one knows dick about coal no more!"

The Manhattan dispatcher transmitted a third alarm to fill out the second alarm for Box 1341 and moved companies from the Bronx and Queens to fill empty firehouses in Manhattan. Captain McLaughlin was working on assembling his crew for a head count. He made a visual check and double-checked his riding list. "All right, while I got you all in a convoy, is everyone all right?" asked the captain. No one spoke up to state otherwise. "OK, fine," said the captain, not to push his luck. "This looks like an all-night affair. Pace yourself. The third alarm association is here with their coffee truck, and they may have sandwiches. As soon as it opens, we'll get something to hold us over."

The radio transmitted, "Box 1376, Ninety-one, Lenox Avenue, and 115th Street, five-story, occupied, multiple dwelling. Reported fire."

"Cap," said Smithy, "let me go over and talk to coffee people. I know some of them, and I might get a bag of sandwiches and a couple of contents of coffee. There's a better than good chance that they send us to 1376 if it's a real fire. I saw field communication eyeballing companies before with a clipboard."

"Yes on both counts," answered Captain Mac. "I was just taking a head count with that very thought in mind. Romeo, go with him."

Three working fires at one time in Harlem was not that unusual, but the amount of manpower needed at a fifth and a third alarm and now a third working fire was stretching manpower to the breaking point. Units were called as far away as Staten Island to relocate. Tenement companies were often criticized for being too specialized in one type of fire. There was, of course, some truth in this. It was natural to do better at what you do the most often. Sometimes referred to as your bread-and-butter fire, this was how a company earned their keep and stayed in business. So it was human nature to not think of hazards of a different occupancy in their district or when responding to midtown to high-rise or lofts, which were mixed offices and manufacturing fires. This caused problems that officers were always reminding the troops of. The criticism of tenement companies were they were overly aggressive to fault. Companies that worked mostly two-story wooden frames had challenges that were different from tenements companies. Fire load would be about the same, but there was no compartmentalization of the interior with fire stopping from apartment to apartment, nor was there outside fire escapes. The roofs would be gabled and more of a challenge to ladder and open up, plus the whole building was combustible.

So their strategies of operation would be different for them. A good part of Queens and Staten Island were two-to three-story frames. The units operating at Box 1376 were largely from Queens and Staten Island. They were brave units, but they had a different mind-set, and the chief who was supposed be responding in with them and in charge had missed that Staten Island Ferry, and there was now a covering lieutenant in charge of the biggest fire of his short career.

Smithy and Romeo had only disappeared from view when the portable radio barked, "Field communication to Ladder 14, K."

"Go ahead with message, K."

"Fourteen, break all hose connections and respond to Lenox and 115th Street. It's a working second-alarm fire."

"Ten four," said Captain Mac. Captain Mac turned to his crew and motioned for them to move closer. "You know the operation to getting out of this mess of fire hose. We have to run over four or five lengths or more to get out of here. We need all hands to move the hose so we don't run over the hose near the butts and pull the hose apart."

"What about Smithy and Romeo?" asked Terry.

"That's good. Terry, I want you to start worrying about me that I'm forgetting something. There'd be a test on this later. But first, go bust your ass and move that hose like I said so we can get the hell out of here and respond to that building that's burning down as we chat."

"Yes, sir," answered Terry, looking forlorn. "I only wanted to help," said Terry, looking to Tully. "So we didn't leave without them."

"Romeo got a radio on," said Tully. "He heard the messages. That's one of the reason Captain teamed them up together."

"Oh," said Terry, moving a hose. Tully was laughing to himself. "Tully, didn't the captain have a good time today at Eighty-sixth Street?"

"Oh yes, and that's why you're lucky," said Tully.

"Why's that?"

"Because he's got a lot more on his plate than we do, so just be a good soldier, do what he tells you, and you'll be fine," said Tully.

Ducky turned on the gun-ball overhead lights, tapped on the horn, and started to creep ahead. It was eight thirty. The three Harlem fires had occurred within fourteen blocks and in a two-hour span. It took five minutes to get out of the street and tangle off fire hose, which now clotted the street like spaghetti. Smithy and Romeo jumped on the truck as it reached Seventh Avenue. They carried two bags of sandwiches and three milk containers filled with coffee and cups.

Captain Mac slid the window that separated the front cab and the jumps seats to take a cup of coffee. Before taking a sip, he said, "Men, do not self-deploy at this fire. Stay together until I get orders! We are not working with Harlem companies."

The radio transmitted a third alarm for the box they were responding to, 1376. Tully said to Smithy, "This reminds you of anything? I'm thinking Tet Offensive." Tully was smiling.

"I was thinking of the Chinese coming across the Yalu River from Manchuria into North Korea."

"Yeah," said Romeo. "And Captain Mac is thinking when General Custer said, 'Men, we leave the Gatling gun behind. It will only slow down our pursuit of the Indians.'" This got a ha-ha from all.

"Romeo, you don't say a lot, but when you do, you're right on the money, man." said Smithy.

"It's easy to see you were a good field officer, Smithy." said Romeo.

"How's that?" asked Smithy.

"Because you know that the troops travel on the stomach." All of the crew high-fived Smithy for the coffee and sandwich. It would dilute the smoke and acid they had swallowed at the fifth alarm. Even if they would upchuck it all at the next fire, it would carry the debris with it. And for now, it was sitting just right.

* * *

An orange glow could be seen like a beacon in the sky from five blocks away. The fire was issuing out of the third-and fourth-floor windows with heavy brown smoke belching from the fifth floor and turning to black as it traveled over the roof. The front of the building was illuminated by the fire, as it would in daylight, only in a strange way, adding more color to the red brick and shadows of green and blue that played tricks on the mind's eye. The back of the building and side were shaded in total darkness. To a lover of fire lore, it was a Don Quixote moment, to do battle with the dragon one more time. They couldn't resist the call to do battle and save the day. The aches and pains of the last fire were forgotten. They were again ready to fight. For truly, fire was wicked, a sociopath killer with no heart or reason. Its only notion is to feed on all in its path. Firefighters' job was to kill the dragon. And they were ready.

"Ladder 14 to Box 1376."

"Command post, K."

"Any orders for Tower 14?" asked Captain Mac.

"Lieutenant Handcock to Ladder 14. Pull to the front of the building, K."

"Ten four," said Captain Mac. He turned and slid the glass window open between the cab and jump seats. "Tully! There's no chief in, there's a lieutenant in charge of this fire. You take the company and stand fast until we see what's going on. It looks like a tower job." The tower ladder pulled in front of the fire building, and Ducky prepared to set the tower up. The captain dismounted and approached a young lieutenant that was walking to him.

"Captain, would you please relieve me?" The lieutenant didn't mean to say please, but what the hell. Nothing was going right tonight.

"Yes, of course, Lieutenant, relax." Captain Mac turned to Tully. "Tully, have them run two lines into the tower."

"Yes, sir," answered Tully, and he turned and went about his business.

"Lieutenant, give me a brief rundown on what we got here."

"Well, there was a lot of fire!" started the lieutenant. He was having a hard time maintaining eye contact as the fire reflected on his face. White hot zinc dripped from the cornice like snot from the dragon's nose. The lieutenant blinked; the captain didn't flinch. "When I reported in, the lieutenant that had the fire asked me my time and grade, and when I told him, he said, 'You got it,' and ran into the fire building." The captain did a good job of turning a laugh into a cough. "There was a good bit of rescues," added the lieutenant.

"Over ladders?" questioned the captain.

"No. Down the stairs."

"OK, fine, Lieutenant. This is what we're going to do. We're calling in an air strike with the tower ladder. I will do this with the radio. We will back the troops out. Let them leave their hose where it is. After it darkens down on the third and fourth floor, then we're moving back in. Do you have that?"

"Yes, sir," answered the lieutenant.

"And I will be into helping you as soon as we get this set up, if you need it. Good job, Lieutenant. We can do this!"

"Yes sir, Captain," said the lieutenant, and he turned and went into the fire building.

"Command post to all operating forces at Box 1378. Back down to the second floor, leave your hose lines where they are. The tower will hit the fire on the fifth floor first, and then the fourth and third to give you time to clear the floors. I repeat, clear the fire floors and regroup on the second floor. Lieutenant Handcock is in charge of inside operations."

Smithy and Romeo were sent to the roof by the adjoining building to make sure it's open and told, "Be careful. This is burning a long time." Tully and Terry were in the bucket extending to the fifth floor. They then played the one-thousand-gallons-per-minute stream into the fifth-floor windows and up into the ceiling and the cockloft. They knew complete extinguishment was not possible from the outside, but this attack would break the heat dynamic. Then they dropped down to the fourth floor and raked the windows as a warning; the outside attack was imminent. They darkened it down and moved the stream to the third floor in the same way.

"Tower 14 bucket to command."

"Go ahead, Fourteen."

"Cap, we're done with the third floor."

"Ten four. Good job, go back to the top floor and give it bath."

Lieutenant Handcock's first idea after backing the troops down to the second floor, which was not as hard as he thought it was going to be, was to make contact with his engine company and make ready to move back into the third floor on the orders. The tightness in his chest was gone; it seemed to disappear at the captain's orders and remark "Good job." One ladder company and two engines reported into command post from midtown. Captain Mac's orders were as a matter of fact as follows: To the first engine, "Take two lengths of 1 ½ and a controlling nozzle." The plan was to get to the fourth floor, drop the hose down the open stairway, and hook it to 2 ½. This will bypass the hose on the stairway. To the second engine, "Take a 2 ½ line and make ready to stretch into the fifth floor. Prepare to stretch a big line up the aerial." There were no question, only "Yes, sir." As the tower stream was back operating into the fifth-floor window, a fire steam was now issuing out the third-floor windows from Lieutenant Handcock's engine company. This operation put a smile on Captain Mac's face. No matter how good the tower ladder is, someone has got to go in and put the fire out, sooner or later, from the inside.

COD car 5 pulled up to the command post. Chief Mann stepped out of the car. The chief's driver, Howard, danced out from behind the driver's seat. "Oh baby, Mac, you look good as the chief. So, Mac, it looks like you've been kicking ass here," said Chief Mann.

"No, just readjusted the harness, added a new bridle, and the team just started to pull the load."

"Patty, you're telling me this is all just like you were back in the British army driving the army mules."

"Well, to tell you the truth, Chief, you do get a lot more done when you try to gentle things along."

"Patty, you're saying I'm too hard on the men?"

Patty laughed a good-natured laugh. "No, no, this is only one small fire. Chief, we're talking about a horse of a different color for your job."

The chief looked up at the tower ladder with the water now shutting down at the fifth floor and the engine company stretching their 2 ½ hose up the aerial to the fifth-floor window.

"Pat, I'd like to ask you a question. Why didn't you use the tower waterway to take a line off in on the fifth floor?"

"That would have tied up the tower, and after all, Chief, this is only our second fire of the night."

"Good answer, Captain Mac."

A second chief's car pulled into the command post. "Chief Thorn reporting. Do we need an additional alarm here?"

Chief Mann turned away from Chief Thorn and said to Captain Mac, "You can take up, Patty, and take an hour out of service when you get back to quarters." And he added as an afterthought, "Good job to your men, Patty." And then he turned to

Chief Thorn. "Thorn, you're a half ass. How far away need I assign you so I don't see you anymore?"

* * *

It was 2215 hours. The crew was thinking how good it would be to get back to quarters, wash up, dress their wounds, and have a cup of coffee. As they approached Park Avenue and 122nd Street, there was an donnybrook in progress at Crescent Moon that had spilled out into the street.

"Oh boy, here we go again," said Tully.

The truck slowed down. A kid with a slash mark across his bloody face ran up to the cab. "My brother, he's cut bad, real bad."

Captain Mac reached for the cab's phone. "Ladder 14 to Manhattan."

"Go ahead, Fourteen."

"Ten forty-seven, police assistance at 122nd and Park Avenue."

"Ten four, Fourteen."

There were two boys guarding the body of the third boy lying in the street. Smithy bent over the boy. "What you going to do?" said one of the boys. Smithy didn't pay any attention to him but checked the pulse in the boy's neck; it was faint. "Man! I said what you going to do?"

Still Smithy gave no reply but reported to the captain. "We got to transport him fast."

"You're not taking that motherfucker anywhere, he dies here," said a mean-looking man.

The crew of Ladder 14 had started to carry the boy to the jump seat. The bad-mouthed man grabbed Smithy's arm causing him to lose his grip on the boy. Smithy saw the flash of what looked like a knife in his other hand. Smithy delivered a crushing blow to the man's neck. As he fell, Smithy kneed him in the face, which made a sickening bone-splitting sound. He hit the street like a bag of yesterday's garbage. Tully picked up the man's knife by the tip and put it inside his glove and into his pocket. They took the boy and his brother and left an angry scene.

"Ladder 14 to Manhattan."

"Go ahead, Fourteen."

"Transporting one male to joint disease hospital. There are still others injured at the scene. Police and ambulance needed at this location, K."

"Ten four, Fourteen," answered the dispatcher. "We have other calls on this."

* * *

"Man, can I ask you something?" asked the brother, now riding on the running board.

"Yes, sure," said Smithy.

"Is he going to make it?"

"He lost a lot of blood. From the look of things, if you pray. You should start now." The boy started to weep.

The boy's heart stopped beating as they were rolling him to the emergency room. All efforts to revive him failed. The boys' parents arrived as Ladder 14's crew was leaving. Tonight would take years to erase from their minds, the lost of their son, if ever. All for a ritual night of gang wilding that was destined to replay over and over again by the boys in the city's ghetto.

* * *

It was 12:45 AM as they pulled in front of quarters. Ducky had stopped to pick up bagels and eggs, not knowing what condition the pot roast would be in by now. A North Bronx truck company was in quarters.

"OK, Captain," said their officer. "We'll pull out and let you go back in service."

"No, thanks. We have an hour out of service from the chief himself," said Captain Mac.

"Hey, Cap, they let our fire go out," said Romeo. "There're no hot water here!"

"What fire?" asked the covering officer. The duck and the dog were running around the truck, and the dog was baying and barking. Romeo was on the far side of the relocating truck as the duck was coming by Romeo. He made a lucky grab of the duck's neck and, in one motion, opened the truck's compartment door and put the duck in their saw compartment. This was the best he felt all night. Ducky sliced all the meat and poured gravy and veggies over it and put it out on the table with the bread and started to make scrambled eggs. The showers were fast as they were ice-cold.

It was 1:30 AM, and the relocating lieutenant came into the kitchen and asked if they were ready now to go into service. Just then, Box 1465 was transmitted.

"That's yours," said Smithy. "We will be about ready when you get back from this one."

"Does Fourteen respond to that box?"

"Yes, and you're still Fourteen. So you better shake ass and get going," said Smithy.

"Where are these guys from?" asked Terry.

"Right on the city line, they had fifty-four runs last year."

"In a month?"

"No, in a year."

"Oh boy! That's why they wanted to get the hell out of here."

"It's their lieutenant," said Smithy. "Didn't you notice how old they were? They've been to more fires than all of us put together."

The department phone rang. Tully picked it up. "Ladder 14. No, we will go back into service," Tully said into the phone. The captain walked into the kitchen.

"Cap, the dispatcher asked if we wanted another relocating company. He said that we had three here tonight. I said no. Right?"

"Right," answered the captain. "The shower brought Burma back to me. We had no hot showers there for a year."

"What will you have, Cap, eggs or beef?" asked Ducky.

The apparatus door was open, and in walked the fire commissioner and his driver and another gentleman. "Patty, you old son of a gun." The two men embraced. "I just heard what a great job you did from my dear friend here, Jake Turner. He lived in that building next door to the fire."

"Hope you didn't have any damage, Mr. Turner."

"No, thanks to you. Things were going to hell in a handbasket before you showed up. With that cherry picker. That young lieutenant was way over his head."

"Yes, we're all over our heads here most of the time," said Captain Mac with a laugh.

Chief Walsh came back into quarters and entered the kitchen. He saluted the commissioner, and the commissioner offered his hand and introduced his comrade. "Fine job tonight, Chief."

"Thanks! But it's my men, of course, that deserve the credit. They make me look a lot better than I am."

"I love modesty. It's a lost art," said the commissioner. "How is everyone holding up, Chief?"

"Well, it's like the commercial said. They can take a beating and keep on ticking. On that subject, Captain Mac, I need Tully the rest of the tour, Skitter got a nail in his foot."

"I hate to part with him, Chief."

"Yes, I can appreciate that! But I need experience from this point on tonight," said the chief. "This has been one of those nights that has a life of its own. I will replace him with a trucky from Ladder 26." Tully went and put his turnouts in the chief's car. "Captain Mac, I meant to pass on a thank-you from Jackie Robinson's widow, for your thoughtfulness in pulling out the tower ladder on the apron and saluting when their car passed the day of the funeral."

"Yes, that was a fine thing to do, Captain," said Jake Turner. "And Jackie was a fine man," he added.

The commissioner was no stranger to Ladder 14. He had been fireman there thirty years before and stopped in from time to time, but he always had his driver call first.

"Commissioner, would you like coffee?" asked Terry.

"Yes, and a cup for Mr. Turner too, please. I saw your father-in-law-to-be, Chief Mann," continued the Commissioner to Terry, "at a party, and he said you were doing good up here."

"Yes, it's a lot more than I thought it would be, but I like it," answered Terry. The bells tolled. Box 1428.

"Truck and chief, get out," said Tully.

* * *

Tully pulled the chief's car back into quarters. The last four calls were two MFA 10-92s and food on the stove and a car fire. Ducky had been able to find and retrieve the duck off the roof with the tower ladder bucket off the poultry center where fresh-killed chicken were sold. The duck was like a lost child to Ducky. It was an impulsive thing for Romeo to do, and he felt bad about it. He thought the duck would be safer transported to the North Bronx and the country and away from the unsavory types of the Harlem firehouse. Romeo would later say, but of course, no one would have believed him or blamed him. Romeo wisely diverted attention away from himself as the perpetrator. But he generously focused on relocating the Bronx truck company and, at the same time, tried to cool the ducky's temper off by telling him that this company stole the duck out of the goodness of their heart, knowing fully well fine duck breeding when they saw it. This was why they were hightailing it, trying to get back to the Bronx, only misfortune struck and they got nailed with a run and a worker. But the cleverness of the duck to fly to the poultry house and ghoul a few young chick was unmatched.

"Look this way, ducky," he said.

"Our duck is now a man," proclaimed Romeo.

It was all winding down now; it was 4:30 AM. Tully took an Alka-Seltzer Gold with no aspirin in it, and he walked up the stairs to the chief's office and put the run slips on the desk, walked out to his cot, and lay down with all his clothes on, or what was referred to as "full field pack." It was said that Napoleon's most endearing trait to his men was he could lay down anywhere and sleep alongside his troops on the ground, the trait of a hardened dog soldier. Tully thought of sleeping in a foxhole in Korea freezing cold. He knew what the captain was trying to do tonight by bringing up his time in Burma and cold showers. It was for those who had not seen that degree of hardship, so they could use that experience to fall back on when times get tough and the tough gets going. Tully thought of the book of James when he spoke of trials and tribulations, or was it temptation? Tully's mind was wandering, looking for a place of rest, as a tired dog turns in a circle before he lies down in between the calls and the duck fiasco.

There had been a call from Mrs. Edwards, the cook at St. Mary's. She needed help finding her son; they drove her to the West Side where he was supposed to be hanging out. Tully knew the car wash owner and his son, who worked 125th Street out in front of the firehouse, lived on this block. He pulled in front of this brownstone and parked. The chief got out of the car and asked some junkie, who was on the front steps to the brownstone, about Richard. The wise guy passed a remark that Richard was the priest's son and he was a stone junkie. The chief went after him, and a small pushing match ensued. This was a bad start, Tully could see, and he said, "Chief, we got to get out of here."

The wise guy didn't know when to stop, even though he was getting the worse of it. The chief had a hold of his collar. "These firemen, what they don't steal, they broke with their wrecking tools." Mr. Sutton, the car wash man, who was sitting on the stoop, came off the wash pale he was sitting on and crowned the wise dude with his pail. "Motherfucker, look what you done to my motherfuckin' head, you ole fool, I'll cut you for that." Hector, Mr. Sutton's son, dropped him with one shot with his pail.

"Chief, we're making the same mistake as this asshole of standing in one place too long," said Tully. "We are going to get nailed by incoming too. Please get in the car, we got to think of this woman. Mr. Sutton's son can handle this guy."

"He's right! You go on, Chief. This dude's all mouth, and if he keeps overloading that jaybird ass of his with that alligator mouth, we're going to tear him a new asshole," Mr. Sutton said as he was dancing around in his Joe Louis fight stance over the prone dude. The chief wisely got in the car.

"Tully, please take me back to the church," said Mrs. Edwards. "I'm sorry I caused so much trouble, but I need to tell you one thing, don't you pay no never mind to that trash talk about Richard and Father. That poor old man doesn't know or want to know the first thing about a real woman. I'm a bad mother, that's the all of it. And a whore to boot." Now she was wailing like a siren as they headed back to the East Side on 125th Street. "I left my baby boy on the church step, and Father tracked me down and gave me a job and a home if I kept the baby. People put him through hell for it, he's a saint, that what he is. I kiss the ground he walks on. But that's the only kissing that poor old man gets. That's him! That's him!" she screamed. "Over there, that's him. Richard, my baby, I love you, baby. I love you, baby."

Tully pulled the car to the curb, and they took Richard and his mother back to their home. The chief was telling her that she was a good woman for doing the right thing and to please stop crying as she gave Richard kisses.

* * *

Tully was now drifting off to sleep on his bed. Only the image of his beautiful wife naked, clad only in black lace panties and wearing red high heels striking theatrical poses was keeping him awake, her idea being if she could do her line naked, she would never have stage fright while dressed. This was such a wonderfully bizarre image; it was burned in his mind, and it played as soon as he closed his eyes when he was away from her. But now he wanted sleep, and sleep alone. His head was throbbing, and his heart racing from the effects of too much smoke and too much lactic acid in his bloodstream, too little sleep. *Please, God, no more fires, I can't do any more good tonight, please. Rock me to sleep, baby,* he said to his dream wife, and his wish was answered. He was asleep.

* * *

It was 0445. They had only one run since bringing Mrs. Edwards and her son, Richard, back to the rectory. The people in the street were in a dark mood tonight; it was hot and sticky. The uncollected garbage from the work slow down by the sanitation department was everywhere, and the people were setting fire to it. The only thing missing was Gershwin's *Slaughter on Tenth Avenue* playing too loud as the background music. Yes, it was the middle of the night, but the kids were still playing with the hydrant the way they usually do. They were using a big soap can open at both ends as a nozzle. The nozzle man straddled the fireplug extending both arms and hands with a firm grip on the can over the hydrant's opening. This produced two hundred – plus gallons per minute stream, which was directed at cars as they stopped for a light; they were having great fun, until they picked the wrong guy, one of their own. He jumped out of his drenched BMW and shot a few people at random.

* * *

The house lights flashed on, awaking Tully from the nightmare of the night being relived. The telegraph bells were ringing; the house lights were on, like the police's infamous third-degree light. "What did you do with your night? Or was the ship going down?" His mouth was dry as a fire pit and his eyes crusted over.

"Tully! We got a job," said the chief. "Hundred thirty-eighth Street and Madison."

Tully's mind asked the questions *Who am I?* and *Why am I hurting?* and *Why do I need more of this?* Tully focused on the wall. The clock said it was 5:30 AM. He slid the pole mindlessly, got in behind the wheel of the chief's car, and started the motor. The front door was pushed open by the fireman on house watch.

"Turn left, Tully," said the chief. "Then right on Madison."

"Thanks, Chief. I think I know that, then again maybe I didn't."

"Are you OK, Tully?"

"Don't worry about me. I'll be fine as soon as my heart starts beating."

"Oh. Is that all?"

"Oh shit, we do have a job, don't we?"

Engine 59 officer had transmitted 10-75, a working fire needing a full assignment upon arrival. The car pulled into the 138th Street block; it was New Law Tenement street with rows of five-story brick buildings. There was heavy smoke in the street; the tenements were brick nonfireproof wood construction for floors and roof and interior apartment wall. Four flats to the floor, fire escapes in the front and rear. The fire was out the windows on the second and third floors. Heavy smoke showing from the windows of the rest above the fire. It looked from the front that the fire was heaviest on the right side of the hallway. The chief gave the message that the Twelfth was at the scene, filled out the Box 1075, but held off with the fire report or called for more additional help. He told Tully to check exposure 4 (the building to the right of the fire building) and added, "Tully, be fast and brief." Tully took a Halligan bar out of the backseat of the chief's car. When he reached the third floor, a man with his frightened wife at his side had their door open. He told Tully there was fire in his apartment. Tully at first thought that the fire was in the common air shaft shared with the fire building and had communicated, at most, to the window frames. He checked it out without comment and was shocked to find the side bedroom on fire. The shaft was an inferno and was sucking the air from the apartment. Explaining why there was no smoke in the apartment, Tully shut the bedroom door and keyed his radio. "Battalion 12 aide to Battalion 12."

"Go ahead, Tully."

"Chief, transmit a second alarm. Report to follow."

Tully told the couple to leave the building and shut the door to the apartment. He was going to the fourth and fifth floors and try and wake the tenants as he ran from door to door and floor to floor. At the top floor, in the same apartment as the third floor where fire was in the bedroom, the door was very hot and locked. Tully made it to the bulkhead door, opened it to vent the hallway, which was now filling with heavy smoke.

"Battalion 12 aide to Battalion 12."

"Go ahead, Tully."

"Chief, it looks like the fire is in three apartments off the shaft of exposure 4. I'm on the roof now, 30 Truck is cutting the roof, K."

"What do you need in that exposure 4 now?" asked the chief.

"Two 1 ½ tenement lines and a truck to force doors."

"You got it, Tully, now come down and meet the engine and the truck. I'll start you off with! And you can bird-dog for them. K."

"Chief, I am going to check the top-floor apartment. It was still locked. I met no one coming down from there."

"Tully, be careful," said the chief.

"Ten four, Chief, K," reported Tully. Tully had only the Halligan tool. He drove the point into the doorjamb baseball-bat style just above the door handle and put his back into the door as he pulled on the tool. He had caught the brass plate, which broke the mortise lock and forced the secondary lock off the door frame. He used his chock to hold the door open. The smoke was blowing out the door, but then it reversed itself into the apartment and into the shaft room where there was heavy fire. He was on his hands and knees, crawling because of the heat. The visibility was fairly good. He found a woman and a small child on the floor; both had a pulse. He dragged them along the floor on a blanket to the hallway. The fire was now coming up the stairway being drawing by the open bulkhead door. He shut the apartment door. He was cut off, but he had a plan. The first thing was to let people know he was in trouble. "Mayday, Mayday! I am in exposure 4, top floor hallway. I have a woman and a child, the fire has the staircase. I will try to get into the front apartment and a fire escape. Tully out." Tully went to the front-right apartment. Ladder 40 was putting up their aerial now. Tully dragged his human cargo to the front flat's door, but the door was locked. It was now too hot to stand and force the door. Tully lay on his back and kicked as hard as he could, but the door didn't bulge. Tully put the Halligan bar under the door and lifted it. The door flexed and something snapped. As he reached for the knob, the door opened on its own. A fireman took hold of Tully and started to carry him bodily into the apartment.

"Hold it, hold it," Tully said. "Get the woman and the kid. In the hall. I'm OK. Did your crew search this flat?"

"No," said the fireman. "I'm dancing as fast as I can." Tully met two more firemen making a search. They found two kids and a woman and removed all to the street, five people in all. Two other firemen helped in removing them to the street. The baby started to cry. Tully smiled. "Thank God, she's alive," he said.

* * *

"Tully, you have the luck of the Irish, son," said the chief. "Are you OK?"

"I think so," said Tully. A second alarm turned the trick. In addition, the engine teams in the fire building hit the fire across the interior shaft way after knocking down the fire flat in the main fire building. This cut the engine work to half in the exposure; only the top floor had heavy fire damage. Three of its four rooms burned out. In exposure 4, the chief left an engine and a truck to overhaul each building.

The chief remarked to Tully, "That was a remarkable transmission, transmit a second alarm. Report to follow."

"Chief, I was only following orders!"

"And what order was that?"

"Be fast and brief! And you told the captain you had to have experienced men."

"It's a good thing you were right, Tully! The deputy rounded in the street, and he monitored your transmission."

"Well, Chief, it's like this. I could see that you could not. The fire was already into exposure 4 on the third floor. That's one engine and a truck, a second truck is need to force doors on the floor above, and a second engine to fight the fire on that floor, and the third engine to help."

"Yes," added the chief. "And of course, firemen trapping themselves freelancing. But you were right, Tully," said the chief. "And the companies heard your transmission and played their line up the shaft and across it. Deputy asked if you were on the lieutenant list, and I said no! And he said, 'He should be.'"

"Matter of fact, Chief, I am on the list, but I don't know if they will reach me. That's why I never say anything about it."

"Well, Tully, being an officer is about making decisions. The fear of being wrong can slow decisions, and that can cost life and limb. I asked for experience, and I got more than I asked for. Good job, Tully."

* * *

Before leaving the scene, they had stopped at the third-alarm association's coffee truck. They would not ordinarily have had responded to a second alarm, but because of the fifth alarm earlier, they were in the neighborhood, so they dropped in with their services.

The chief and Tully met Father Cook. He was renewing old friendships and blessing all he talked with. He thanked them for helping Mrs. Edwards. He was not at home when she needed help. He poured a small shot into their coffee cups of Irish whiskey from a silver flask before wishing them a good night and blessing them.

The effect of the coffee was doing them both good. "Chief, have you ever considered another line of work?"

The chief laughed. "Every year the first ten years on the job. Until Margaret, in a discussion, told me I was doing God's work. It occurred to me at the time I was a sinner and was not likely to change, my only hope I had to be saved was to do more good than bad. 'Faith without deeds is death to the soul,' from the book of James."

"Yes," said Tully. "James being my birth name and the shortest book in the Bible, I can say I know the verse. Chief, might I ask you how the meeting with my mother-in-law, Grace, went with your wife, Margaret?"

"In a word, Tully, *wonderful*. Of course, the whole thing is too far-fetched to be believable. That people would put orphans on a train in New York City and send them out west to be picked over at each stop for adoption. But it did happen, and it did work out beautiful, for all but a small group of children. The case I'm most familiar with happened in Lincoln, Nebraska. There was our last stop. There were three children left, a girl and two boys. Two being a brother and sister. As luck would have it, the boy Joseph had a bad cold. The nuns had him looked at at the stop in Chicago by a doctor, and he was giving a bottle of medicine of the day and sent on. To the stop in Lincoln, there was only one couple to meet them. A nice woman picked a boy and the girl, but not the brother and sister, most likely because Joseph on this day looked like death warmed over. The boy who had been picked gagged himself and spit up on his coat. The sister was trying to keep the brother and sister together, and the nun was telling the woman that Joseph was the picture of health leaving New York and he would be fine in a week. When the picked boy puked on himself, that made the switch easy on the woman. As one nun took the passed-over boy away, the girl ran to him and told him she would never forget him and she'd find him someday."

"And, Chief, you were that boy?" asked Tully.

"Oh yes, and I still need to tell the story in the third person to get it all out."

"Chief, I told this story to Kitty, and she cried for a day. I'm asking this for Kitty. How did you find each other?"

"Well, the family brought up Margaret and Joseph. I was in a very devout home. At eighteen, Margaret went into the convent but did not take her vows when the time came. The mother superior told her to be true to herself first. The order had an orphanage in New York, and she transferred there. The fact that I was put in foster care and not adopted made it easier for her to locate me. She traced me to Our Lady Of Sorrows School in Brooklyn where an older nun did remember a Billy Walsh and read about a Bill Walsh who was a fireman and had made a rescue of a mother and children in a row-house fire. They made a call to the fire department. They were told that a William Walsh was assigned to Rescue 2 and when he would work. Well, here's where it gets funny. Here comes the two nuns in full habit into the firehouse and telling the house watch their business. He in turn calls the captain, and he orders me front and center. Well, I had no idea of what this was all about. Before I recognized her, she lunges at me and throws a lip-lock on me. My eyes felt like they were popping out of my head. And that's when Sister Rita coldcocked me with a right cross. That decked me. The captain was saying, 'Good God almighty! We'll all lose our jobs! Mother, have mercy on us.' Margaret was on the floor with my head in her lap, and she was kissing my face and saying, 'Billy! It's me, your Margaret! I found you, Billy. And I love you.'"

"Was there something else about this Sister Rita?" asked Tully.

"Yes. She said, 'I'll never talk to you again, Walsh,'" and the chief smiled. The chief's car was moving east on 125th Street. The sky was purple, and the sun was breaking through. It was another Harlem sunrise and a new day after the longest night. And unknown to Tully, he had just clocked his first ten thousand alarm as Box 1385, Fifth Avenue and 116 Street, was transmitted.

The end. Of part one.

Made in the USA
Columbia, SC
08 September 2021